For Nicky, Eve and Poppy

caveo obsideo libri

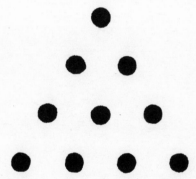

There's a wonderful paper by Schopenhauer, called 'An Apparent Intention of the Fate of the Individual', in which he points out that when you are at a certain age and look back over life, it seems to be almost as orderly as a composed novel. And just as in Dickens' novels, little accidental meetings and so forth turn out to be main features in the plot, so in your life. And what seem to have been mistakes at the time turn out to be directive crises. And then he asks: 'Who wrote this novel?'

Joseph Campbell, *An Open Life*

Introduction
The Hand of Glory

When I was thirteen years old, my greatest wish was to see a Hand of Glory. I must have been a pragmatic boy, for here was a wish that could come true.

For those who don't know, let me explain what a Hand of Glory is: an occult item – the mummified left hand of a hanged man, specifically a murderer, severed below the wrist at midnight by the light of a full moon. One wonders how easy it would be to fulfil these criteria, but fulfilled they must be for the object to acquire the powers accorded to it. And those powers are impressive. Any candle made from the fat of the dead criminal (combined with virgin wax and sesame oil), placed in the Hand and lit, will render all those in its presence, save the bearer, totally unconscious. Nothing will wake them until the flame is doused with milk (dousing it with water will have no effect). The Hand can also unlock any door it comes upon, thus making it of great value to thieves. Those who possess such a potent charm could surely help themselves to the contents of whichever property they fancy. (There is another, more alarming, piece of folklore connected with the fate of the Hand's victims: if they are not woken by the second cock-crow of morning, they will die, and not only that, their souls will be taken to hell, whether deserving of that fate or not.)

I say I must have been pragmatic, but there was an otherworldly drive behind the desire to track down this ghoulish item. It was not purely a matter of having a taste for the macabre. Since the age of five or six I have been fascinated by the supernatural. How this enthusiasm began I find it difficult to remember – as difficult to remember as my entry into the world itself – but it is core to my earliest conscious memories. My parents, and indeed my friends' parents, were aware of this, to judge by the presents I received on birthdays.

More often than not these gifts were anthologies of supernatural stories, mostly fictional but occasionally collections of supposedly factual accounts, too. The titles are still vivid in my mind, as are their covers: *Ghosts and Hauntings*, *Great Ghosts of the World*, *The Encyclopedia of Witchcraft and Magic*. One of these, perhaps my favourite, was a volume called *Haunted Britain* by the delightfully named Anthony D. Hippisley Coxe. This took the form of a travel guide, with a map at the front replete with different symbols and accompanied by a complex key: a star for wishing wells, sacred, magic and mysterious places; a skull for hauntings, ghosts and poltergeists; a little sea-monster for a location identified with the appearance of spectral and mythical beasts, and so on. I would spend hours, my head bent over the map, cross-referencing it with the entries, identifying possible destinations, studying it as if it were some kind of escape route, although at that age I had no idea from what I might be trying to escape.

Some of the destinations were tantalisingly close: Burton Agnes Hall, wherein resided the skull of Aud Nance, separated from her remains in order to quell her unquiet spirit (which screamed in the night until her dying wish to be interred in the house itself was carried out). Bramham Park, where a phantom coach and hounds were said to charge through the gardens by the light of a February moon. Brimham Rocks, with its mysterious tipping stone, a huge boulder carved by ancient watercourses, which was balanced precariously on an angular base. Supposedly it could be tilted by a truly honest man. (I knew this would be beyond me. I was a habitual liar, often concealing my culpability for various accidents around the house beneath a convincing blanket of denial.) All these places were geographically close, but there was no destination more tantalising than Whitby. The famous harbour town sported three symbols. One of them – a black cauldron ('witchcraft, sorcery and curses', according to the key) – referred to the Hand of Glory itself. According to Mr Hippisley Coxe, this item was no mere figment of imagination or legend. Not only did it exist, it was on display at the Whitby Museum. Well, here was an achievable goal. A trip to Whitby was entirely practical.

Often – during the school holidays at least – my parents would arrange trips to Yorkshire locations. It wouldn't be difficult to suggest a day out in Whitby. It was a seaside town, it had an abbey, and doubtless its share of craft and antique shops, too, which would be a lure to my mother. Indeed, I cannily led with this, saying I'd seen a piece on TV about teapots from the east coast and maybe we could go there? Robin Hood's Bay was apparently very nice – or Whitby? I mentioned that there was supposed to be a good museum, too, as if this fact were only of the merest passing interest to me. And so the excursion was arranged and my excitement grew as the day approached.

The skies were fine as we set off down Wigton Lane towards the ring road and the A64 beyond. What would the thing look like? What colour would its desiccated skin be? Would it have a candle fixed between its bony digits? Had it ever been used?

'This is typical of you.'

'What?'

'How are we supposed to walk up hills like this with your father's back?'

'I didn't know it was up a hill.'

'Yes, well. That's the point. It's not up a hill. For God's sake, where is this place?'

My mother turned to my more stoic father, her face drenched with the salt-smelling freezing drizzle being driven by a cruel wind relentlessly into all our exposed areas.

'We're not walking another step. Melvyn – !'

My father was expected to be the enforcer of this decision. My sister was crying from tiredness. The steep Whitby side streets seemed to hold nothing but blank-faced houses. The shops had trailed off some way back. The vague directions in *Haunted Britain* had suggested that the Whitby Museum would be the simplest of institutions to find, yet there was not a hint of anything intended for tourists or travellers on this road. Just rows of ordinary properties, their quotidian paths and blank front doors no different from those I saw every day.

'I don't know what's the matter with you. How difficult would it have been to find a map? I don't think this place even exists. Have you made it up? Is it another of your stories? You've got so you can't tell the difference between what's actual and what you invent. Did you make this whole thing up to scare Jayne?'

My sister cried even harder. I could feel disappointment swelling within me. The promise of the excitement and mystery I had yearned for, yearned to see with my own eyes, was about to fade into a fog of banality and disappointment. Of course the Hand of Glory, or its accommodating museum, didn't exist. Of course there was nothing to see. There was nothing there at all. There never had been. Or if there was, it might as well not be since it was not, nor ever would be, for my eyes.

But the yearning didn't fade. Still there was this need to experience directly the supernatural. Perhaps 'need' is wrong; it was closer to desire. I could function without it, but I craved it nonetheless. It was an ache, a wish, a hankering for something more mysterious, something larger than that which I could perceive around me with my five unsatisfying senses. The failure to locate the Hand of Glory and gaze upon it became emblematic of the encroaching cementation into a material life that seemed to be happening, year on year, as childhood fled and adulthood approached, ready to ensnare me in its hard, plain, boring arms.

But the books remained on the shelf, round the little corner of my cramped bedroom, which was increasingly becoming a shrine to this yearned-for world I couldn't touch.

There were some nights still, if I'm honest, when they frightened me. Maybe this fear was the next best thing to the sense of wonder that was at the centre of my longing. Fear and awe are in close relationship, particularly the kind of fear associated with the supernatural. The Germans call it *ehrfurcht*, a semi-religious word meaning 'reverence for that which we cannot understand'. But it's odd to be frightened of a book. Or maybe not. Books are powerful things. Perhaps it was an inversion of my Jewish upbringing, where ecclesiastical volumes are hallowed objects. If one drops a prayer book, one has to kiss it after retrieving it from the floor. And at the end of their span of use, such books are buried in Jewish cemeteries since religious law prohibits them from being destroyed. It's not much of a jump for a child to think of this power spilling over into non-religious books, too. One collection I owned, *Stranger than Fiction: 50 True Tales of Terror*, filled me with an irrational fear. It might have been the cowled skeleton embossed into the front (the book had long since lost its dustjacket). Or it might have been to do with the contents themselves. Either way, on a dark, windy night, or when I was alone in the house – even in my early teens – I would place that book in another room before I went to sleep.

Written by a number of different authors, *Stranger than Fiction* took a variety of dark and terrifying legends from around the world and fictionalised them as short stories. Imagined interior monologues and motivations for their protagonists lent them an immediacy and vividness that the bare summaries in other books of this type simply didn't possess. It was a kind of magic trick, I suppose: the author, by creating characters on the page – fictional versions derived from actual individuals – enabled the reader to enter into their original experience, feel what it might be like to have faced the terrifying (and impossible) phenomena they apparently encountered. Favourites included: 'The Gytrash of Goathland', a yarn about a werewolf-like creature that haunted the North Yorkshire moors; 'The Campden Wonder', a chilling story of witchcraft in a Cotswolds village; and 'Tapu', a tale of a young man tormented by Maori demons.

In recent years, as a sceptical adult, I still find myself drawn to the memory of *Stranger than Fiction: 50 True Tales of Terror*, even though the book is long gone. What pleasure there might be in writing such a book myself, I thought – in returning to that expansive world I used to inhabit, even if that pleasure is essentially nostalgic. The thought was always idle, however, because the supposedly true stories of this nature I was aware of were already overly familiar. And I did not have the inclination to go and search out new ones.

Then, in defiance of my own scepticism perhaps, synchronicity stepped in. My agent forwarded me an email from a journalist called Aiden Fox. He wasn't known to me. At that time he worked on the *Bath Chronicle*, but he'd been employed by various local newspapers and radio stations in the south-west for more than thirty years. He had an interest in myths and legends of the British Isles and for many years had run a column, interestingly enough also called *Stranger than Fiction*, which briefly summarised a different eerie story or supernatural tale. Over the years he had amassed a number of these accounts and was keen on compiling them into a book. The email explained that he was looking for a writer of fiction to collaborate with, someone who might be able to articulate the stories more fully than he himself felt able to. Typically, his column ran to no more than two thousand words and was written in a bright and breezy style. But now he was interested in fleshing out these 'real life' pieces into something fuller and more literary. What he was actually talking about was a modern-day version of *Stranger than Fiction: 50 True Tales of Terror*. I don't know if he was aware of the earlier book. If he was, he never mentioned it. Ordinarily I'm wary of such enquiries (not that I'm inundated with them, but they come occasionally, as I'm sure they do to many writers), and often they are speculative. One is aware of the fact that the importuner has perhaps made blanket approaches. In Mr Fox's case, I didn't get that impression. It felt like, for whatever reason, I had been selected as his writer of choice. Attached to the email was a document containing a number of the original stories as they'd been sent to him. If I was already predisposed to his idea, it was the accounts that clinched the matter. Within a few minutes, I was ensnared. Mr Fox clearly had an eye for the uncanny. There was such a strange particularity to the letters and clippings he had sent me that my imagination couldn't help but respond.

Aiden was jolly and friendly. At first glance he was physically nondescript. You might take him for someone who works in IT rather than journalism, in his neat grey suit and unbuttoned white shirt. But he was possessed of an immediate and ebullient charm, and an intriguing sense of purpose, as if his mission to disseminate stories of the unexplained had some hidden, higher motivation. He wrong-footed my offhand and slightly self-regarding suspicion with his own intelligence and affable wit. He wasn't an idiot and he wasn't a weirdo. And I was relieved. Relieved because I was already intrigued, in spite of my lofty instinct to dismiss his initial approach. There was something about the clutch of supposedly real-life stories he'd sent me that had me hooked. The truth was that some of them frightened me. I took this is a good sign. That frisson is always what one hopes to find in a tale of this type.

Unlike me, Aiden was a believer – but that only added to the appeal. I was coming at these accounts from a writer's perspective, captivated by the metaphorical possibilities of their impossibility. Aiden was closer to my junior self: desirous of touching something that he felt was just out of reach.

I've always been bewitched by an eerie location. Some of this may go back to *Haunted Britain*, where the dustjacket proclaimed that the book's photographer 'was overcome by such a sense of evil at Saddell Abbey near Campbeltown that he could not bear to stay longer than a few minutes'. It was remembering that bit of jacket blurb that sealed the decision and my subsequent *modus operandi*. A number of the stories had filled me with a weird sense of dread, a sense that lingered after first reading them. That strong response felt like it was worth more exploration. Unlike the child who hid the book that frightened him in the next room, I am now drawn to explore things that engender fear, to look more deeply into them. Here was a golden opportunity to do some actual fieldwork. I decided that I would visit as many of the places that appeared in the stories from Aiden Fox's collection as I could, in emulation of Hippisley Coxe (particularly given that a good number of them were in my beloved Yorkshire). And I suppose that decision put the seal on the format I've adopted, too.

In many ways, this is a record of a voyage – the journey of discovery undertaken by a rational adult into the child's fascination and compulsion to lose himself in the irrational. In youth I yearned for the mystery itself, I wanted to enter it, experience it. As an adult I want to know what that mystery is, what lies behind it, what it really means, and as a consequence, perhaps discover what is truly real. So this is also a guidebook. It's intended to take you, the reader, on a journey literally as well as figuratively. And there is something seductive about the possibility that a number of readers, however small, might be impelled to set off on an expedition themselves; that, somewhere out there, other captivated children might be standing next to their own shrieking mothers as they go in search of a mystery, tantalisingly just behind the veil. Maybe they'll tear through to the other side as I was never able to. Sceptic I may be, but who am I to deny another an encounter with the ineffable?

Jeremy Dyson,
Yorkshire, 2012

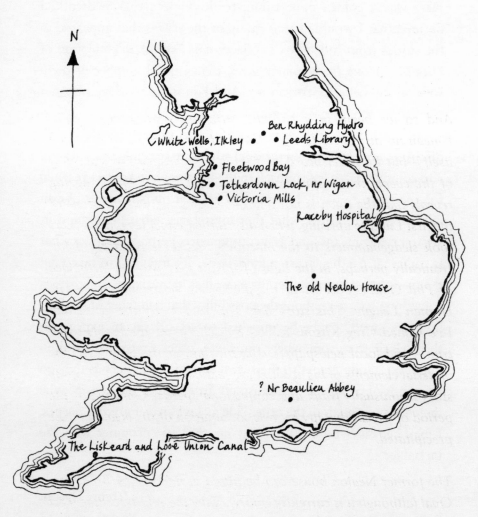

N

Ben Rhydding Hydro
White Wells, Ilkley • • • Leeds Library

• Fleetwood Bay
• Tetherdown Lock, nr Wigan
• Victoria Mills

Raceby Hospital

The old Nealon House

? Nr Beaulieu Abbey

The Liskeard and Looe Union Canal

The Selected Hauntings

And so we begin in a perhaps surprisingly anonymous place I mean no disrespect to the citizens of Hinckley, or to the town itself – but I'd never heard of it until I read Aiden Fox's account of the events that inspired the following story. A bit of digging reveals that the town is not without interest. It was the scene of the first Luddite uprising, when disgruntled Hinckley mill workers took sledgehammers to the machines that were replacing them. Ironically perhaps, in the light of this, it was also the birthplace of Phil Oakey, vocalist of the pioneering electronic group The Human League. This story was sent to Fox by the gentleman I've named Greg Kitson. Kitson himself claims the events to be true – and local newspapers confirm that, at the very least, the material elements of his account are factual. His own telling of the story is unusually frank and confessional, perhaps inspired by the period of psychotherapy his brief occupation of the Nealon house precipitated.

The former Nealon house can be found at number 24 Broadgate Oval (although it is currently empty). Take the A47 travelling west from the M1 (easily accessed from Junction 21) for about 6 km. Take a left on the B4468 for about another kilometre and you will find a turning on the left just after Hinckley Golf Club. This is Broadgate Oval, a circular street of 1930s detached and semi-detached houses. Hinckley serves as a dormer town to Leicester, which is less than 20 km away, and contains many such prosperous and attractive roads. You or I would walk or drive past the former Nealon house without it even registering on our consciousnesses. Its pleasant 1930s aesthetic has definite appeal, a certain style evident in its green-painted timbering linking it to a once recent, now increasingly distant. inter-war past. It was the kind of house my grandparents lived in, the kind of house I grew up in; as far removed from the metaphysical as one could imagine.

Before we set off, it's worth adding two things pertaining to the book you're reading, even at this, the earliest part of our journey together. My wife, who I run most things past, wondered why Aiden Fox wasn't writing this book himself, given that he was, after all, a journalist. Why wouldn't he want to claim full credit for his own research? I explained what he'd told me: that the kind of book he'd imagined wasn't the kind he felt able to produce, and that my guess was that he'd tried already and either got nowhere or had the thing knocked back. Something about this explanation didn't satisfy her, however, and if I'm honest it didn't fully satisfy me either. But I was already intoxicated with the prospect of what I was about to start work on, so I avoided probing any further. I was happy to share a credit with Aiden, and felt that in itself would surely resolve any potential material issues the situation might throw up. The second thing is more amusing. I'd decided to begin my journey to the Nealon house as early in the day as I could bear. The best route from Ilkley to Hinckley meant going via the M1 and driving past Sheffield, so I wanted to avoid the rush-hour traffic. It was still dark when I got in the car, and as I sat in the driver's seat about to put my key in the ignition I glanced in the rear-view mirror. The car is a hatchback, an old Peugeot 307, with a removable interior cover for the boot. The cover was in the house, where it had been since a trip to the recycling centre a couple of weeks earlier. This meant that the boot was uncovered, though I couldn't see what was in it in the mirror. Why did I want to see what was in it? Because I was abruptly gripped with the thought that there was somebody curled up in there, waiting to climb out – and that they would do so, once my journey was under way. Whilst I knew that this was the most absurdly clichéd straight-to-DVD horror-movie scenario my imagination could throw at me, that knowledge was not enough to negate the urge to get out of the car and check that the boot was actually empty. I was about to do it, too, until pride kicked in. I was an adult now, and a parent. I was no longer dictated to by such irrational urges. Of course, there was nobody in the car with me, hiding unseen in the back. This feeling was nothing but an atavistic remnant of some caveman need to check dark spaces for predators. I was above being governed by it. By an act of will, I turned the key in the ignition and reversed out of the drive. My faith in reason alone would be my guarantee that the car contained no concealed psychopaths, spirits or murderous ghouls.

But if I'm being honest with you – and I feel I should be – I wasn't actually free of the sense there was somebody there until I reached the M621, and the sun was rising over the Stourton interchange ahead of me.

Kitson from Nealon

Greg saw the house in the supplement that came with the local paper. He'd been renting a flat until he was sure that this job was going to be for him – after all, this was quite a change from his life in Brighton – but the job in Leicester was perfect: a senior marketing position with a company who produced the free gifts attached to the front of children's weekly magazines. When Greg was a boy magazines were called 'comics' and free gifts were a rarity coming once, at most twice, a year, perhaps to mark the launch of a new title or the merging of one title with another, or maybe even a notable anniversary such as a hundredth issue. Nowadays, the gifts came every week and were seen as a necessary part of the children's purchasing experience. Occasionally Greg caught the scent of disapproval in his attitude towards this development. The current generation would never know the thrill that came from the limiting of gratification. How he himself had looked forward to the second issue of *2000AD*, with its Bionic stickers that, placed on the reader's arm, created the illusion that he was in fact a living computer. Now such pleasures came weekly, no more special than a Sunday afternoon.

The job, however, was a good fit for him. Four days a week (and in truth he could get by doing three and a half), of which an amount could be done from home. The rest of the time he would be at the office in a pleasant part of Leicester, less than thirty minutes' drive away. This left half the week free for Greg to spend at his discretion.

He liked to go to London. He liked to go the gym. He was not unattractive – a fact he was comfortable admitting to himself now he was forty-one. He enjoyed wearing good clothes, and would travel to Nottingham to buy his suits, shirts and shoes from the big Paul Smith shop in Willoughby House. His marketing skills had given him a reasonably sophisticated understanding of human nature and this enabled him to pursue another of his favourite pastimes: the seduction and bedding of younger women. Because of his full head of blonde hair and good all-round physical condition, he could pass for mid-thirties. This easily gave him access to women in their early twenties, and sometimes younger. His favoured diversion would be to go to London on a Thursday evening, check into one of the more stylish hotels in the West End and then head out into town. He had definitely developed a scent for those in need of company. Girls from other countries, away from their homes, lonely in their offices and retail outlets. He knew the secret of attracting another was to become genuinely interested in them. It's true he never revealed that he wasn't looking for a long-term liaison, but he never felt he was being completely deceitful. He was respectful, generous; a skilful lover. The worst any of these women would be able to say was that they had enjoyed their time with him. Perhaps the fact that the phone number he gave them would prove useless was mendacious, but it was hardly abusive. He'd long ago discovered who he actually was and how he liked to live. Once he'd accepted this fact, he was free to carry on with the business of living.

When it came to family, he saw his mother several times a year. She lived in Dundee so distance was a legitimate reason for the restriction on these visits. As for his father, he could go fuck himself. He'd cut himself out of Greg's life when the extent of his infidelities – and what they'd done to Greg's mother – had become apparent.

There was much to occupy Greg's life beyond these amorous adventures. For one thing, there was his burgeoning collection of twentieth-century design. It had started in a small way, desk lamps, vases, glassware; but as his resources had grown it had extended into furniture, too. It was this sensibility that had led him to purchase the Nealon house and, albeit indirectly, to the disturbing events that followed.

The vendor – one Isaac Nealon – had lived at number 24 almost his entire life. He was born in Coalville, but moved to Hinckley with his mother and father in the early 1950s. Nealon's parents were both academics: his father an economist at Leicester University and his mother an art historian. Had Isaac Nealon been born thirty years later, he would have been diagnosed with autism. But at that time such classifications were reserved purely for schizophrenics, and so there was no label attached to Isaac Nealon other than the abusive ones used by the children on his street. His parents had tried to send the boy to school, but within two years it had become apparent that this was not going to work out, so they decided on the radical approach of educating the boy at home. Isaac had definite artistic ability, particularly as a draughtsman.

When Greg had bought the house (for what he considered to be a bargain price) the first thing he did was get it cleared and steam-cleaned from top to bottom. However, the company had neglected to attend to the attic. It was only when the plumber had to go up into the loft that Greg discovered the stash of what turned out to be nearly three thousand drawings. There was no indication how long they had been there. Some of the paper crumbled in his hands; some seemed to have been drawn on yesterday. More disturbing than their number, however, was the narrowness of focus of the drawings' subject. Almost exclusively, Isaac Nealon had produced studies of his own back garden. There was some variation in the viewpoint, but most of the scenes were framed by one of the upstairs windows. The later ones emphasised the overgrown rockery, to the rear of what had once been the lawn.

It wasn't just the dilapidated appearance of the house that had contributed to its catchpenny status, but also the aroma of derangement that clung to it even in the Nealons' absence. They had lived increasingly private lives after the parents' retirement. Isaac's mother had died in 1978 and his father had become as reclusive as Isaac after her death – apart from occasional bursts of seemingly random travel. When he had not returned after seven years from one of his sporadic excursions, the property legally became his son's. Then, when Isaac himself was committed to a care home in 2001, the house was put up for sale by a cousin.

By the time Greg actually moved in, the place had been transformed. He hadn't wanted to be there for the cleaning. The first time he'd viewed number 24 the smell had made him feel sick. But he'd been assured by the contractors that the house could be made as new and something about this literal whitewashing had been immensely appealing: to take something so evidently dysfunctional and make it clean and uncorrupted. While the house was undergoing its metamorphosis Greg travelled to London for a spot of recreational activity. There was an antique design fair in Islington; in addition, it had been several weeks since his last visit so Greg felt it was time for another foray into the bars and pubs of the West End. It was interesting to note that these intimate encounters were now firmly associated with travel in his mind. It did not occur to him to attempt them near home. He would no sooner have had one in the house itself than he would have taken a meal in his toilet.

It's worth making a diversion to describe the liaison that followed as it may cast some light on Greg's state of mind when he returned to Hinckley. In Greg's view what happened with Jasmin was not so different from any of his previous affairs – and maybe it wasn't – but it may just be pertinent to what occurred next.

Greg had refined his method over many years, more than two decades perhaps. Of course, he wasn't confident when he began, but gradually his self-assurance had grown and with it he found he'd acquired some kind of technique. Much of it involved acting 'as if'. He generally felt he was not worthy of serious attention, but it seemed that if he behaved counter to this, women would respond in kind. Deep down this did not convince Greg there had been any actual change in his essential character. But the physical encounters were gratifying enough in themselves for him to persist with them.

Greg met Jasmin in the American Bar at the Savoy, a location that satisfied his aesthetic sensibilities. Its very nature guaranteed a certain kind of clientele. The women one met there were often, as has already been noted, in their twenties, not promiscuous, in long-term relationships. The thrill for Greg, if he gave it any thought, though he was more comfortable not reflecting on it, was that he was persuading someone to do something they normally wouldn't – and, more importantly, that they were choosing him over some present partner. There was no doubt that the American Bar attracted a particular kind of romantic. A woman who perhaps wanted an escape from the everyday, from her routine dissatisfaction.

'Hi ...'

The girl looked up at him.

'Hello.'

'Are you alone?'

This approach hadn't been made cold. Greg was not stupid. Before he exchanged any words there had to have been a period of casual glances that escalated to the point of a shared smile. Once he had that information the conversation that followed was, as far as he was concerned, a mere formality.

'I'm meeting someone later,' she said.

Greg could tell this was a lie but nodded politely before continuing.

'Would you do me a favour?' he smiled sincerely. 'I'm *not* meeting anyone later. I'm utterly alone. Would you be kind enough to let me buy you a drink?' He could see suspicion in her dark eyes, but that was OK. He knew what to say to allay it.

'I don't think so.'

'What about something you wouldn't normally have? A Sauterne Cup?'

'What's a Sauterne Cup?'

'One of Harry Craddock's finest.' Greg had already caught the barman's eye.

'This isn't what I do, you know.'

'What?'

'Let pushy older men buy me drinks.'

She had black hair, cut into a short bob. She was small. On the edge of plump, definitely pretty, but with an air of sadness about her.

'So I look old?'

'Yes.'

She had some mischief to her. Some spirit. That could only be a good thing.

Her relationship was not in a good state. She worked – not happily – in the Space NK shop in Covent Garden. She'd studied Design History in Manchester. This gave them a good deal to talk about. Greg's travelling persona did not work for the toy company. Rather, he was a buyer for a small chain of design shops that sold historical and classic household items ranging from kitchen equipment and desk lamps to chairs, sofas and cabinets. His fictional job, which gave him great satisfaction, was to scour jumble sales, car boots and house clearances and organise the restoration of anything of interest he found. As he spoke, he became so enthused about this imaginary version of his life that he found himself wondering why he did not actually live it. But there was a price to be paid for everything – an attitude that was the one thing of his father's he'd allowed himself to keep. If he had followed the former path he would doubtless be earning half his current salary and would not be able to play the game he was now engaged in playing. Of the two possible freedoms, he preferred this one.

A few more drinks took them into the Banquette restaurant, where Greg switched from enchanting her with his enthusiasm to a more focused form of listening. Listening, being seen to listen, was the key to progressing matters to the next stage. He sensed that things were not good with Jasmin and her boyfriend. She said 'boyfriend' rather than 'partner'. If Greg was being honest, this excited him further. It made her feel younger. She'd been with him since college.

She desired a deepening commitment, but the longer they spent together, the more he seemed to want to please himself. He would devote hours to his Wii but would not take seriously her request that they share more edifying activities. Greg nodded throughout this account. Strangely, she never asked him whether he was married. Maybe she didn't want to know. Of course, he had no ring. Greg carefully judged her alcohol tolerance and ordered the drinks accordingly. He didn't want her insensible, desiring instead that she remain just below the peak of her alcoholic high.

'I need to call Neil.'

'Sure.'

Greg sat on the end of his bed, giving her some version of privacy. Her voice was low. She turned away from him, facing the elegantly exposed brick of the hotel wall. He tried to focus his attention elsewhere, unwilling to bear the discomfort of her troubles.

'I can't. No.' A pause. 'At a friend's. It doesn't matter. It doesn't matter. Why does it matter? Just a friend's. Someone from work. No. No. Neil. No. Why? Because I don't want to. Because I can't. I just can't.'

Overheard in this way, there was a madness to the conversation. Eventually, Jasmin pocketed the phone. Greg turned to her. Her eyes were wet with tears. He cast the observation from his mind, opened his arms to her. Held her.

'It's all right.'

'I'm really tired of him.'

'I know.'

'He doesn't – '

'It's all right. I promise you.'

Greg moved a lock of her dark hair out of the way and over her ear. It was a large ear, given the smallness of the rest of her head.

He kissed the side of her neck as gently as he could.

The following morning he ordered breakfast, but she'd said she had to leave; that she needed to get home to change, wanted to be there before Neil went to work. She asked Greg for his number. And Greg did the slightly eccentric thing he did now after any of these encounters, when it became apparent that the other party wanted this information. He dialled them so they had his number in their phone, and then – the minute they were out of the hotel room – he threw away the pay-as-you-go mobile that he'd bought at Euston Station, removing the sim card and snapping it in two. There was an element of ritual about this action, he knew. As for the expense, it was relatively minor and more than worth what it bought in peace of mind.

When Greg arrived back at Hinckley, the house was ready for him. As he approached the green-painted front door, he caught himself referring to it as the Nealon house. He had to stop that. It was his house now. The Kitson house. He'd owned flats before – two flats – but they were cells within a larger organism. This was an organism in itself. It felt like he was finally established. Inevitably, as he inserted the key into the lock he thought of the small semi in Glossop where he'd grown up. His mother waiting, more often than not alone, her husband away on one of his 'business trips' or 'golf weekends'. Nothing would ever be said about them.

Greg saw the telephone as soon as he walked into the bedroom. The decorators must have found it in one of the cupboards. Perhaps to the less-educated eye it would have been unremarkable, a dusty relic of the 1930s. But he immediately recognised its value. It was a 200 Series model manufactured by Siemens. Fashioned in Bakelite, rather than the later cellulose acetate models. It was not uncommon to see them in black, or ivory. But this one was red. Bright red. It must have been made around the time that the Nealon house was built. It even had its original jack-plug. Sadly, that would have to be replaced with a contemporary connector, but that was an easy job.

Pleased with this unexpected bonus, he took it downstairs, pausing by the stairwell window. It was only as he stood there, his forehead against the cooling glass, that he registered how clean everything was. The interior design company had done a fine job. The whitewashed walls and polished floorboards made it feel like a new-build. He looked out into the garden. The lawn had been mowed and the beds – if one could dignify the narrow strips of earth with that description – had been weeded and turned over. Even the rockery had been lent new life, its small whited boulders now clearly visible, standing out like knuckles against the shrubbery behind.

He sat the red telephone on the kitchen table and stared at it for a while, wondering where to put it. In an age of soulless, ugly, grey handsets here was something solid from a more substantial past (the past had so much more substance than the present, thought Greg, of course it did – it was already defined). The eccentricity of the thing pleased him. Yes, he wouldn't have the modern luxury of walking around the place conducting phone conversations – but the truth was he didn't like talking on the phone. Better to let the apparatus serve as ornament. He wandered out into the hallway, to see if there was an obvious place to put it. Maybe he'd have to purchase a small table to place the thing on, but that was hardly an imposition. It was as he had this thought that he noticed the telephone socket. It wasn't one of the new ones. They'd been placed over in the corner on the narrow wall at the back of the kitchen. This was one of the house's original sockets – a small box with rounded edges that rested atop the skirting board. It had been painted over more than once. His decorators must have missed it, for the paint was yellowing and a small patch of it was flaked in its lower corner, revealing an earthy brown beneath. A sudden thought made Greg laugh. It was silly, but why not? He went to the kitchen, came back with the red phone. The old cable felt hard and brittle resting against his fingers as he carried it through to the hallway. He held up the jack-plug, admired its nippled end, the two circles of dark ceramic embedded within a bronze cylinder. He sat on the floor, placed the phone down and, despite being aware of the action's perversity, he inserted the jack into the redundant socket. There was only a little resistance requiring a brief, effortful push to oppose and then the jack clicked into place, the sprung mechanism of the socket closing satisfyingly around it. Greg sat cross-legged on the floor of the hallway, his back against the stained-oak panelling of the stair-wall. He moved the red telephone onto his lap, picked up the receiver; it was possible that the old telephone cabling was still connected to the line. He listened for a dialling tone, the plastic circle of the receiver cold against his ear.

Nothing.

Actually, not quite nothing. There was a low hiss of white noise. Electrical. Distant. Maybe the new line hadn't been connected yet. As if in answer to the thought, the telephone started ringing. His modern Panasonic handset. It was plugged in upstairs in the bedroom.

When Greg returned five minutes later, having taken the call from work, the old phone was waiting for him on the wooden floor, the receiver expectantly uncradled. Reflexively, he held it to his ear once again. The gentle hiss remained, undulating slightly, like a far away sea. Or a breath. He put the receiver down, the twin black terminating buttons clicking loudly as they were depressed.

There was one more job to do in the garden before Greg felt the house was his. He'd asked the landscape company to clear the shrubbery at the rear of the rockery but they had left a note to say regulations forbade it because they'd found the remains of some asbestos panelling that would have to be dealt with by a certified disposal company. Upon investigation this turned out to be two small pieces of insulating board that Greg could put in a refuse sack himself and take down to the recycling centre. No one would know what it was once it had been thrown in the household-waste skip. The cost of professional collection could be better spent on a telephone table he was watching on eBay.

He held his breath as he picked the boards up, irritated to discover that there was quite a bit of other stuff left to clear. He wondered exactly what he'd been paying the landscape company to do; it seemed that they'd mowed the lawn, weeded the beds and that was all. It was late afternoon and the sky was already darkening. This small unkempt area of trees and bushes felt clogged and enclosing, closer to wild woodland than a garden. Greg pulled at some weeds, revealing an uneven pile of bricks and a small mortar spreader, cemented into a rusted roasting tin. He kicked at the detritus with his foot. There was something else behind it, a cardboard grocery box, puffy with damp and mould. He prodded at its surface. The cardboard gave way immediately, dissolving like a ghost and revealing a line of tins with rusted tops and faded labels. Greg suddenly wanted to be back in the house. He turned to look over his shoulder. The squat bulk of the rockery sat between him and the comforting amber glow of the living room. Reluctantly he turned back to his task and bent down, gingerly picking up one of the decaying cans.

'It was all he ate.'

Greg jumped up, scraping the side of his cheek on the scratchy finger of a hawthorn branch.

'I'm sorry.'

It was an elderly woman speaking. She had a happy, red-cheeked face.

'I'm sorry. Oh – I didn't mean to startle you.' She was holding a dish covered in cling film. Her hair merged with the scrubby thin branches around it. 'Forgive me. I've been meaning to say hello. I came round last week, hoping to find you. Your workmen said you were away. I promise I won't be round every day. I really wanted to say hello. It's so important to greet people properly, don't you think?'

Greg stood upright, moved round so the light wasn't behind her.

'I'm Margaret. Margaret Day. I'm next door.' She rebalanced the plate on her left forearm, freeing her other hand to hold out and shake. Greg put down the rusting can of beans, began to formulate his response. Before he could speak she was off again. 'It was all he ate, you know – Nealon the Younger. He only ever walked round to the Spar. He survived on what you could buy at that shop.' She nodded down at the rusting, sodden tins.

'Hi.' He smiled. 'I'm Greg. Greg Kitson.'

'Oh. Mr Kitson. It's a pleasure to meet you. It really is.'

Greg shook her thin, age-mottled hand. It was warm in the cold damp air. 'There's a gate, you see. Not that I habitually use it. But I saw you in the garden. I so wanted to catch you.' There was a moment of expectant silence. She was hoping he would invite her in. In that moment he resented her. 'I baked you this.' She withdrew her hand from his so she could pass him the cake. He took it.

'That really is very very kind of you,' he said. He could see her face more clearly now. It was smooth-skinned, round-cheeked. Her body was hidden in a dark blue raincoat that continued almost all the way to the floor.

'Oh, it's nothing, I assure you. Baking is all I do nowadays. I'm widowed, you see. I fill the hours with patisserie.' She laughed again. Greg laughed, too.

'It's still very kind.'

More silence. He wasn't going to yield. If he did now, even though there was part of him that welcomed her warmth, he would never be rid of her. He could see her coming round every day. The weary thought of it stretched ahead, suffocating him.

'You would see him there. Younger Nealon. Sometimes in his pyjamas. He was quite shameless.' She was babbling to fill the silence. 'I don't think there was anything really wrong with him. He was odd. But not sick. Not like people said. When the father took up and left – and he was an odd man, let me tell you – a committed socialist – a communist actually, I think. Of course, he was terribly unhappy after Mrs Nealon died. Hardly a surprise he went off like that. He thought he'd become a burden to the boy, you know. Old people do think they're a burden. Though I promise I shan't be to you.' She laughed enthusiastically. Greg made himself echo her laughter. Another moment's pause.

'Well – it's been lovely to meet you,' Greg heard himself saying. She would go now.

'And you.'

'And thank you for the cake. I'll bring the plate back round.'

'That's so kind of you, Mr Kitson. Very kind. And I'll introduce you to Molly. My pup. She'll be no bother either, I assure you. She's a King Charles – very even-tempered.'

Greg watched the old woman push off through the undergrowth, disappearing into the twilight. Holding her cake, he turned back to the decomposing tins of beans. He bent down to pick them up and placed them in the refuse sack, pulling his sleeves over his hands as he did so. He didn't want to touch them with bare skin.

The house was unusually quiet at night. It's true that Greg had never lived in a detached house before, but he was surprised at the silence that enveloped him when he climbed into bed. He lay there trying to ignore it, if one could ignore silence. With the television switched off the house had fallen almost immediately into a cavernous hush, encouraged by the wooden floors and sparsely furnished rooms. He was discomfited by the cluster of feelings that emerged when he turned out the light. He didn't bother naming any of them, but they were unpleasant. He would strain in the darkness to hear signs of life beyond his heavy curtains. Strangely, even a passing car brought comfort. On the third or fourth night, as sleep began to pull at him, unravelling consciousness, a sharp crack reverberated somewhere off in the emptiness of the house and it was enough to snap Greg awake, his heart suddenly racing. He became so alarmed by this, he set out to discover the source of the noise. It turned out to be the refrigerator – something to do with its cooling mechanism. He had the problem fixed and, for a week or so, the silence became just silence. Until, that is, the following happened.

It was somewhere around three o'clock. He'd lain there for some time, listening hard. Once more, he'd been woken by a click. Not the loud, echoing crack like the fridge had been making. This was softer, more delicate. He lay there, alert, tense, his breath caught, to see if it recurred.

Click.

Then silence.

He started breathing again, but in short shallow bursts. He was cold all over, lying with his cheek against his wrist. He could feel the scamper of his pulse – like vermin pattering, trapped in a box.

Eventually he got out of bed. Turning on the lights helped. He went to the curtains, pulled them to one side. The street was dark, with occasional pools of orange light revealing wet pavements. Nothing moved.

Click.

Greg whirled around. He forced himself to relax, to breathe. What did he think it was? Be rational. An intruder? He moved out into the lightless landing, his hand reaching ahead of him for the switch. The light bulb dispersed the darkness, but not the dread. He peered down over the banister to the empty entrance hall. The stairwell light-switch was about a metre away. Moving slowly and silently, he flicked that, too. Of course, there was nothing to see. Greg stopped himself from calling out 'hello'.

Quietly, deliberately, Greg descended the stairs. He switched on a light in every room, from each doorway. The house was empty. He stood in the hallway, feeling foolish, a slice of cold air hitting his bare feet through the bottom of the front door.

Click.

Greg spun around. There was the red phone, semi-forgotten, its black cable coiled serpentine beneath it.

It was only an electrical fault. He knew already there was current passing through the old cabling because of the hiss on the line. Fluctuations in that current would be enough to trip the mechanism inside the telephone. The solution was to unplug it. He was not going to do that. Because to do that would be to admit to or be governed by an irrational fear. So he left it plugged in. Back in his bed, a dim thought came to him as he hovered uneasily on the edge of sleep: perhaps there was an even less rational fear behind that one – what he didn't want to risk hearing was the click still occurring with the phone disconnected from its ancient socket.

Although it had been less than three weeks since he had made his last visit, Greg started thinking it was time to go to London again. He could feel it calling him. It helped him deal with the discomfort of lying there in bed: imagining the thrill of meeting someone he didn't know, visualising the game of it, intuiting their personality, their weaknesses, their foibles, manoeuvering himself mentally into a position where he could use what he'd perceived to persuade them up to his hotel room. The quickening excitement of getting them to undress, lying with them – feeling their vulnerability at his side.

He began to use these thoughts more frequently than usual, as an escape pod from the now-nightly fear he was experiencing in the dark. Sleeping with the lights on didn't help. Perversely, it made things worse, as if by lying there, fully illuminated, he was somehow drawing attention to himself.

During the day, on days that he wasn't working, he found himself in the garden. This was a surprise, but he realised that he was more comfortable out of the house, looking in. The leaves were beginning to brown and thin. Shrunken, prematurely fallen conkers lined the bottom of the fence, their curtailed spikes broken in places revealing unripe white testes within. Greg stood, holding a rake, staring at the rockery. It was an unusual shape looked at straight-on; more of its silhouette had now been revealed by the barer branches of the trees at either side. It was hump-backed, like a tortoise's shell, but sliced off abruptly at one end. This flattened side was surrounded by a small clump of hawthorns and rhododendron bushes – a shrub Greg had always disliked, reminding him of the tight, plain parks of his childhood. Leaning the rake against the fence that backed onto Mrs Day's, Greg walked towards the bushes, pulling his gardening gloves down tighter over his wrists. Reaching out as he approached the rhododendron, he pushed its dark, plasticky leaves to one side. The bushes had been planted tight against the flattened end of the hillock and it took some effort to prise apart the thick branches and expose what was beneath. The end of the little hill was lined with dark rocks arranged like a dry-stone wall, except they had been crudely cemented together. It was an odd arrangement because it looked amateurish, whereas the rest of the mound had been quite neatly and professionally laid out. Greg leaned forward, the smell of moist earth cold in his nostrils. The mortar had come away between two of the rocks. Something else was visible behind it. Then the phone started ringing from the house.

Greg turned sharply. It was a sound he hadn't heard for twenty years. A metal bell being struck at speed by a vibrating mechanical clapper. Without thinking, he was running towards the open back door. Almost as he entered, the ringing stopped. There was the phone, now on its little Deco table. Even in these circumstances Greg found a beat in which to appreciate how beautifully the shiny scarlet Bakelite stood out against the polished walnut of the table's surface. He gripped the handset, held it to his ear, even though the phone had stopped ringing. Maybe he hoped that he might just catch the caller, whoever they might be. He pressed the earpiece harder against the side of his head and frowned. He placed his left forefinger into his left ear to concentrate all his listening attention into what was coming out of the seven pepperpot holes on the other side of his head.

Ffffffffffffffffffffffffffffffffffffffffffffffffffffffffffffffffffffffffffffffffffffffff . . .

A low and constant drift of nothing – perceptible nothing. But nothing.

Wait.

Ffffffffffffffffeeehhhhhhhhhhh.

It was a slow-moving alteration in the tone of the sound. Like something ancient and ossified and dead trying to force itself back to the memory of life.

Eehhhhhhhhhhhhhhhhhhhhhhfffffffffffffffffffffffffffffffffffff.

It was gone. Wasn't it?

Fffffffffffffffffffffffffffffffffffffff.

He pressed the earpiece harder against his head, with enough pressure to hurt. The hiss remained constant. The line alive, yes, but only with the sound of its own disconnection.

This was madness. And with that thought, Greg unplugged the cable from its socket, wrapped it around the old telephone and threw it into the back of the Josef Frank cabinet in the lounge, shutting the door on it with a satisfying click.

That night he did something he'd never done before. He knew he wouldn't sleep. Or rather, he knew he wouldn't be able to turn the light off in his bedroom and that in itself would prevent sleep. So he got in the car and drove out towards Leicester. He ended up going further; Leicester felt too close. He drove on up the M1 as far as Junction 25, thinking he'd head into Nottingham. But there, glowing green in the night, just off the motorway, was a Holiday Inn. He pulled into the car park, feeling suddenly comfortable and safe again with the thought of the possibility of a thrilling encounter. It was different from his usual MO, but that was OK. There was nothing wrong with shaking things up a little.

The bar was quiet, the decor awful. All polished wood veneers over MDF, offset against a hideous black carpet. Nevertheless, he was hooked by the chance of an adventure. He ordered a Jack Daniels and Coke to help things on their way. If necessary he could book a room, stay for the night. He didn't have to drive home at all if he didn't want to.

A group of other men came, older than Greg, in their fifties, their shirts pulled tight against the swell of their tummies. One of them glanced over and Greg looked away. He got his phone out of his pocket, pretending to check his emails. He ordered some bar food, Cajun Spiced Chicken on a Herb Focaccia. An Americano coffee would take away any flavour that lingered too strongly on his breath. It didn't have to be a young girl. He was prepared to give himself some headroom. Someone in their thirties would be fine. And when the women walked in, he thought she would be perfect.

'Hello.'

'Hiya – '

'Are you alone?'

As usual, this approach followed a non-verbal preamble. It was notably easier than usual, or at least it happened at a faster pace.

'I'll say.' The woman beamed at Greg. The sun of the Jack Daniels he'd been downing was still rising within. She was bathed in its benevolent glow.

'Would you do me a favour?' He felt like a wedding DJ, parroting his shtick; the same every gig, regardless of the venue. 'I'm utterly alone. Would you be kind enough to let me buy you a drink, share ten minutes of your time?'

She laughed. 'Darling, you had me at "hello".'

She was called Liza. She worked as an on-the-road rep for a workspace services provider ('Sanitary products, darling, between you and me, but we're not allowed to call them that any more'). She laughed a lot. He wasn't looking too closely but he guessed she was in her late thirties. She liked to drink, more than him. And she wondered if he'd like to continue the drinks in her room? Although there wasn't a mini-bar as such, she kept a bottle of vodka in her bag and they could ask for some ice to take up.

He waited in the bed while she was in the bathroom, the blanket scratching at his bare arms. He wondered if blankets were used anywhere other than budget-priced hotels nowadays? The wardrobe to his side was mirrored. He turned, saw his face, his pale hair. He looked like somebody's father. He turned away, pulling the blanket up further. Suddenly squeamish, he leaned his right ear against his shoulder, pressed his left hand against his other ear, hummed slightly in case he heard her urinating. When she emerged from the bathroom she was in her underwear. She was drunker than he was. She fumbled for the light-switch, to turn it off. He caught the line and sag of her bulging midriff. It reminded him of the middle-aged men in the hotel bar. There were the threads of veins visible in her legs. She was older than he realised, maybe even older than him. She was on the bed before he could speak. He smelt soap. Felt a hint of her cold bulk.

'Shove up.'

She would warm up soon enough. He was simply warmer than her because he was under the covers. But the cold spread within. Any possibility of excitement or arousal had fled. What was he going to do? He would persist. He couldn't leave. She lifted the blankets a little in order to unstrap her bra. She pulled at her knickers. In the low light he caught a glimpse of a thick mat of

44

pubic hair. She was on him, kissing him wetly. It was all right. He could use her like a hand.

He ended up leaving. She'd pulled at his semi-erect penis, but been unable to coax it into anything functioning. He'd rubbed at her crotch in a desultory manner and then said he felt sick and he would have to go. She'd started shouting. He pulled his trousers on in the hotel corridor. She came after him, standing in the hotel corridor wrapped in a towel, screaming, and he left the premises with his shoes in his hand. He drove off barefoot.

When he got back home, Greg turned on all the lights and sat there in the front room staring at the undulating black lines of the Marimekko curtains. He ran a bath but was too tired to actually get in it and rolled into bed without putting his pyjamas on.

He woke abruptly, having heard a loud noise in his dream. All he could remember was the last part of it – it was him as a child, a boy of seven or eight. But it was confusing because he was the father of the child, too. The child was naked, slick, covered from head to toe in his father's semen. The noise was a metallic, mechanised ringing, amplified almost beyond endurance. At least it had been in the dream. Now he was awake, there was a noise but it was much quieter. Was it there at all? He had to strain to hear it. Was it not the wind, blowing against the double slice of the telephone cables fastened to the junction box outside the bedroom window? Or was it even less substantial, some kind of tinnitus deep within the mechanism of his ear? For the second time that night he pressed a hand against the side of his head. There was a definite timbre. A definite clangorous ring. But then it got louder when he pulled his hand away.

Reluctantly – but knowing he had to, for sleep would not come again until he did – he climbed out of the bed and went to the door. He turned on the light. The ringing was louder still. The sound continued growing as he descended the stairs.

He knew where to go. Perhaps he was still dreaming. The dark wooden cabinet in the corner of the living room waited for him. It felt like a hutch – something alive in it. The feeling was confirmed when he pulled open the door and saw the red phone in the back corner coiled in its cable, curled up, needing him. He reached for it. It didn't vibrate. Of course it didn't. Nevertheless, he unwound the cable, took it out into the hallway and plugged it into the old socket. He didn't want it to ring in actuality, so he lifted the receiver first. He pressed it hard against the side of his head. Impossible to tell now, in the thick of nighttime, whether the soft burr was electrical or merely blood rushing through the capillaries and veins around his auditory nerves. Whatever it was, his mind assigned it sense, found meaning forming out of the inchoate chaos. First a long, drawn out sigh – like a final breath reversed. Ayyyhhhettttthhhhtttttt. Then five distinct sounds. Geehhh. Meeeeeeeee. Ouuuuuuuu. Ohhhhhh. Heeeeeeeeeee.

Greg was unable to stop his instinctive response.

'What?'

How he wished he'd been able to keep silent, though, when his question brought a reply. The sound of it alone seemed to burn his ear. It had told him exactly where he needed to look.

He stood in the garden, having turned on every light in the house, opened every curtain to fill the outside with as much light as he could. He had no torch, but did have a book light. A line of five LEDs that cast a piercing whiteness into the dark. He'd balanced it on a hawthorn bush facing the flat side of the rockery. It was relatively easy to pull the stones away. What mortar was left crumbled like sand. Soon what was behind was revealed. Seven planks of wood – sawn-off floorboards – shoring up the side of the rockery and dotted with thick-rusted nail heads. There had to be some kind of wooden frame the mound was built around. Greg went to the boot of the car, which held a rudimentary toolkit. Finding a little crowbar meant for levering tyres from wheels, he returned, possessed by a sense of urgency he didn't understand. Working fast, he inserted the chisel-shaped edge in between the gap in the first two planks and pulled. The wood, though old, was thick and well-preserved and at first he didn't feel he would have the strength to shift it. But then, with some exertion, the first plank began to move. Greg worked the chisel back and forth and, once there was space, used both hands to free the arrangement further. The harsh brightness of the LEDs revealed the more regular tessellation of a brick wall.

It had the look of a DIY job. The bricklaying was imperfect and uneven. Was there something behind it? He already knew the answer to that question. He chipped at some of the mortar where it seemed loosest. A clump came away, enough for him to wriggle a finger within and feel what was behind. Something with a shiny surface. He pulled at the brick. It came loose with ease. Then it was a simple matter to remove some of the others. More planks of wood, but these were finished, painted with green gloss. Soon most of the wall had come away and he was faced with a door, although one from which the handle had been removed. There was a bored hole, filled with plastic wood. The door sat within a frame and it had been nailed shut around its outer edges. Taking up his crowbar, and with even greater urgency, Greg found a gap to insert it. He pushed the iron in with the grim determination of someone forcing themselves into a doctor's surgery for a feared diagnosis. He pulled hard. The wood snapped, effectively making a little unevenly shaped window. Greg reached for the book light, swinging its piercing beam within. He caught a glimpse of a bowed, ridged roof. It was an Anderson shelter, from the Second World War. The rockery had been built over it. There was the edge of a bunk bed. He tried to swing the light to reveal it further. There was material on the bed, folded. He baulked at the smell, like sewage. Using his hands, he pulled at the wood to try and make a bigger hole. He succeeded in breaking some more off; it fragmented like balsa in his fingers. He pushed the light against the hole, driving out the darkness. Something was in the bunk bed. Twisting his hand, Greg followed its line with the beam. The flash he caught made him yell out loud and he dropped the booklight. However brief, the glimpse was enough to have created an image he would take with him to his own death. A face. Or the remains of one. What was left of the eyes were wide – in an eternally silent scream.

The police came quickly. Young Mr Nealon had already passed on, the care home informed them, only a few weeks earlier as it happened; so he couldn't be questioned, not that he would have been much help anyway. Mrs Day next door, it transpired, was more useful, particularly when it came to the dates. The discovery of the body told its own, clear story. Old Mr Nealon had never left. He'd become ill and Young Nealon didn't want the responsibility, for whatever reason. He placed him in the rockery and sealed it up. Had he been dead before he went in there? Probably. No one could say for sure.

Greg didn't want to spend another night there. His first thought was to go home to his mother, but he couldn't face that either. As quickly as he could, he found rented accommodation. He took nothing from the house with him at all. Nothing. He was going to buy everything new. Two suitcases full of clothes and that was all. Although his first thought upon moving in to the new place was to disconnect the phone, he fought against the urge. Something had to change.

This thought brought him comfort when he threw back the lid of his largest suitcase and found, though he had not placed it there himself, the red Bakelite telephone cradled within – the rotten black cable coiled around it like a conquering worm.

My *childhood interest in the supernatural came with certain assumptions, chiefly that encounters with the metaphysical took place in the past, somewhere in the previous fifty to two hundred years. Without realising it, this was most likely because my idea of the paranormal was entirely formed by the literary and media conventions I had been exposed to. Almost exclusively these ghost stories were historical in nature. I think the only contemporary portrayals of these phenomena I'd come across were in children's TV programmes. One series called* Shadows *specialised in creepy stories, often involving schoolchildren of my age and in lonely and abandoned places. Another one,* The Georgian House, *involved contemporary children becoming ghosts themselves by going back in time.*

One of the appeals of Aiden Fox's collection was the abundance of current encounters. The Nealon story took place in the twenty-first century, as does the next account. Indeed some of you may even know of Ramon Huld, not through any associations with the uncanny, but simply because of his background and the manner of his disappearance. Perhaps unusually, the 'haunting' associated with Huld (and he is still only missing presumed dead, as no body was ever found) is not connected with the place of his disappearance.

As I drove north-west to the coast, I was still musing on the fact that this, my second journey, must be a tacit acceptance that I was now writing Aiden Fox's book for him. For a few days I'd been trying to remember what that situation reminded me of. At first I thought it was M. R. James' story 'Casting the Runes', where an unfortunate academic is unknowingly passed a curse by a black magician whose paper on alchemy the academic has rebuffed. But the shape of my encounter hardly fitted this template. It was only as I was writing up notes from my visit to Hinckley that I recalled, with a smile, what I was actually thinking of. My great-uncle, Jack Hirst, had been a keen teller of Chassidic tales and one of my favourites was the story of Eleazer of Worms and the Sefer ha-Razim.

Eleazer of Worms was a thirteenth-century German Jewish mystic known for his visions and magical acts. He was as wily as he was learned. When the remains of a legendary book of magic known as the Sefer ha-Razim came into his possession, both these attributes proved beneficial.

The Sefer ha-Razim (or 'Book of Secrets') was, according to legend, King Solomon's most prized possession: a text that contained a much older text hidden magically within it, one supposedly revealed to Noah by the angel Raziel. When accessed, this work gave the possessor access to the power of creation itself; but, as might be expected, for Eleazer there was a catch. The version that had come into his hands via the ancient synagogue of Fostat, near Cairo, was in such a state of decay that many of its sections would only survive being handled once. However, if the complex rituals and incantations it contained were to be performed correctly, they would have to be referred to many more times than that. The scroll would therefore have to be copied as soon as possible, and by a biblical scholar, too. Of course, Eleazer himself could do the job, but he had enough learning to know that to do so would be fatal. Part of the wisdom the Sefer ha-Razim contained detailed the holiest of all knowledge

– the so-called 'twenty-two paths of wisdom' derived from the twenty-two letters of the Hebrew alphabet. This knowledge teaches that these very letters of the alphabet are the building blocks out of which God constructs creation itself, and that for a mortal man to write the specifics of such information down – even in a coded form – is a blasphemy of such a great order that upon completion of the task a 'Ruchim' or dark spirit would immediately appear and transport the blasphemer directly to Sheol (the place we might call the 'afterlife'). How was Eleazer of Worms to solve this conundrum? The parchment was rotting by the day, in the damp German air, and he needed a biblical scholar unscholarly enough not to know of these dangers. Now, it just so happened that there was a learned Rabbi in the town who, shall we say, did not have a low opinion of himself. Knowing this, Eleazer went to speak with him.

'Reb Yochannan,' said Eleazer, making himself appear as humble as possible in his entreaty. 'I need some advice from a wise man, so naturally I must come to you.'

'Of course,' said the Rabbi, already kvelling (we might say 'glowing with pride'), for he was easily flattered.

'I have an old Sefer I need transcribing, but it is beyond my skills to decipher the text. It is in ancient Hebrew and I thought you, of all people, would know of a scholar in Ludwigshafen or Mainz who might be up to the task.'

'Eleazer,' said the Rabbi, already smiling. 'Why subject yourself to a day's ride unnecessarily? Let me have a look, for I studied such Sifrim in my time as a student in Lodz. I may be able to fill the gaps in your knowledge.'

'Thank you, Reb Yochannan, thank you. I would be honoured if you would look for me.'

Three mornings later Eleazer came into his front room to discover that Reb Yochannan had indeed completed the task. Of course, the old Rabbi himself was never seen again, and Eleazer had his transcription. Even better, the work had been carried out free, for to feed a man's pride never costs the feeder. It is the sinner himself who pays.

Leave the M55 at Junction 3, taking the A585 signposted 'Kirkham/ Fleetwood'. Head towards the town centre, staying on the A585 until it becomes Dock Street and then the Esplanade. Take a right onto the outer promenade and you will see Fleetwood Bay on your right.

Fleetwood itself is a quiet seaside municipality about fifteen kilometres north of Blackpool. Until the latter part of the last century it was a thriving fishing port and its architecture exhibits much of the same faded Victorian grandeur to be encountered at other points around the British coastline. What hasn't changed – for tens of thousands of years at least – is the topography of the beach itself. Like the rest of that north-western coastal region, low tides are extreme and the sea will retreat for a mile or more, exposing huge flat expanses of mud-brown sand.

Walking these great stretches can be an intimidating experience. There is something profound and overwhelming about the emptiness one feels there. Without landscape, distance becomes impossible to judge. Without sun, under a grey sky, the sands feel like an abyss.

It was on this beach, and under such conditions, that – according to Aiden Fox's notes – reports of an occurrence came not once, or even twice, but on five separate occasions. In the first account, the 'apparition' was observed walking some five hundred *metres from the shore by an individual who knew Ramon Huld personally. They were shocked to see him, given it was more than two years since his disappearance. The second and third times the witnesses did not report knowing Huld but recognised him from local newspaper reports. For those that aren't aware, Huld was a round-the-world yachtsman; or rather, a would-be round-the-world yachtsman. He was an enthusiastic amateur who'd crossed over into the realm of the professional and entered the Route du Rhoum in 2002. His solo round-the-world attempt began in 2007, but he was never to return.*

His boat was eventually found – extensively damaged – off the coast of South Africa, near Port Elizabeth, washed up in a private nature reserve. There was no sign of a body and none has ever been recovered.

For a time, Huld was in touch with his team via radio and email, though his communications became increasingly sporadic and confused. It seemed that he suffered some kind of breakdown under the relentlessly brutal sailing conditions, which must have contributed to his ultimate fate.

What follows is my extrapolation from the fragmented journal entries recovered from the vessel.

The Diary of Ramon Huld

DAY ONE: 13/11/07

Well, here we are – the first day. It's hard to believe it has arrived. On occasions, as a child, I would appear in school plays and there was little pleasure in this for me aside from a sort of perverse enjoyment of the slow build-up of tension over the weeks that preceded the performance. At first this took the form of a revelling in how far away it all was: 'Oh, I can enjoy myself today – it's so long before I have to appear on the stage.' As the days passed, the balance of this cosy, pleasant thrill would shift towards a more uncomfortable feeling. I would glance at the calendar that hung next to the telephone and count the days, seeking respite in the cushion of their number. As they diminished, the fear would become overwhelming. It reached such a pitch towards the end that I couldn't believe the time would ever come when I would be on that stage. This, I imagined, must be how the condemned man feels in his cell. Ridiculous, of course, because I was in no physical peril; the worst thing that could happen would be that I forgot my lines. Why did the possibility of that humiliation feel like death? It was madness, really. Nevertheless, the relief when the ordeal was finally over contained the rush of a reprieve.

This voyage will be different. I love the sea, I adore it. Every single aspect of it. Even when the waves are like mountains and there is no end to their rise and fall. I love the smell of the salt. The constant roar. Even the cold and the wind become friends. Because it is just them and me – and nothing intervenes. I know myself in those moments. That is what I seek, that communion.

But this is going to be hard. It is the furthest I have ever sailed. The furthest anyone can sail. It will be tough. I will be tested. The *Ashray* – will be tested. (The boat was named, incidentally, not by me but by Franz Breuggemann, one of her designers. An Ashray is a creature from Scottish myth. The word means 'water lover', and it describes a being that is completely translucent and lives submerged beneath the waves. It is nocturnal and if captured and exposed to sunlight it melts, leaving only a puddle of water. My *Ashray* is more substantial. She is a multi-hulled vessel – a trimaran – and Breuggemann says she is the finest boat he has ever built.)

As I sail up the Wyre, away from the yacht club, there are a few people gathered to watch my passage. There was more fuss at the club itself, with the local radio and television. The people here, however, are genuine spectators and they are strangely silent as I pass. I wave, feeling it my duty to do so. How wonderful that soon I will be completely free of all social obligations. Just me, the *Ashray* and the ocean.

The wind is changing. I can feel a Genoa-to-Solent approaching. And so we begin . . .

DAY THREE: 15/11/07

Less than a hundred miles from Cape Finisterre. The wind is being very unpredictable. It's gone from ten knots to more than twenty and the sea has just built and built. I've yet to regain any kind of appetite, despite the sense that the voyage has unquestionably begun. I know another of the real challenges I face will be sleep. I have to move into that state of mind that accepts there are no more seven- to eight-hour stretches. I'll be lucky to have a night with three or four hours unbroken. In my days as an architect there were times when we stayed up many nights in a row to get a competition project completed. To keep going, I perfected a technique where I'd lie under a table and nap for fifteen minutes. Mike always said this won us more than a few big contracts. He was never able to manage it himself. It was all or nothing with him. My grandmother told me about being in Dresden during the bombing. She would have to sleep under a reinforced table. She would lie staring up at the lines of steel and imagine she was sailing alone in the most watertight boat that had ever been built. It brought her such a sense of peace that, no matter what was going on in the air above, she would be able to float off into the most serene slumber.

This is something I think of when I'm lying in the cuddy. I had a similar fantasy as a child in which I imagined I was in a space capsule drifting across the galaxy. All my needs were met, the universe was peaceful and miraculous outside the window, the stars alive with luminous beauty, and I would float, float, float on alone. Such calmness. A joyful calmness. As a child, there was no such thing as loneliness. That is a concept that comes later. It requires other people and the neurotic need for them. One has no such needs as a child.

The wind is still all over the place. It made a sudden turn through a hundred degrees, which was somewhat alarming. It's odd because it's in the clouds. We will be out from under them soon enough.

DAY FIVE: 17/11/07

About a hundred and eighty miles off Lisbon. Have seen no life for many hours. I was getting used to the gulls, swooping and crying. When the cloud is low, they can echo in the most peculiar manner, quite dissimilar from how one hears them on land. Then there is the noise of people – of everyday human life – surrounding them. Even the way the cries reverberate off architecture affects their tenor. But here, where there is only the roar of the sea and the noise of the wind against the hull and the sail, these calls sound filled with strange intention. Of course, there is no intention. A gull's cry is an animal sound. It is spontaneous and pure. It is not possible for it to be corrupted.

This life I am living is so different from any other's. If I were religious, I would say I was blessed to be able to partake of it.

DAY SIX: 18/11/07

What is this voyage about? I think it's to do with a group of likeminded people – who have had what they might call 'former' lives – starting again, claiming something back for themselves. Breuggemann was an industrial designer: he used to create bathroom suites! I was an architect who preferred theory to practice. The construction site is a place of compromise. Of make-do and mend. One must deal with contractors who often have no love for their craft and outright contempt for you. Why? Because you set the highest standards for yourself, and work to achieve them, and they

– who at best work to the median – become intimidated. And this emerges as hostility, resistance to your standards, your requests. Ultimately, I felt like I was between the wheels of a mill – one being the politics of running a practice with a creatively gifted but deeply flawed partner, the other the relentless imperfection of the industry. And so sailing became a therapy; a cleansing agent. This voyage – this voyage is the final stage of healing. It is a personal challenge, a physical ordeal, yes. But it is also a gift to myself. Two to three months without compromise. Two to three months of being the pure version of the entity that I am. Yes, the environment and circumstance demand responses – but they can be truthful. I will not have to argue my case against the shifting sands of someone else's unreliable opinion.

Conditions are more stable now. We're about a hundred miles south-west of the Canaries and my goal is simple: to stay in the breeze and south of the high. When the wind becomes as changeable as it was yesterday there is a danger that everything starts to fall apart. It becomes fatiguing just to maintain one's forward momentum. But now I have about fifteen knots of breeze and I'm surfing between twelve and eighteen knots. And it is wonderful.

DAY SEVEN: 19/11/07
When I was a boy, I would go and stay with my grandparents near Alicante. Their house clung to a cliff like a cormorant's nest, and if the night was warm I would be allowed to go to sleep on the balcony, staring at the stars, with the breeze carrying the tang of the salt from the sea. I loved my grandfather. He had been a fisherman in his youth and later a captain in the merchant navy. He would sit me on his knee and tell me tales of his voyages – some truthful and some fanciful, rich in the lore of the ocean.

Sadly, this love affair was not to last. I discovered, when I was about eight or nine, that Grandpa was not my grandpa. I had been lied to. My true grandfather had perished in the war. Grandma hooked up with the man I had known as my grandfather in the late 1950s. It had been thought better to deceive me, rather than expose me to the supposed sordid details of their unmarried tryst. The unfortunate victim of this deception was my love for the man, which I was never truly able to recover. He retreated from being the warm, cuddly old fellow who would dandle me on his lap to a slightly tarnished and distant figure who had no real connection to me. I tell you this because whenever I am at sea I find myself thinking of him. He died about twenty years ago. He spent the last portion of his life in a retirement home where I rarely visited him.

DAY NINE: 21/11/07

The wind has gone crazy, absolutely crazy. It will be best to keep the Gennaker up for now. It's hot, too. The last of the fruit went this morning. I had to throw two bananas overboard. They'd gone black overnight. Of course, this is no surprise. The temperature has risen as we've headed south. (When I say we, I mean me and the boat, of course. But she is everything to me at this moment in time. She is a friend, she is a parent, she is a lover – at least in the sense that I have to be constantly attentive to her.) I've taken to sitting in the galley, because it's coolest. I like it there. It reminds me of the kitchen area at Guildea and Huld, which was a pleasant place, at first – before things went sour. People said to me again and again before I left on this voyage, 'But how will you cope?' Of course, they were never referring to the physical difficulties, which, to me, are the source of the real challenge. No, the thing other people consistently baulked at was the very thing I embraced: the fact that I would be totally alone; no one to second guess, no one to please but the *Ashray* – who could never have an agenda, and could never lie. That's what I love about it out here. Everything becomes so simple. It was simplicity I always yearned for before – in my designs and in my life. It was easier to get them into my designs. The practice seemed simple at the start. I hadn't known Mike Guildea that long, but he was affable and I thought his work was very good. At first we seemed a good fit, complementing each other. And then, almost over night, he went mad. It was a demanding project; we had to work long hours. He would descend into moods; a darkness and heaviness would settle upon him.

Once, after we'd been out at a client meeting (we were always hustling for business, as any new practice must), he came into the office and confronted me.

'Why do you do that?' he said.

I had been in for some time already, working on revisions.

'Do what?' I asked.

I felt a terrible chill, my stomach iced. There was something irrational about his question – a bitter edge full of irritation, hatred even.

'Mock me in front of clients.'

'I – I'm . . .' I struggled to find a response. I didn't know to what he was referring.

'You said "I won't have another drink, but I'm sure Michael will." Implying to them that I'm an alcoholic – that I'm immoderate – unlike you, of course, always so impeccable.'

His eyes were wide. There was a seriousness about him that I had never seen before.

'I – I certainly didn't mean that.' I was struggling. This was extraordinary. I felt like a child with him. A child being chastised by a fierce parent. 'I was just trying to entertain them. It was a light-hearted joke.'

'Funny how the jokes are always at my expense.'

There were tears in my eyes. I was horrified I was going to cry. How I hated to be made to feel so vulnerable by a professional colleague.

'There was no malice intended, Michael. I'm sorry. It was supposed to be good-natured.'

'I haven't got time for this, Ramon. For you behaving like that. You understand? You need to try a little harder.'

There was a dangerous creeping noise coming from the rudders earlier. It will mean a full examination of the cassette box to be sure everything is OK. Each difficulty is another drain on one's ever-depleting energy.

DAY ELEVEN: 23/11/07
It feels like we've been at sea for a long time, but in truth it's a week and a half. I am pleased with our progress. The *Ashray* is turning out to be a fine companion. She exceeds Breuggemann's promises. We're about four hundred miles north of the Equator. Considering we're in the Doldrums, to be heading south at thirteen knots – which is what we were doing last time I checked – is very pleasing. Very pleasing indeed.

Leaning over the side of the hull, I saw something large shadowing us. When I say large, I mean about the size of a dolphin, maybe bigger. The shape was somehow more elongated. Perhaps it was a whale calf. I'm no biologist, so it's ridiculous really that I'm even typing this. When I looked again an hour or so later, it seemed to be still there. It couldn't have been a whale calf – they wouldn't swim that far alone. Maybe it was some kind of optical illusion, some wash or turbulence caused by the rudder.

It's the aloneness I'm cherishing, as much as the environment. How I trust the *Ashray*. She is part of me – while being her own entity. I respect her, and I know she will support me as I support her. This is a beautiful relationship. It's true that, as we sail towards the South Atlantic, I'm moving ever further from the chance of human companionship. There have been occasions where I feel a tiny snag of panic. It's just the ocean and me, and I answer it with a thought – 'If anything went *really* wrong, I could radio for help. It would probably be here within hours.' A human being is never really that far from another human being.

Part of this challenge is to show myself I can achieve something on my own. Perhaps it was just cowardice that led me to start my practice with another person. Funny how my architectural heroes – Renzo Piano, Norman Foster – all made their names with their own practices, yet I chose to be with someone else. So now I've put myself in a position where it is only me. To find out what am I made of. To find out if I have what it takes to do it on my own. That I am, as it were, enough. This voyage will demonstrate the matter beyond any doubt.

DAY THIRTEEN: 25/11/07

Just after I crossed the Equator I ran into some life – some confirmed life, that is, above the water. Whatever it was that was following the *Ashray* before had dissolved back into the surrounding ocean. Today it was a booby that came to visit. As I say, I'm no biologist, but I think it was a masked booby. It seemed curious about us and flew behind and around us for at least two hours. They only live in the equatorial area. They look unreal, like drawings. There was a definite intelligence in this one's eyes. Like it wanted to know something about me. It settled on the sheet rope quite still and

I gradually moved towards it. At first I thought it was staring at me. And then I realised it seemed to be looking straight past me. Ludicrous, but it made me turn and take in the whole length of the boat. There was nothing there, of course. When I turned back, the booby was gone. It made no sound whatsoever. I've no idea what a booby's call is, never having heard one. But seabirds are not usually silent.

I have got too used to the flatness of these warmer oceans. I need to prepare myself for the coming turbulence of the South Atlantic.

DAY FIFTEEN: 27/11/07

I knew today was going to be bad. I began it in the cuddy with a silent prayer. I have no religion. But I stood facing myself in the small mirror that hangs opposite the door and remembered something I heard on a radio interview with a ninety-two-year-old priest: 'God is being able to look yourself in the eye while you shave every morning.' I looked loose-skinned, tired, but very much alive, very much gathered into the moment, doing what I was supposed to be doing, investigating my depths – with only myself to carry.

As soon as I hit the deck I was grateful for the three hours' uninterrupted sleep I'd been able to manage. The pitch and the roll was already such that it was necessary to hold on to something just to make one's way along the hull. I felt a growing hum of fear – a dentist's waiting room, pre-hospital surgery kind of fear. It was in the wind, in the flap of the Genoa, in the increasing roll of the boat beneath me. I immediately set about focusing on the numerous practical tasks I would have to complete to simply ensure we stayed upright in these increasingly violent waves.

DAY SEVENTEEN: 29/11/07

I'm writing this retrospectively. It's hard to be clear about the last twenty-four hours. I'm tired. I ought to sleep. But I don't want to. For the first time, yesterday, I wished I wasn't here.

This is what happened. The temperature had dropped sharply. The water temperature was down to about fourteen degrees. The sky a vast grey lid draining all life out of the sea ahead. We'd crossed into the Southern Ocean about 1300 hours. I knew I'd be down here for some time, faced with nothing but this endless colourless vista. All the romance, all the pretence of my great expedition seemed to leak away, sucked out by the undeniable emptiness before me.

The vastness of this world has wrapped itself tight around me. The sailing was OK at first, but then the waters began to stir. Soon the sea was transformed. First into hills that rose up around me, cutting me off in a bowl of dingy, lead-coloured water. And then the hills became mountains. We tore up them, we raced down them, and I began to feel I had lost all control. The sudden turn in speed meant I had to fight my way through a sail-change – and halfway through I thought: 'I will not be able to complete this voyage.' I wondered what would happen if I just let go. Suddenly I was staring into the reality of my own limitations. I wanted to give up. I didn't give up, but I wanted to. I fought my way through the rest of the change until my throat burned with the cold and the salt. As I manoeuvered along the hull, all I could think of was Mike Guildea. These thoughts would not have surprised him. He would have predicted before I began that I would not be capable of completing what I had set out to do. When we were working together he saw straight into the heart of me and perceived exactly what my weaknesses were. I think he got them the first time we ever spoke. He saw my ludicrous grandiosity, which masked the hollow reality. He saw the childish nature of my ambitions and aspirations, and perceived I lacked the skills to fulfil them. Now, as I slunk towards the cuddy, my heart shrinking in my chest, I knew, without a fragment of doubt, that Mike had been right about me.

And it was then I saw it.

The air was thick with spray. And the spray hung in a mist that bit at every exposed area of flesh. Nevertheless, despite the limits of my vision, it was clear there was something there. A figure clinging to the rigging where it met the freeboard. Except it wasn't clinging. It was hanging – insouciantly swinging with the motion of the boat. Like an ape. I could make out no detail, only a silhouette. But it was staring at me. It nodded its head at me. It jumped up a little as the hull was hit by a wave. And then it was gone. It had leapt into the sea.

DAY EIGHTEEN: 30/11/07

I lay in the cuddy until it got light. I did not want to be up on deck in case it came back. Of course, there was nothing to come back – it was an optical illusion, some conglomeration of moisture and haze. It is cold enough here for the spray to freeze in the air, if it gets caught in a sudden gust of Antarctic wind. And I know this in my head. But here, in the ever-moving boat, tossed by the unpredictable wind and conditions, it's harder for the head to rule. All right. What did I think I saw? A man? Where would a man come from? Pirates? Not in the South Atlantic. I've not seen another vessel or picked one up on the radio for over forty-eight hours. I don't even know why I'm writing this. And what was it, if it wasn't a man? Some kind of . . . primate? At sea? Four hundred miles from the nearest landmass?

I am going to sleep. Even if I don't sleep, I'm going to close my eyes for an hour. This is the real problem. Intermittent and deficient sleep. I have taken for granted the fact that I can function like this – on brief bursts of sleep. I cannot.

Got up again because I wanted to write something down. It was a memory that came in a dream. Of course, this explains a lot. My grandfather ('grandfather') used to delight in telling me stories from his time sailing the South Atlantic. There was one story in particular that I simultaneously always wanted to hear and would beg him not to tell me. The story of the sailor boy and the Dwendymar. Even now, as an adult, I do not want to tell it. It is enough to have made the connection. Remembering this alone will lay the fear.

DAY NINETEEN: 1/12/07

Drifted in and out of a sleep state. Burning with tiredness. Remembering in my head is not enough. Let me write the story down. Forgive me if I do so inelegantly. This is for my own benefit. Not the readers' – whoever they might be.

'The Story of the Dwendymar'

Once there was a young boy who wanted nothing more than to be a fisherman. He had never even seen the sea. But he would dream about it. Sometimes he would stand on the dry savannah and think that he could catch the smell of salt in the air. Gradually, the more time he spent in his imagination, the more real this world of the sea became, and the less vivid the everyday world of his farm and the earth seemed. 'I think,' the boy would say to himself, as he lay in his cot at night, 'I think the sea is calling me. It is calling me and I must go to it. I must leave the farm and the earth and everything I have been told, and find out for myself what nobody has taught me.' And so the boy gathered his things: a rod and a net that he had fashioned for himself from a hoe and rake; a bag of bread and a flask of water. And at the darkest point of the night he set off across the fields, following the breeze, searching the air ahead of him for the scent of the ocean.

Sooner than he thought, he arrived at the coast. He heard water breaking against the shore like the world breathing in its sleep. The sand glittered in the moonlight and he took his sandals off to feel it, soft damp and cool against the soles of his feet. Before he knew it, he was at the water's edge and for the first time in his short life he gazed at the ocean. There was no end to it. He could not see where it joined the blackness of the night sky, only where the lacework of the stars faded into it. A soft bump-bump made him turn. There was a small wooden boat floating free at the edge of the shore. The boy knew it had been sent for him. He threw his things aboard and pushed it off, into the waves. Soon the boat had been caught in a current and was pulled sharply away from the coast.

He fell into a deep sleep. When he awoke he found he was in a turbulent churning ocean; it surrounded him, walls of blackness tipped with smiles and frowns of foam. It was so dark he could barely see and the stars had disappeared. It was everything he could do to stay in the little craft as it was thrown about. He himself was almost tossed overboard, and he ended up with his hand trailing in the sea. In his fear he cried out for help, and he felt the water close around his fingers, compressing them like a grip. Suddenly, sitting on the prow ahead of him was a translucent figure, a little bigger than himself. It spoke and its voice was the muted roar of ten thousand waves. 'I will help you child – but there is a price.' 'What is the price?' asked the boy, fearing that he had nothing to give. 'The price?' whispered the creature. 'You must listen to my song. It is the song of all things.' 'That does not sound too terrible.' said the boy. If the watery creature could be said to have smiled, that is what it did, and a gust of wind blasted the boy's face with freezing spray. 'No, it does not sound much. But it may rob you of everything you hold dear.' The boy had little choice, but he also had courage. 'I will accept your bargain,' he said. The creature pulled itself upright, towering over him like a curling wave. 'Take my hand and pull me aboard. I will sing to you as I guide you home.' The boy reached out and it was as if he was burned and frozen at the same time. He was thrown back into the craft as the creature crouched over him, dripping. And it began to sing its song as the boat drove through the waves towards the land.

Many days later the boat washed up ashore. Its only passenger was an old, old man with the eyes of a child. His life was nearly gone and he spoke six words before he passed: 'Beware the kiss of the Dwendymar.'

DAY TWENTY–TWENTY-ONE: 2/12/07–3/12/07

Losing track of day and night. I must force myself to be present. It's not just a matter of completing the voyage. It's a matter of survival. The sea has calmed to a more manageable roll, but it is still rough. I have to remain watchful because in these conditions all it takes is a strong gust, too much sail, and the *Ashray* could flip and that would be that. I made an inventory of supplies. I do not want to die of thirst. I do not want to die.

It is later now. I spent most of the day/night in the cockpit – staring ahead – the *Ashray* being hurled down the waves with winds gusting over fifty knots. The fear has become a constant presence. There is no respite. I remained taut – not knowing what was going to happen beyond the next wave. Would the craft survive? Another thought tugged at me. An unwelcome thought: that that is not the thing I am afraid of.

Later still. I am inside the cockpit as I type. I did not want to retreat as far as the cuddy in case I have to make a sail-change. But I am exhausted. I cannot sleep. I am writing this for want of something else to do. I do not want to lie, unoccupied. It is true I am attuned to every single sound the boat makes. I have been since we set out. That is why I am lying so still. I do not want to announce where I am. Because there is an alien noise. It started about twenty minutes ago. A splash – like water being dropped onto one of the hulls. A wave breaking. Except the waves have subsided and we're down to twenty knots. And it was followed by something else. A more rhythmic splashing. Like someone trudging about in water. It would stop. And then start up again. It receded. And then became louder. It was coming towards me. I am losing my mind because it is above me and I am white with the fear of what is going to look in at me around the door.

DAY ?
The sky is a perpetual grey. The waves a perpetual roll. When the noise had ceased – and it must only have been the water slapping between the hulls – I left the cockpit and walked all around. What did I think I would find?

I ate some powered milk with a spoon to conserve water.

I have a confession to make. I went to shave – to show I was in command of myself. I broke the mirror. On purpose. Because there was something in the doorway behind me. Instinctively, I turned.

There was nothing there. When I turned back to the mirror, there it was again. I threw the mirror on the ground. I trod on it to break the glass.

The boat is running free. I could not find the strength to steer it. Or the will. Because I can hear singing. If you would call it singing. And I do not want to hear its song.

DAY? NIGHT?

I am hiding. I am hiding. I am hiding. It is with me. I hear it sloshing behind me. I write this to fill my mind with something other than the terror. I am not alone. And I am utterly alone.

I caught sight of it reflected in the cockpit window. I broke the window with a grapnel anchor.

I will stay like this hiding in the corner. Typing.

Something will happen.

Reports about the wreck of the Ashray do confirm that every window and reflective surface on board the boat was broken.

The accounts of those who claim to have seen Huld walking the exposed seabed out at Fleetwood Bay had the following unusual detail in common. What they initially glimpsed they took for a large bulky shape,– until they realised it was, in fact, two figures, one in step with the other, barely a pace behind it. One report said Huld looked hunted, in shock – a man caught in a moment of terror. Another that he looked at peace. As Huld passed, the perspective shift carried both figures into the mist before the face of the accompanying figure became apparent. Two of the witnesses reported hearing a cry in the wind. It could have been the words: 'Save me', possibly 'Saved.'

Or maybe it was just the call of a booby, carried on the wind over some unimaginable distance from the flat abyss beyond the horizon.

I accept I have a predisposition for stories relating to the music industry. I used to play in bands, and still would, given the opportunity. So naturally, I was drawn to the following tale.

It's true that the players here could best be described as being on the fringes of the music industry, rather than being within it. But they aspired to be there – or their youthful selves had aspired to be there.

I should confess that I was grateful to be returning to dry land after wandering the open expanses of Fleetwood Bay. Of course, this was nothing to do with any supernatural encounter but rather because I'd been unsettled by my decision to walk for myself the flat, empty sands – a conscious rebuttal of my naturally agoraphobic disposition.* Just before travelling to Fleetwood I'd received a greetings card from an actor friend in Australia, which said on its front (quoting Eleanor Roosevelt): 'You should do one thing that scares you every day'. Fighting all those instincts that instructed me not to, I pushed myself out into the vast and colourless emptiness, away from the

---

* In my early twenties I contracted TB and, following that, experienced a bout of anxiety and agoraphobia, during which I was unable to leave the house without severe panic attacks. Although I recovered from this unpleasant situation within nine months, there are still rare occasions when I feel its residue.

safety of the promenade. To enable myself to do this, I clung to my identity as a writer. 'Just observe' was the mantra I kept repeating as I walked, and I attempted to catalogue the feelings that accompanied my irrational anxiety: a sense of imminent obliteration by the immense unbounded space was the closest I could get to articulating the idea behind it. And then there were the physical feelings: searing white flashes of primal terror, as if the emptiness were tangibly dangerous; as if one were walking along the narrowest of tightropes, a deadly drop into an abyss on either side. And worse than that even was the sense of loneliness, or isolation – characterised by a feeling of being beyond the help of any other agent – utterly vulnerable and utterly alone.

The feeling came back to the shore with me. Doing what I could to maintain my analytical faculties, I attempted to self-talk myself away from these overwhelming sensations. 'This is a flaw in my perception, a crossed wire.' And I could sense this physiological quirk as it played around the edges of my peripheral vision. Shapes would come into being there only to disappear as I swung my head first one way and then the other to free myself of them.

Walking back to the shoreline, I was grateful as the security of the promenade approached, and resisted the urge to run towards it (although the word 'grateful' underplays my relief, which was closer to the quenching of a terrible thirst).

I wondered if there was another clue in this experience that might lead me towards understanding why I should want to take on this book. The anxiety and agoraphobia that marked my entry into adulthood were in many ways an inversion of my childhood fascination with fear. Was there a fundamental connection between the two?

I was perturbed to find my discomfort lingered as I drove back toward the motorway. A distortion persisted around the edges of my eyesight, the sense of a shape behind me, which disappeared when I turned my head. The weirdness of these ocular phenomena was that they made one feel as if one were being accompanied on a journey one had chosen to make alone.

Victoria Mills – the former home of the Redbrick Sound recording studio – are best approached via the M62. Exit at Junction 22, taking the A62 Oldham Road. Cross the Hulme Hall Lane A6010 interchange and take the first left onto Varley Street, followed by the third road on the right. This is Lower Vickers Street. You'll find Victoria Mills about halfway along on the right-hand side.

Although it finally closed in 2010, Redbrick Sound thrived in various incarnations for more than thirty-five years. It began life as a small 8-track recording studio before becoming a 16-track in 1979, and then, by the early nineties, a fully developed 24-track facility.

Ultimately it was the digital revolution that finished Redbrick. Its typical clientele were now able to access equivalent technology on their laptops, and the bookings began to dry up. Neither luxurious enough to offer any added value on top of the technology, nor lo-fi enough to provide a fashionably retro sound, Redbrick went the way of much else in the music business, swept aside by the democratising tide of cheap (or free) software. The studio has been converted to as-yet-unoccupied office space; but a hint of its romance remains in the exposed Victorian brick and heavy industrial doors that cover the entrance to the redeveloped mill's lower level.

This account comes via a group of people who hadn't been assembled in one place for more than twenty years. When they last sat in the dark environs of Redbrick Sound they were little more than children – though they would not have said that about themselves at the time. When they returned (or those still alive had returned), they were firmly in mid-life. What they describe occurring (and Aiden Fox found the report – or had it recommended to him – online via the band's MySpace page) may be read in an entirely non-supernatural way and still affect the reader.

I must admit that, even in its re-rendered form, I find the post-industrial environment of central Manchester oppressive and perturbing. The treeless labyrinths of monumental brick edifices that line streets both narrow and wide cannot help but make one feel hemmed in. The dark line of the Rochdale Canal that backs onto Victoria Mills provides relief only in the imagination, with the knowledge that the water could carry one into open countryside a few miles to the east.

Standing there, looking at it, feeling what these people felt, entering their lives, I turned because there was a figure behind me. Something little with long hair? A child? There was nothing there. Only the empty tar-coloured ribbon of the canal and a relentless cliff face of solid bricks.

A Wire With Gain

There were four surviving members of Zurau: Richard Clip, Glen Pressfield, Ray Kirk and Gyp – though nobody called Gyp 'Gyp' any more, outside of this context, not even other friends who had known him in his youth. None of these people had seen each other for many, many years and this made them all nervous, albeit nervousness covered with a more clubbable bonhomie. As they hugged, shook hands and laughed in the car park – their breath hanging in front of them in the still, cold air – there was one imbalance that was evident in this first greeting, even as the group tried to conceal it: Ray Kirk was now famous and the other three weren't. This statement should perhaps be immediately qualified in that Ray was famous in Canada, and that 'famous' was an overstatement. But he had a successful career as a broadcaster with a public profile and Richard, Gyp and Glen didn't. The discomfort this fact brought was further tempered by the fact that Ray's success had nothing to do with making music. That might have killed the others. It's true that Ray wasn't what one would call a celebrity and certainly he wasn't well-known in the UK. He had started working as a music journalist in the early nineties and relocated to Canada. It was there that he began broadcasting, at first on radio with his own late-night series on the public service channel and then with a number of one-off documentaries for CBC television. In fact, it was because of this that the four of them were meeting up. Ray had pitched a piece both to the CBC and the *Globe and Mail* about a man approaching mid-life revisiting his rock and roll years. The *Globe and Mail* had commissioned the piece without hesitation; the CBC needed a little more convincing and were waiting to read the article.

'Raysy – Raysy Raysy Raysy!' Richard pinched Ray's cheeks excitedly, grinning broadly as he did so. 'Little Raysy.' Ray caught a burr of something alcoholic on Richard's breath. He smiled.

'Place hasn't got much warmer then,' Gyp exhaled through pursed lips. Even though they were standing in the reception, his breath continued to cloud. Still slender, though taut and muscled rather than willowy, Gyp rubbed his hands together. Ray noticed the fingernails were now clean and manicured rather than black with engine grease.

'You can go and bring the gear in. That'll warm you up,' said Glen to Gyp, winking.

Of course, Ray was already composing his article – he could hardly help it, though he didn't want the others to perceive him so nakedly at it. Part of his technique was to be as invisible as possible whenever he was with his subjects. There was plenty of time to make his presence felt on the page.

'So when's this piece coming out?' asked Richard, hauling his own gear in. Ray noticed that while Richard's guitar case was scuffed and tatty, the black tolex peeling away from the plywood in places, the neat little Vox amp was new.

'Oh, there's no deadline as such,' said Ray, lying. He wanted to take as much emphasis as he could off the article. Just let it all unfold.

Richard, Glen, Ray and Gyp. They were Zurau. They weren't always called Zurau. For a short while they had been Dot Dash Dot – but there was a consensus that this was actually a tongue twister and would be an impediment to anybody buying their records. (Mrs Welsch – who owned the garage where they used to rehearse on Saturday afternoons – had a mild cleft palette and it only took two painful conversations with her to end the usage of that original name for good.) It was Richard who offered up Zurau. Glen thought it too heavy metal. He was normally very even-tempered, so this in itself was alarming. Ray thought it was more prog-rock; he imagined an album with a Hipgnosis sleeve in the Pink Floyd style. Unlike Glen, he kept this to himself. It was Gyp who tipped the balance. Because he was the one with working-class credentials – he lived in a council house, had a single mother – somehow his opinion carried the decision. He liked it. He thought it sounded like Bauhaus. So Zurau stuck. The air of mystery it carried was deemed a plus. It also worked for Gabby. And, in the end, this carried it for Ray. Another fact he kept to himself.

'Well, this is very swish. Very swish.' Richard took his coat off, throwing it at the hat stand in the corner of the room.

'It's a live room,' said Stouty, the engineer. He had silver thinning hair, cut severely into a flat-top that he ran his hand through as he talked. 'We had it decked-out about two years ago.'

'Didn't this used to be where the mixing desk and shit was?' Gyp was stood on a little stage area at the back of the room.

'All got moved around. When we got access to the back there...' He pointed to an area behind glass at the far side of the room.

'What about the little place you could go and sing in? The weird echo place?' said Gyp. He was sitting on the sofa, rolling his drumsticks lightly across his thigh.

'Sorry?'

Stouty looked at him blankly.

'There was a little room with its own acoustic. Wasn't that where that was?' Gyp nodded over at the new control room.

'That wasn't this studio,' said Richard quietly.

Ray knew that it was this studio. Gyp was right. It had been down some little steps at the back.

'Was,' said Gyp, like a surly teenager.

'That was the place in Todmorden, at the top of the hill. The "Jive Bunny" place.'

'Was it fuck,' said Gyp. 'It was here. It was the place that gave Gabby the heebies.'

'It wasn't here,' said Ray. Everyone turned to look at him. 'It was the Todmorden place.'

Everyone let go the fact that Gyp had been the first to mention Gabby's name; that it had been mentioned at all.

It was funny, thought Ray, or notable enough for him to imagine putting it in his article, that they had set up their gear almost exactly the way that they used to. Not just at Ma Welsch's, but as they did on stage, too. Gyp's drums were at the back, Glen stage-left of him, bass amp on an old red plastic milk crate (it could well have been the same red plastic milk crate he used to use twenty-five years ago). Ray himself had erected his keyboard stand on the opposite side from Glen. He was the only one who seemed to have invested in new kit (Richard's new amp aside), and now he felt slightly uncomfortable about it. The Korg Oasys he'd bought from a dealer in Toronto, even though it was an ex-demo model, probably cost about a quarter of one of Gyp's mechanics' salaries. What had seemed stylish in the magazine photos, and indeed the music shop's demo room, now had a whiff of mid-life Harley Davidson about it in the more down-to-earth environs of Redbrick Sound. The idea was to have an all-in-one unit that could create and handle any keyboard sound Ray wanted, and the Oasys would certainly do that. But as he remembered his old Moog Rogue (what had happened to that?) and Arp string machine, with its dodgy phaser pedal – they seemed to have considerably more style. In those days he didn't even have a keyboard stand. He used four port boxes paired on top of each other to make two pedestals. They had pictures stapled to the front – a Hieronymus Bosch print and a still from a fifties Hammer film, *X – The Unknown*.

'Nice board,' said Gyp, who'd ambled over. 'What's it do?'

'Everything,' said Ray, without meaning to sound like an arsehole.

'Is that what being on Canadian TV buys you?'

'It's what being a middle-aged man without children buys you.'

'Show us something,' said Gyp, ignoring the self-deprecation. He always did have a good bullshit-detector. In his youth Ray had thought this a working-class trait. Now he knew enough to realise it was a mark of Gyp's character – and it was only Ray's own inverted snobbery that had labelled it as anything else.

'Shall we have a talk about a plan?' said Richard, who was sitting on the back of the sofa. He seemed rejuvenated by the company and the situation, already appearing ten years younger than he had down in the car park ninety minutes ago. He looked more serious, more focused. Like a leader. There were times in the past when he'd come across like that. When he hadn't seemed inhibited by his own anxiety and self-negation.

'Well it's simple, isn't it?' said Glen. Was he resenting Richard taking control so assuredly? Glen ran his own design business now, and despite the first such enterprise going under, his latest company was thriving. Maybe he didn't like suddenly being subordinate to Richard, who, after all, was essentially an unemployed guitar teacher. 'We finish the four tracks. Re-record what we need to re-record. Mix it. Will we get all that done in three days?'

'I can stay longer,' said Richard.

'I thought we were only doing three days. That's the point of it. Ray?'

This was Gyp, who sounded wounded, or maybe just alarmed that his long weekend of time travel might already be spreading beyond its allotted boundaries. He too had a successful business, a car dealership. Not to mention a young family from his second wife. He was understandably anxious at the thought of being sucked down into a time pit.

'We should try and stick to three days,' said Ray. 'Better to be disciplined about it.'

'You always preferred having done your homework when it came down to it, didn't you, Ray?' said Richard, looking a bit older again. Ray just smiled. But he felt like he'd been cut. Why on earth should a typically caustic remark from Richard hurt him like that now, aged forty-three?

He was the successful one.

It had been Richard's job to bake the tape. In truth he was the only one with knowledge of such arcane practices. Magnetic tape begins to degrade after a certain amount of time, particularly magnetic tape manufactured before 1984, even more particularly Ampex 456. The polyurethane in the tape absorbed water over time and became sticky. It created a form of gum that glued the tape surfaces together. It looked (and felt) disastrous – to come across an old, cherished recording and discover all the surfaces seemed to be dissolving into a liquefied goo. But there was an easy remedy. Warming the tape on a low and constant heat for a few hours was enough to reverse the problem and make the tape playable again (though it would be wise to make a digital copy of it and work with that from there on in). It was difficult to do this in a conventional kitchen oven, because it was hard to keep the temperature so low; but it was relatively easy to improvise a system with a hairdryer, a cardboard box, some duct tape and a meat thermometer. If Gabby had been there, thought Ray, she would have been the one not only to have done this, but to also then give everyone a detailed lecture on the physics of it, including details of the relative lengths of the urethane molecules involved.

Richard handed Stouty the Ampex box. The biro writing on the outside had faded, ghosting in places where something had dripped on it, though it was still legible: 'Zurau session – Sep 26th 87 – Profane – 4.22. The Houses of the Russians – 3.57. Wake Up – 5.11.' These were the last three songs they ever wrote, and the last three they ever recorded. And nobody had heard them for twenty-one years. Normally, when a demo tape had been recorded individual cassette copies were run off at the end of the session, or at least one was and the job then devolved on whoever took it home to make further copies for each member. But this tape had never been completed. The band had broken up before the end of the session. No one had wanted to go in on their own and unilaterally complete the songs. It had been Richard who'd retrieved the quarter-inch master tape, paying for a rough mix himself despite the fact that the session remained incomplete and he wasn't talking to Gabby any more.

'First thing,' said Stouty, 'is to get it into Pro Tools. Just so we're safe.'

His voice was soft, the vowels rounded with that form of northern effeminacy that was no indicator whatsoever of any equivalent femininity in the speaker's character. He carefully laced up the narrow brown ribbon onto the machine, his attention fully focused on each individual stage of the operation.

'Fingers at the ready, boys,' said Gyp, 'because this could be one stinky nappy full of shit.'

He extended his own forefingers and held them under his ears. Everyone had a version of the same expression on his face. A tense grin of concentration – a state of readiness – a shield against what? Disappointment? Embarrassment? The disinterring of ancient pain? Not just a shield, thought Ray. Their eyes spoke of something else, something oddly inappropriate on their ageing faces and in direct opposition to all the default cynicism and sarcasm and self-deprecation. Hope.

Stouty threw the faders on his mixing desk, pressed buttons, settled himself in his swivel chair. The band members leaned forward on the sofa. Of course, this wasn't the first time Zurau had heard themselves at all in twenty-odd years. They were there because recently there had been a good amount of listening – and not just by themselves. For all the limited nature of their releases, the single-figure national airplays, the handful of music-press reviews in the brief span of their existence, it seemed that Zurau had fans – perhaps more now than they'd had then. And all because of the Internet. The worldwide web was a strange resurrection man capable of leaking life into long buried, long forgotten powers. It seemed to only need the merest wisp of a memory for something to start there, in that virtual representation of actual space: a fragment of a song posted by someone who loved it at the time, an individual recollection recounted in some blog or tweet; and if enough people read it, or were caught by it, that original fragment pulled other particles towards itself, via a link or a comment, and soon these tenuous veins and ligaments gathered together, refleshing themselves into something of substance – a MySpace page, a YouTube channel. Despite their own self-inflicted death, Zurau found they lived again through the passion and love of others. The fact that this was the case after more than two decades apart was enough to remind these waning men of what they felt about what they had once done together.

The song began. Rolling tribal tom-toms, very much in the mid-eighties style. Ray looked at Gyp, expecting him to start tapping his sticks in time on the edge of the sofa, a habit he remembered vividly because it used to annoy him. But the sticks Gyp held remained rigid in his hand, his face taut with concentration. A huge spiky stab of keyboard came and Ray remembered everything about it. Discovering the sound messing about on a Saturday afternoon at Ma Welsch's. Having to recreate it by hand every time 'Profane' was played, because the synthesiser was entirely analogue and had no digital memory. Richard's vocal next, no words to begin with, instead a percussive, repetitive 'ah ah ah' that the engineer at the time (Mike? Geoff? Tony?) had echoed-off with a delay line vaguely in time with the rhythm of the track. Now Richard's face looked ageless, his eyes fixed in concentration, following every beat, every breath, sucked back into the memory and the time itself. Ray felt a huge flash of warmth rising from his belly to his chest – the memory of the raw creativity of that time, that activity – swimming free in the ocean of it, gulping in the endless oxygen of it, finally released from the airless aridity of a decade of exams and school. Smelling life ahead, his life, not the life his parents wanted for him, wanting to weep in excitement at the sense of ecstatic possibility he was now immersed in, so wonderful was the sense of what might be out there for him. He put his middle finger to the corner of his eye and felt a tear.

'So what's the plan?' said Glen, a cigarette drooping from between his lips.

The decision was made, counter-intuitive but smart. Ray always thought Richard was cleverer, more able and adept than he believed himself to be. Rather than just completing what was there on the tape, he suggested that they all play along with their own parts as they originally recorded them, lay them down afresh. This would allow them to get a new dynamic going, something that was alive in the here and now, and also serve as an exercise, getting themselves back into the muscle memory of where they were when the song was written. Back then, this approach would not have been technically possible, as track counts were so limited. Fourteen of the original sixteen were taken up with what had been recorded, even in its incomplete state. Now, thanks to digital recording, track counts were unlimited. They could lay down as many takes as they liked and all of them could be kept. Nothing had to be perfect either, as the best bits from each take could easily be compiled into one super-performance.

'How very, very odd,' thought Ray as he stood behind his keyboard, adjusting the sound. There was Richard in front of him, and with a woolly hat now covering his bald head, the view was the same as when Ray had been nineteen. He vividly remembered standing in this same position on that September day, attempting to play the twiddly riff he had devised, knowing it was technically beyond him to perfect it. In the dustbin clamour of Ma Welsch's rehearsal room the odd duff or mistimed note would disappear with Ray perfecting it in his head. Here (or there, from the perspective of the now), in the stark light of the studio monitors, each mistake had been a jag of shame twisting in his belly. 'Let's go again,' the bearded engineer (Tony? Mick? Keith?) had said, and each attempt had whittled another sliver of patience away, revealing the contempt underneath. Worse, worse than any of it, was Gabby's stare. Gabby had sat staring at him from the sofa with an eye that saw through all Ray's superficiality and pretension, deep into his hollow core. 'Out there,' she seemed to be saying with her contemptuous gaze, 'out there, you may breeze through life with your smile, your giggle, your quickness with words – but when it comes down to it, you don't *mean* it. I *mean* it. I know what it costs to actually *do* it. Or worse – face up to what I can't do. And it *hurts*.'

Of course, she hadn't said any of this out loud. Barely any of it ever was verbalised. Occasionally, there was a flash or spark that hinted at what she really thought, and it would genuinely sear you. For example, Ray had said how good he thought the soundtrack album of the *Absolute Beginners* film was and Gabby had fired back like a pistol, 'Why don't you listen to some proper jazz, Ray?', and Ray had not known what to do other than smile as if this were a joke he could share. Gabby listened to proper jazz. Gabby had the most extraordinary record collection Ray had ever seen (and he was proud of his own). But his own was made fat by things bought for effect, covers that he would display at the front of various piles for the benefit of visitors. Gabby's record collection spoke only of a fierce and deep and authentic commitment. Gabby could not care what visitors thought, because there were no visitors. The only time Ray had gone round was to pick her up. She lived with her mum in a neat semi in Cheadle Hulme and Gabby's mother had sent Ray up to collect her, perhaps delighted that a boy was finally in the house, asking for her. The room had been immaculate.

The exact opposite of Ray's hope-for-the-best keyboard-playing style, which was emblematic of every other aspect of his life. Ray remembered a shiny polished linoleum floor, which seemed odd for a bedroom, eggshell-blue walls, and nothing but the records, face-out in neat rows resting at inch-spaced intervals against the wall. Gabby must have been in the bathroom and he could not help but browse through them. Names he'd never heard of, covers that spoke not of a debt to fashion, but only of taste.

'What you doing?'

Ray had turned, shocked at the fear in Gabby's voice.

'Looking?'

Gabby had said nothing, merely pulled on her Harrington jacket, zipping it all the way up to her neck as she picked up her bass.

And then there were the arguments. Gabby, whilst being quiet and sweet, could sometimes start arguments for no reason and with people she didn't know. In fact, in that last session she'd been surprisingly aggressive with the engineer (Tom? Mark? Rick?). Somehow, as Ray remembered it, some idle conversation had begun about recording technology. This was another area Gabby exhibited a perhaps surprising amount of expertise in. How old was she? She was older than Ray – twenty, twenty-one? She'd been bright at school, apparently, but had not gone the university path. In fact, she was working at a baker's at that time, because there were odd hours that affected when they could and couldn't record. And there was sometimes the impression that she would have to go straight from a session to work, although she never really spoke about it. But despite ceasing her education, Ray was aware that she'd achieved an intimidating amount of A grades at both O and A levels. (How was he aware of this? Through Richard?) She was an autodidact, and whatever she was interested in, she made it her business to find out and learn everything and anything she could about it. So when she started talking to the engineer about amplifiers, and the theory behind their construction, no one in the band was surprised. But the engineer was. And he didn't like it. The argument had run something like this.

'It's beautiful pre. The best pre-amp I've ever heard. A perfect piece of engineering.'

'Perfect?'

You could hear the glee in Gabby's voice. Well, glee wasn't the right word – because that implied a smile, and she wasn't smiling. Satisfaction maybe. Satisfaction at being presented with an opportunity to demonstrate her knowledge.

'Just turn it on, listen to how it sounds. Pass anything through it and it sounds better,' said the engineer, still gloating.

'What do you mean, "better"?'

'It just adds a – ' The engineer made a little kissing gesture against his fingers.

'And how does *that* sound?'

She was sitting on the edge of the sofa now, taut with a furious and contained energy – like a fighting dog tied up outside a shop.

'Sweeter. Warmer.'

'And by "sweeter",' (and the word emerged coated in disdain) 'you mean with some kind of high-end gloss. Some additional frequencies around 14000 kHz that weren't present in the original signal?'

The engineer looked bemused at this attack, both in its content and who was delivering it.

'And by "warmer", do you mean some kind of boost to the mid-frequencies? Around the 4000 Hz range, with some associated harmonics?'

'If you say so, sweetheart.' He was cross and was content for his anger to show itself.

'So what you're describing is certainly not a perfect amplifier.'

'Really. Is that so?'

'Of course. By your own admission. A perfect amplifier would add nothing, take nothing away. No distortion. No filtering. A perfect amplifier – in engineering terms – is merely a wire with gain.'

'A wire with gain?'

'A wire that merely amplifies whatever signal is run along it – adding nothing – taking nothing away. Only making louder what was there. What you are admiring in your beautiful and perfect pre-amp is distortion. Not perfection.'

She sat back on the sofa, satisfied at the unequivocal way she had disproved his statement. He stared at her as if she was mad, beneath his contempt. Gabby? Gabby didn't care. The engineer looked at her, his mouth slightly open, deciding whether to defend himself, then merely shook his head slightly and turned back to face his faders.

Perhaps it was the argument that triggered the incident that followed – the loose brick removed that brought the whole tottering tower down.

It had been time to record the backing vocals. Richard wanted her to do them before he replaced his guide vocal with the final performance. The song already had a haunting ethereal quality. Ray had set his Arp Quartet so its notes had a stupidly long release, floating on for ten or fifteen seconds after he played them. And the engineer had a suggestion.

'You know what we could do?' What? said everyone, responding to the dark glee evident in his question. 'Record her down there.' He pointed to the floor.

'Down where?'

'In the slubbing room?'

'The what?' These questions from Richard, who was perhaps suspicious that someone else was providing a creative idea.

'From when it was a mill. Something to do with the cotton. Like a chamber, long, stone-lined. We use it for reverb. Got a mic and a speaker down there. But she could sing down there – put the mic at the other end. Sound great.'

'Excuse me. Firstly, I can't sing so . . .' said Gabby. She was immediately drowned out, overruled by everybody else in the band – even Gyp.

'Gabby, you've got a fucking beautiful voice. You stupid mare.'

'Secondly, I think it sounds like a lame idea. Better to record it up here where it's controlled. That way we can add reverb if we want. Take if off if we don't.'

'Yeah, we can do that anyway, darling,' said the engineer, sounding like he was already in thrall to his own suggestion. 'Why not do it this way first? It'll only take ten minutes.'

Gabby was always arguing her way out of her own contributions. She'd been taken into the band as a second guitarist partly because Richard knew she had a clutch of songs, and he was always hoping to get her to throw them into the pool of material the band could draw on. Whenever the matter was raised, she would shake her head and dismiss them as 'utter shit' that she couldn't bear to play. But sometimes you would catch a riff or a snatch of melody, at a sound check, or when she was tuning up her guitar, and you would yearn to hear more. But nothing was ever good enough, according to Gabby.

And so, and Ray couldn't quite remember how, Gabby was pushed, bullied even, into doing what everyone else wished. The engineer disappeared through a door in the corner of the control room, a rusted, iron-clad door that Ray had never even noticed because it lay hidden in shadow, offset in a small alcove. He returned after a few minutes with a roll of cable, which he unfurled, connecting the terminating jacks into his patch bay.

'Come on then, darling, we'll set you up. All right?'

And a defeated Gabby had been led through the door and down the stone staircase beyond.

Had there been an argument with Richard? Had Ray heard a muffled disagreement from the little kitchen area behind the orange curtains by the sofa? Did Richard use the weight of their by-then-apparent tryst to get Gabby's vocals onto tape? Or had Ray added this embellishment in his memory afterwards? At this distance, it was very hard to distinguish between memory and story. As a journalist he often thought the two were interchangeable. Memory was a story you told yourself about yourself, extrapolated from a tiny dot-matrix of facts.

And now it was his own memory that was dim. How was one supposed to recollect a series of events after that length of time? Or was that guilt blocking his memory? He could remember now. Looking at the backs of his old friends was enough to draw the memory forth. He had called them friends at the time. Friendship flowed easily and uncynically to him then. If you liked someone, they were a friend. What was wrong with that? It was Richard whose own cynicism and defensiveness refused to label things that way. Everyone had an ulterior motive in his worldview. Everyone was self-serving and therefore a potential instrument of pain. The world was a lonely, awful, brutal, terrible place. Gabby slotted right into that worldview, too. She tacitly agreed, though Ray had never heard her speak of it. And why now was he dismissing a part of himself as facile for having thought of

Gyp and Glen as friends, as well as Richard? Why had he himself let that cynicism in?

Thinking about it, this is what had happened. It wasn't on the first attempt to get the backing vocals that Richard had argued with Gabby. It was on the second. The first time, she had gone. And the engineer had started fucking with her. They'd all sat there, listening to it unfold over the talkback, like it was a radio play.

'Can you hear me?' The engineer was at his desk. He'd lit a cigarette.

'Yeah.' Gabby's voice sounded far away, almost lost in the natural reverberation of the stone chamber.

'In a moment – '

'What did they use this place for? It smells.'

'Originally I think they did the spinning down there, teasing out the yarns. Later, other things. Shall we have a run for levels?'

The engineer pressed play. In the control room Gabby's voice came back unaccompanied. It sounded pure – resonant – affecting. Ray remembered thinking she should have been singing the lead. She stopped singing.

'I don't like it down here.'

'Sorry, love?'

'I said I don't like it down here.'

'Well, they do say it's haunted.'

'Fuck off.'

'No – well, you know, it does have kind of a bad atmosphere. Because of what went on in there, probably.'

There was a pause in which Gabby didn't speak. Then her voice came, echoing – distant – hardly there at all.

'What went on here?'

'You know. With the kids.' The engineer turned, winked at the others.

'What . . . ? Fuck off. I'm coming up.'

'Gabbeee,' said Richard, irritated. 'Just get on with it.' He seemed more irritated by the fact she was allowing herself to be so easily manipulated than with the engineer for fucking around with her.

'What happened with the kids?'

'Mate . . .'

This was Gyp appealing for the engineer to stop. But the engineer was a good fifteen years older than the rest of them; an adult with a beard that made him look like a member of 10CC. In that studio – on his patch – he was his own authority.

'It's an old mill, this. All kinds of bad shit happened here. You're in the slubbing room and that's where they sent the kids who misbehaved. You know they had loads of kids working in a mill – six, seven years old and up. It was noisy in there. The main machine room was next to it. That was supposed to be the punishment. The noise. But there were people there who'd use that noise to mask what they'd do to the kids.' He left a moment of silence before continuing: 'Shall we roll again?'

This time he played the track back in the control room, too. They could hear Gabby moving around, brushing the mic. When it came to her part, she didn't start singing. There was only a rustle. Something being thrown down. A few minutes later she emerged through the iron-covered door and into the control room.

This was when the argument with Richard had occurred. This was what Ray had heard from behind the curtain.

'What's the matter with you, huh? Having him pull your chain like that.'

'I don't like it down there.'

'Don't let him fuck with you like that.'

'I don't want to sing, all right?'

'Gabby.' The exasperation in Richard's voice was genuine.

'I am not a good singer. I cannot sing. Do you understand?'

Richard's voice was low. Ray couldn't hear what he was saying.

'No. No, Richard. No.'

Ray – in his youth, in his naivety – thought he had something to offer. He put his head around the curtains. Richard had stared at him, glowered at him.

'Gabby, your voice is beautiful.'

'Shut up, Ray.'

'Really. You sing beautifully.'

'Just get back down there,' said Richard, now ignoring Ray. 'All right? This is costing us twenty-five pounds an hour, all right? It's like a taxi meter going round and I'm paying most of it. So do me a favour.'

Ray had withdrawn after that. He just remembered Gabby reluctantly heaving open the metal door, the back of which he had registered at that time was covered with faded green baize.

'All right, my darling, we can go again. Can you give us something for level?'

Gabby muttered something that echoed softly from the back of the stone chamber.

'What was that? We didn't catch that?'

'I said' – and she was shouting now; it sounded like she was in a bathroom at the back of a cave – 'that this will be the shittiest pile of shit you ever heard and it's coming from the shit-smeared mouth of a walking, talking shit. All right?'

'We'll just give it a go, shall we?'

The engineer reached for a button on his remote unit and the silvered circles of the tape machine began their slow and tempered turn. It came to the section where Gabby was supposed to start singing. Nothing happened. The engineer stopped the tape. Richard's guide vocal snapped off, followed by the briefest tale of an echo.

'Can you hear the foldback all right, darling?'

'I said, "Very funny".'

'"Very funny" what?'

'Yeah. I'm coming up – and are you coming up too, Gyp?'

Gyp didn't speak. But he looked around the room as if to say 'what's she talking about?'.

'So you're not going to answer me. You're all pricks.'

And the sound of her headphones begin thrown off echoed in the unseen dark space beyond the monitor speakers.

When she emerged into the control room, she clearly had words readied in her head. She was about to speak them when she saw Gyp and the rest of the band sitting in the control room. She looked confused. Or worse than confused.

'Yeah. Who was it then?'

'Who was what?'

'Touching me?'

Everyone looked around at each other.

'No one,' said Gyp softly.

'Yeah. Fuck off.'

'No one was down there, Gabs.' This was from Richard. Was that a conciliatory tone in his voice?

'And this is what you are like, isn't it? This is what you are all like.'

'No one was down there. You must have bumped into something.'

'Someone came up behind me.'

'No, they didn't.'

'This is – yeah. You can all just fuck off. All right?' She was white-faced.

She went to sit in the car park. She wouldn't come back in. The others sat there in silence in the control room. Ray expected Richard to go out there and use some kindness to get her back in, but he seemed to be sulking himself. Perhaps he was cross with the engineer for fucking with Gabby's head in that way and was not bold enough to say something to him. In the end Ray heard himself saying, 'I'm going to go out there and see if she's all right.'

There was no response initially until Richard said, 'Yeah. Great.'

'Gabby?'

There was no answer from her. Ray could see her now – in his memory – on the lone stone wall that backed onto the canal. The water was unseen, rushing somewhere deep, below and behind her. For a moment, seeing that she was facing the water, Ray feared she was going to jump.

'Gabby.' He called again. It was hard to see in the unlit gloom, but there was movement. Taking this as a sign that he was allowed to approach, Ray moved towards her. 'Why don't you come back in, record your bit in the studio? Just put normal reverb on it.'

'Go away, Ray.'

The end of her cigarette glowed bright – a point of fire making everything go black around it.

'Gabby, you're too good to not do this. You're too good at everything. Not just the singing. But the bass playing, too. And guitar playing. You're better than all three of them. You're a better pianist than me, too.'

'Go away, Ray.'

Ray tried to understand what was the main thing upsetting her. Was it that she thought they'd been fucking around with her? Or was it coming from somewhere else?

'He's just a bearded prick. You can't – '

'It's easy being you, isn't it, Ray? Because you're not that bright. You think you're a lot cleverer than you are. And a lot better than you are. You don't just *think* it, you believe it. And that's an easy way to be.' Ray felt liked she'd scooped something out of him. It was a very plausible story. 'Being worth something isn't just being able to do a rough easy version of something – you know that, don't you?'

'Come on.'

He was close enough to see her now. Behind her glasses, behind her long straight unstyled hair, she had a strong, angular, beautiful face – though it was made ugly by her expression – but Ray could see beyond that. Always saw beyond it. He felt a craving for her. A need to be with her. It was his secret – the one he never voiced.

'It's all shit. This shitty little studio. This shitty little band that thinks it's going to be something that will never – be – anything. Because it isn't anything. It's just pretending. Not real, Ray. Not real.' She paused, breathless – then started again. 'You'll never be anything. I'll never be anything. It's shit. I'm shit. I am . . .' She struggled to find the word. 'Disgusted. Disgusted.' And she did look like she was going to be sick. Ray stood there for a time, looking at her burning face. He felt burned up himself, from the inside, by what she'd said. She turned away from him, moved into the shadows. The water rushed nearby, below, dark and dirty.

There seemed little point in saying anything else to her. He trudged back inside, pushing the rusted bar of the old fire exit to, not closed, in case she wanted to come back in.

'Do you want to try a take?' said Stouty. 'We can do it however you want to do it. We can track all of you, then go back and pick you up one by one. Or comp bits in, if you want? Whatever you want to do.'

There was something seductive about stepping back into one's past this way, thought Ray, feeling the shiny new keys of his Oasys beneath his fingers, even given the upsetting things he was remembering. A paradox – the past – even an uneasy one – could be more comfortable than the present. Particularly if the present is faced honestly. What lies ahead? Decline? Pain? Loss? Uncertainty? Even with these distressing memories that had been playing – in this story of the past – there was a known future ahead of them, and the future at least was full of warmth, joy, excitement. 'For you,' came the thought, like a slap. 'Not for Gabby.' And, as if cued by the thoughts, Richard spoke. He turned to Ray and the illusion of a young man he'd had standing in front of him earlier was ripped up by the old face. A man, skin lined with care and disappointment. Ray searched again in the clay of it for the youthful person beneath, that this was surely moulded atop. There was nothing to be found, now. Just the man. In the moment. Which was all there really was.

'We need those BVs,' said Richard, looking stern – as if it was somehow Ray's fault they never got them in the first place.

'Can't you do something on your fancy techno slab?' said Gyp.

'It's the tune she was singing. That's what makes it,' said Glen.

'I'll do it,' Ray heard himself saying.

'On that thing?' Richard sounded sceptical.

'I'll sing them. In the place. Down there. It's the only way to get that sound.'

Imperfect as what Gabby had recorded was, it was true that it sounded extraordinary. It was the best thing about the track.

'You'll *sing* them?'

'I can sing, you know. I sing in the Toronto Bell Arte Singers.' This was a partial truth. He had done it once, for an episode of his radio show.

'Hang on, everyone. Don't want to put a kibosh on things – but when you say "down there", what do you mean?' said Stouty.

'The funny long stone room – the reverb chamber.'

'If you mean where I think you mean, we don't use it as a reverb chamber. We've got the Lexicons.'

'What is it used for?'

'Assuming it's where I think you're talking about, not for anything. Well, storage.'

'Is it still wired up?'

They'd had to move a fire extinguisher and a broken MDF shelf unit to get at the iron-covered doorway. The others had waited in silence while Stouty went down to check. Ray wondered what their memories about the last session were. Of course it wasn't anything they'd talked about. Not that they'd really talked at all. But an atmosphere had arrived in the room. Reflectivity? Regret? It was more like fear.

'It's doable,' said Stouty, emerging from behind the metal door. His messy hair was covered in dust. 'The junction box's live. It might be as simple as plugging in a mic and some cans. You might want to put a fleece on or summat.'

It hadn't taken long to patch everything in.

'What I can do is sample each phrase we've got of her, and play it back to you before we go for a take, so you've got what there is of her melody. That sound all right?'

Ray nodded. Richard looked at him sceptically. He seemed suddenly tired.

'Don't matter if you fuck it up, does it?' said Gyp. 'No pressure or owt. Just something else for you to put in your article.'

The door creaked as Ray passed through it; the protest of unused hinges. There was a narrow arched descent, with tight, small steps, each one not quite big enough to take a foot. It felt safer to walk down side-on, pressing the cold stone of the opposite wall for support.

The air was cold; it got colder as Ray descended. A patch of darkness lay ahead, engulfing the next few steps. That was OK. It dispersed again in about three metres, shifted by a small spotlight imperfectly mounted on the low arched ceiling. The mill couldn't have been constructed much earlier than the early nineteenth century and yet somehow this passageway felt much older, almost medieval. He noticed his heart beating faster than usual. How could there be anything threatening down there? Stouty had been in there twice in the past half hour without a flicker of emotion. Maybe engineers had an empirical bent that protected them from the lash of a vivid imagination.

Ray was grateful to reach the bottom. But the gratitude soon evaporated when he rounded the dog-leg corner and was faced not with the stone chamber he was expecting but an extension of the tight passageway that had surrounded the staircase. If anything, it seemed to narrow. He wouldn't be able to stand upright. Ray looked around to see if there was a turning or doorway that he had missed. Stouty hadn't mentioned anything about this. The narrow passage was so far beyond the bounds of a conventional egress that Ray couldn't believe this was the way to the slubbing room. If it was, surely Stouty would have given him some warning. With effort, he turned around and considered climbing the stairs again, to return for clarification. But the incline looked alarmingly claustrophobic from this angle, and something about climbing back the way he had come seemed more terrifying in the moment.

'Stop it,' he found himself saying aloud. Who was he addressing? The ancient Mancunian stones? No. He was talking to himself – attempting to arrest the rising sense of panic. JUST MOVE, for God's sake. And so Ray moved forward, aware with every step of the stone walls pushing in on him and down on him. At one point, he had to turn sideways just to fit. As he kept going, a thought entered his head. They might shut the door for a joke. Or he might get stuck down there, like a pot-holer caught in some subterranean tragedy. It was not possible to see where the end of the thing was. There were three receding patches of light – and a greater sense of darkness beyond. And then, just when he thought he'd reached the limits of his endurance of the terror, the corridor abruptly opened up around him.

The slubbing room was about three times the width of the corridor; not spacious, but nevertheless it was a huge relief to be there. He could touch the ceiling. It was damp and soft, lined with some kind of doughy lichen. He nearly knocked over the mic stand Stouty had put up. The headphones had to be at the other end. There was one light bulb in the centre of the chamber. A number of fluorescent bulbs were screwed at uneven points to blocks of wood, but they didn't seem to be working. He looked for a switch, but found only one and did not want to risk flicking it in case it was the wrong one and took the whole space into darkness. Moving slowly, he made his way towards the headphones, which were resting an upturned milk crate, not unlike the one Richard used to balance his amp on. He thought of Gabby, down here on her own, twenty-two years ago, coiled up, bound in her own self-loathing.

He picked the cans up, pulled them over his head, turned to face the length of the slubbing room. He began to walk, closer to the microphone, but the cans jarred his head backwards. Their lead didn't stretch more than two metres from the socket they were patched into. He was going to have to shout across the six metres between himself and the microphone, which was on a stand positioned and bent in such an odd way that it seemed to have an attitude – like the Anglepoise lamp at the start of a Pixar film. Ray inhaled to calm himself, not wanting the others to hear the tremor in his voice. The sharp scent of the damp stone caught in his nose. Did something just move at the far end of the room? He shouted towards the microphone.

'I'm here.'

'You took your time.' This was Gyp. Chirpy – bright – seemingly unaware of anything troubling at all.

'Stouty hadn't told me it was an expedition to get here.'

No answer. He heard the control room in his cans. A rustle of a crisp packet. The talkback mic had a heavy compressor on it, which meant it picked up everything. 'Do you want to have a run through?' This was Stouty. Ray could feel his breath against his own ears.

'Can we just go for a take?' he shouted, trying to sound reasonable.

'Bit much for you down there, mate?' Gyp again. The crisps were his.

'Cold,' said Ray, lying.

The sudden movement came again, making him jar his head in its direction in an attempt to catch what it was. It felt huge. Like something in a cloak or a cape dropping down from the ceiling. He kept his eye fixed on the direction where he had picked up the movement. The irregular checked pattern of the pointing in the brick wall seemed to shift momentarily. The movement came again. It was a shadow. An abrupt amorphous swipe. Ray's eye moved to the lone light bulb in the centre of the room. Water droplets were dripping down the side of the bulb, making the shape on the wall.

'We can go for a take,' said Stouty. Was there a delay on this line? He might as well have been on the other end of a satellite link to Australia. 'I'll play back the original. For reference, yeah?'

The click of Gyp's drumsticks striking each other signalled the start of the song. Was that what they'd recorded this afternoon – or was it the original? The tape hiss told him it was the latter. He strained to hear Gabby's vocals and couldn't. Until they began, just over halfway through. He listened, hummed to himself. Tried to focus his attention on the task he had to fulfil. Just as he was getting the point where she'd cycled through the simple melody enough times for Ray to think he'd absorbed it, she seemed to sing something different. And then there was some kind of interruption – a physical interruption – and she stopped singing altogether. It didn't matter. He had enough of it in his head to make an attempt.

'OK,' he shouted across the room. He didn't like the echo that came back at him in the headphones. It was disorientating, like being high, all the dimensions of the space felt suddenly wrong. 'OK. Let's go for one. I've got it.' Another moment of silence – as if the control room was in an aeroplane, thirty thousand feet away. And then:

'OK.'

Four clicks from the drumsticks. Brighter. Clearer. This was now. Ray tried to call the melody to mind – Gabby's breathy wordless cry – a fluid collection of 'ahh's and 'ohhh's and 'oohhh's. He held the model of them in his mind, felt the connection of his intention to the muscles in his throat. He began to sing, attempting to thread his idea of the melody around the guide vocal that Richard had laid down. It had been years since he'd attempted anything like this, finding the emotion, expressing it through the inflection of his voice. Thinking this, though, was enough to disrupt the flow of what he was doing and this first attempt spluttered out before it had begun. The music in the headphones jerked to an abrupt halt, slicing off halfway through a struck guitar chord. Ray was about to apologie himself when Stouty's voice interjected in the headphones.

'Sorry. Ray? We're having a problem up here. Something's humming. Bear with us.'

There was no comment on what Ray had offered up, either from Stouty or from his fellow band members. He stood there, alone in the stone chamber. He shivered, clutching himself, rubbing his upper arms with their opposite hands. He took the cans off. Was that someone on the stairs? He thought he'd heard a noise. A soft step. Or was it someone muttering? Had Gyp come down to join him? Or to try and play some lame practical joke on him? Would he really? With the memory of Gabby now so present? There was a strong compulsion to go and see who was on the stairs. But he would have to move away from the headphones. Fuck it. He was going to. And just as he began to walk off there was a crackle of noise and Stouty's voice came miniaturised from the floor. Ray picked the phones up, pulled them on. He really didn't want to cover his ears now. Whichever of them was in the stairwell would be able to enter without warning. Nevertheless, Stouty was calling and Ray was now quite keen to get this done and get out of there. He might even run up the stairs with his eyes closed to get around the feelings of panic.

'Yeah. Ray? Can you hear me?'

'I'm here,' shouted Ray, hearing a vague and distant version of himself coming back into the centre of his head.

'Yeah. We think it's some kind of ground-loop hum. Probably the circuit the light's on.'

'Yeah.'

'Are you all right if we turn the lights off just while we go for another take?'

A pause in which Ray said nothing.

'Is that OK? Ray?'

Was this a joke? Was this something the three of them had cooked up together, with Stouty deadpanning the instruction down the talkback mic? Gyp waiting to leap out at him from the shadows, once it was dark? Ray took a moment to consider what his response might be? Lose his temper with them? Express anger at their childishness? Stand up to them? The one thing he would not tolerate as an adult was being bullied. Or was it better to give no response at all? Just go along with the request? Wasn't there more dignity in that? There was always the possibility that Stouty's request was bona fide.

'Ray?'

'Yeah. That's fine, mate.' He listened for some kind of response. Nothing came.

'All right. I can isolate the circuit up here. Just bear with us. It'll go off in a minute or so, OK?'

'Yep.'

Then, after a moment. 'Just stay where you while you're singing. Soon as we've got a take we're happy with, I'll switch the circuit back.'

'Yep.'

Ray wasn't going to react. He contained himself. The click of the talkback shutting off. Silence. The dense silence of dead headphones. He took them off, rested them round his neck, waiting for Stouty to come back before he put them on again. If there was going to be a minute before it went dark, should he go and peer out into the corridor, up the stairwell – to see who was there? Yes – go on. Now. He was about to pull the headphones off when his mind started to make the calculation. What if he was halfway through the chamber when the darkness came? He would be stuck, lost. He imagined himself caught in the blackness, unable to move as if it were a kind of jelly. He'd rather be on the headphones, so he could talk to them and hear what they had to say – there was comfort in that, wasn't there? But then he wouldn't know if someone was there. Before he could reason further, the light went, taking thought and calculation with it. He stared into the blackness, expecting his eyes to adjust, that there would be some glimmer from the doorway. He realised the door was shut at the top of stairs. *Put on the headphones* was the first thought, when thought returned. But thought fought with instinct. Instinct was to remain as alert as possible, with every sense primed, waiting to see who was going to come at him through the dark. His ears strained for sound. He moved his head to the left. The slight noise that his skin made turning against the collar of his shirt was picked up by the reverbatory walls and thrown back at him. There was nothing else. He moved backwards groping for the wall behind him, just to feel something, to ground himself in a physical space.

Calm. Be calm. This is surely one of the advantages of middle age. One could draw on one's life experiences and insights to puncture the childishness of instinctive fear. There was no threat in the room. There was nothing that could hurt him. (Spirits? Ghosts?) Ghosts of who? (Ghosts of children. Lives unborn. Think of all the lives here that never flowered.) There are no ghosts. (Think – each one of those children – who worked in this mill from the age of what? Six? Seven? They were the same as you – the same spirit – the same capacity of mind – encased in non-possibility by culture and circumstance – taken into this dark place and . . .) This is just a story, Ray. You are telling yourself a story. (Who else might be in the darkness with you?) Nobody is in the darkness with me.

I am alone in here with nothing but air and stone. (Gabby might be. She's dead. Would she come back to see you? What would you see?) Nobody comes back from the dead. (Then where do they go?) They just stop. (You just stop then. What will it be like, when you stop, Ray? What will that feel like?)

A thump from the headphones. He pulled them on.

'OK in there?'

'Yep.'

'Shall we go for another?'

'Yep.'

The four clicks came. The song began. Glen's bass melody snaking round Gyp's rolling tom-toms. Focus on the rhythm. Focus on your task, Ray. Time to make some noise. Time to open your mouth. He began to 'ahhhh'.

Something was circling him. There was no breath, but there was movement. He could feel the air moving around him. It was deliberate, predatory. It only came up to his waist. Was it a child? Or an adult on all-fours?

He reached out, groping the darkness around him.

Something pulled at his leg.

Then something pinched him.

He screamed.

'Fuck off,' he shouted into the darkness. 'Fuck off. Who's there?'

'Ray?' in his earphones, but he'd pulled them off.

'Fuck off. Gyp? I know it's you.' Ray lashed out with his arms.

'What?' That was Gyp in the headphones.

'Ray – are you all right?' That was Richard. It was hardly going to be Glen. Who was it? His mind was throwing up images. Something unborn, a misshapen thing, lumbering through the darkness. Something that would never come out, because it couldn't. Circumstance wouldn't let it. Something full of primal rage.

Ray suddenly found he was standing completely still – paralysed – all will frozen or gone. If he had had to leave that terrible place to save his life, in that moment he was unable to.

'Put the light on,' Ray heard himself shout, 'put the light on.' For an instant, the tiniest of instants, when the light returned Ray wished that it hadn't. For he imagined that he'd caught sight of something, something little and black and human-shaped, scuttling into the wall.

He sat upstairs, on the edge of the reception's uncomfortable sofa – recovering. He found that a cloud now surrounded him – a fug of failure and self-rejection. 'I am nothing compared to what I should be. Why am I nothing? Because I have failed. Because of my lack of ability. Because of my lack of willpower. Because of my basic, inescapable laziness. Because I am not good enough. Because I don't apply myself. Because I won't do the work. Because I go too easy on myself. Because because because I have wasted it all. If there was ever anything there really to waste. I have wasted it through fear. I have wasted it through not being as good as any of the people I admire, though in my grandiosity I have fantasised that I am. Well – now we see the truth. The truth cannot be eluded for very long. I am not up to much. I never was, never will be, never could be.' Whose words were these? They weren't his. Or were they? Were these thoughts that usually swam unnamed and unarticulated in the depths of him that his time in the slubbing room had brought to the surface? He was wrapped in something now. He couldn't feel his way through it. Or had he been simply unwrapped and shown the truth by whatever had milled around him, Rumpelstiltskin-like, in the dark?

He sipped at a can of Heineken that Gyp had passed him.

'You all right, mate?' This was Glen, sat next to him – an arm tentatively laid over his shoulder. Was he twenty-one again? Had he come out of there twenty-one? He searched inside for some more recent memory of his various adult achievements to blank out these dark cries and calls now surging up from within. He thought of his CBC show. His international radio award. His first television broadcast. But it was like a trying to warm himself round a photograph of a flame.

Richard was at the door now, sober-looking, pale.

'What?' said Ray. Instinctively, he'd expected mockery from the others but there was none.

'We found something. On the tape,' was all he said.

They sat together in the control room, all the intervening years having fallen away now. Four men who knew each other when they were much younger. That fact alone bound them together. Having shared youth was like sharing a parent. Stouty was sober, too, though he had no connection to any of them or their history. But he was sensitive enough to have picked up a hallowing in the air. He pressed play on the Otari machine.

The reels began to turn. And the song began. Gabby must have recorded this . . . but when? Stouty had found it at the end of the tape. Her voice was beautiful. Accompanied by nothing but a mournful bass played through a delay. The melody was beautiful.

And now Ray was crying. Gabby's ability, Gabby's talent revealed beyond all doubt. There would be no more songs as beautiful as that ever again. No more with that specific mix of voice and melody ever anywhere in the infinity of the universe, ever again. Its moment was gone. And it never even really came. Apart from in this brief flowering – unheard until now.

Ray had run away from it, too, just as Gabby had. Run away from something vital within him because of some story he'd told himself, which he couldn't even remember. He'd run away from making music, from his first love, and there it was, frozen in his past. Oh, he could hear its burning memory calling to him now, though. He could hear it so very clearly. The passing of time was a wire with gain.

Everybody likes a good asylum story – at least they did when I was growing up. The recent changes in policy towards the mentally ill in need of long-term care have meant that most of these buildings have disappeared or are on the edge of disappearing from the physical landscape, and thus the inner landscape of new generations of children. But once . . . once they cast a large, dark shadow fuelled by their expanse, their often ornately gothic architecture, their positions on the edge of town.

The Leeds of my childhood had not one, but two such institutions. High Royds out at Menston and the larger Meanwood Park Hospital just off the ring road. Of the two it was the former that haunted the minds of Leeds schoolkids. High Royds' name, and indeed Menston, the name of the village where it resided, became synecdoches for madness, lunacy, or more often what was then labelled 'mental deficiency', and these names were used as playground insults, usually accompanied with an extravagant physical pantomime of the invoked condition: tongue thrust hard against the lower lip, making it protrude into the jutting disfigurement thought, by schoolboys at least, characteristic of the insane. Now, like most of these facilities, both High Royds and Meanwood Park have been redeveloped into private housing estates, although retaining their more impressive architectural features – a clocktower here, an assembly hall there – presumably in the hope that their grim provenance will be forgotten and ultimately the structures will invoke nothing but appreciation of the grace of their design.

For those of a certain generation – that is, mine, or older – this could never be the case. There will forever be a particular horror connected with these buildings, glimpsed from the car (perhaps on a trip to Harry Ramsden's in Guiseley for fish and chips), more extensively in the winter months when the curtain of leaves fell, revealing the hidden castle of the insane behind. What happened in there? What happened to you that sent you there? Or how badly had you come out when you were born? What was wrong with you? What did it smell like? What did it feel like? What did it sound like? What hopeless cries of terror echoed down its tiled corridors? What subterranean trenches of despair must be felt by those incarcerated therein upon waking every morning to remember where they were? However miserable you'd felt at your most despondent, would it be but an inch of the mile-deep anguish of the unfortunates held behind those dark, unwindowed walls? What was it like to go mad? There was a blackness, a shade you felt inside yourself even as you contemplated these things from a distance. The bravado of the playground was one thing, the reality of this nightmare world another. It was no piece of theatre or fiction, but a living reality, mere feet from the car, where you sat wrapped warm and safe with your (when it came down to it) loving parents. There were such things, and they weren't that far away.

Given all this, was I afraid or excited when I came across the inspiration for the following story in Aiden Fox's files? Now these terrible places were no more, did it make their contemplation any easier? The idea of these buildings retained a certain horrific romance – and they were rapidly disappearing – so the excuse to visit the remains of one was welcome, at least in the abstract.

Sleaford is as easily approached by rail as it is by car. Connections from Grantham on the East Coast mainline run reasonably frequently and the railway actually travels past the back of the grounds of the old Rauceby Hospital. Tantalisingly, some of these remains are visible from the train itself: large redbrick structures linked by unusual wooden bridging corridors raised twenty feet off the ground.

At the time of my visit, the redevelopment seemed to have come to a halt – perhaps a victim of the economic downturn. Neat townhouses and semis in the contemporary style were visible at the far side of the old grounds. But there was enough of the hospital (originally known as the Kesteven County Asylum) to gain a sense of its character. Most imposing was the old admin block – with that pointy, Edwardian redbrick gothic style I personally associate with the monkey houses at Regent's Park Zoo. One is used to seeing it in town centres – libraries, museums – and there it seems mundane and ordinary, no more worthy of attention than a public baths or a junior school. And yet the change of use to something darker somehow throws its towers and cupolas into a more sinister relief.

I say sinister, but the truth is – upon walking from the railway station – I was actually relieved to be here. My time on the abyssal sands of Fleetwood, and the primal anxiety it had stirred, still burned in my memory. That feeling I took to the urban, brick-made cliffs and channels of Manchester had been a constant presence on and off. I realise now that my adult rationalism is a source of self-esteem and personal power. Because I'd been fearful as a child and young man, to have triumphed over that fear in adult life has become central to my identity. If I wake from a dream in which myself or a loved one dies, I am quickly able to manage the anxiety that such a dream may be literally prophetic with the thought that no one has ever had such a dream and that it is not possible to predict the future. If I wake hearing a noise in the night, any sense that the source may be supernatural is quashed in less than a second as I bring to mind all I have learned about the functioning of the fight-or-flight response and the evolutionary advantage of a vivid imagination. Actually the best account of the ghost phenomenon that I've yet come across, at least from a psychological perspective, is Professor Richard Wiseman's. Wiseman is a brilliant and rightly celebrated academic who has devoted much of his career to the study of so-called paranormal phenomena. He maintains that evolution has left us all with a genetic predisposition to see faces in dark places, particularly when we are alone (and thus potentially more vulnerable). The thinking is this: there is a huge evolutionary advantage in perceiving a face at the back of a dark cave, or in a forest. The fight-or-flight response is engaged, pumping adrenalin into our system so that, if there were a sabre-toothed tiger or equivalent predator in front of us, we would have the energy to flee as fast as we could, thereby increasing our chance of surviving to pass our genetic material on. If, however, we merely misperceived what was there – making a face out of a couple of rocks and a bit of moss – we would have fled from nothing, but incurred no evolutionary disadvantage because the fear doesn't harm us enough to kill us. Therefore, we have been bred to see fearful phantoms in the dark, and, given that physiological evolution runs somewhat slower than social evolution, we have yet to grow out of this proclivity. As soon as I heard this rather elegant and beautiful piece of reasoning it made absolute sense and I felt I'd finally found an answer that explained and satisfied.

But for the first time in many, many years, the experience of visiting these supposedly haunted places, deliberately allowing them to make play with my imagination, seemed to be challenging my hard-won equilibrium. It was ridiculous, of course. Merely a fanciful response to the material I was working with. This was no more than fear, fear that had caught me and revived something habitual. I was determined to control my thinking and thus I decided to consciously invert my responses on the next visit – to look for the comforting and the familiar in whatever the environment was. I'm sure you, reading this now, if you were so minded, would be able to scare yourself. If I were to suggest to you that there was a figure behind you, about six feet away, and it was staring at you from a shadowed corner of whatever space you were in, you would start to feel something – a sensation of presence that would impel you to turn around and look.

Go on . . . You can feel it looking at you . . .

This is how our minds work. Well, they can be made to work in the other direction, too, and it was this facility that I was going to draw upon as I explored the remains of the Rauceby asylum.* The road was visible, with suburban houses beyond. The sky was blue and, though cold, the bright late-morning sunlight gave some cheer. I could happily walk the perimeter of the remaining buildings with no obligation to explore within. So when I rounded a corner and saw, sitting on a large pile of bricks, a small figure with long hair over its face, in a light-coloured coat – I was, I have to say, thrown back into a state of alarm.

I immediately brought all my rationalism into play. I'd primed

---

* I've since discovered that there are warnings to would-be urban explorers about asbestos remains, which it would be irresponsible not draw the reader's attention to.

myself to see something – and there was nothing there. Look again. It would be a sack, with a piece of torn bin-liner flapping out of it, distorted by my expectations into something anthropic. I looked again. It was a small figure with long brown hair falling over its face, in a light-coloured coat. It squatted on the bricks, looking down at me, seemingly studying me through the hair fallen over its face.

I turned, as slowly as possible, and walked back the way I had came, propelling myself – without running – towards Rauceby railway station.

It's funny. When I began this book, everything about the realm of the supernatural was metaphor to me – a metaphor I relished as a writer because of where it allowed me to go, because, in simple terms, I find it is so entertaining. It had never occurred to me for one moment that I would be challenged in the process. But now I did not want to go back to Rauceby.

I did go back. I made myself. Thinking of the Eleanor Roosevelt quote. Thinking of my own battle with agoraphobia – where the only way to overcome unreasoning fear was to face it down.

I went back. The figure was gone. And then I wrote up this story.

Ward Four Sixteen

'What do you think?'

Mara looked at Hal so directly, asked the question in such a matter-of-fact manner, that her motive could only be pure.

'Sounds good. It'll do me good,' said Hal, smiling.

'It will do him good, won't it?' said Mara, turning to Ridwan. Again, so open, so free from guile.

'I think it would do him good,' said Ridwan.

Of course, there was no question about Ridwan needing any such purgative. He was about to fly to Malawi to spend the rest of his summer holiday with orphaned children. This kind of thing came easily to him. Less so to Hal. Not that Hal thought he was himself bad, or particularly selfish. He was within the normal spectrum of these things. Which is to say, generally, he didn't spend much of his time with orphans or the handicapped.

Mara was seventeen. She'd be eighteen in November. She and Ridwan had been together for nearly a year now. She was Ridwan's first girlfriend. Hal could see why Mara would want to be with Ridwan. He was good-looking, half-Nigerian, long-lashed and delicate-eyed. Mara was half-Jewish and maybe that gave them an affinity. Hal had thought, cynically perhaps, that what would have been most attractive to her about Ridwan was the act of visible rebellion that came with dating someone possessed of such obvious ethnicity. Mara lived, after all, in the nice end of Sleaford, in a large detached house on Sovereign Street in whose conservatory they were now sitting. Her parents probably avoided describing themselves as Sleaford residents, despite the fact that Mara went to Kesteven and Sleaford Girls' High School. They would have described themselves as living in Folkingham. The name evoked a more picturesque image, with its historic buildings, pretty church and village greenery, whereas Sleaford was a market town with a Superdrug and a mental hospital.

'You want me to get you home, big man?' This to Ridwan, who was not a big man, at five-nine was only an inch taller than Hal. Ridwan didn't drive and Hal had access to his mother's Renault Clio – not always, but he did today.

'Better had,' said Ridwan. 'Haven't finished packing.'

'Come on, then.'

'Oh, babes,' said Mara, scrunching up her face in protest.

Reasonable, thought Hal, given she's not going to see him again for a month. Reasonable, but it still irritated him. If felt like a juvenile gesture. Yes, she was seventeen, but he felt she was as old as anyone he knew.

In the car on the way home there was silence for a while, or rather an absence of chat filled with a compilation tape, Kitchens of Distinction, The Happy Mondays. It was Ridwan that broke it.

'Will you stay there tonight?'

'Hmmm?'

'Will you stay at Mara's tonight and tomorrow, while her mum and dad are away? She asked me to ask you.'

'Well – '

'If you're doing her voluntary service thing, it'll make it easier. She didn't want to ask you herself. She was embarrassed.' A little pause then Ridwan added, 'It'd be a favour to me, man.'

'I'll stay.' And Hal felt a little rush, a little wave of adrenalin that tightened his belly.

He pulled over at Ridwan's, a more modest semi on Cranwell Avenue.

'You coming in?'

'For a bit.'

Hal liked Mrs Adebeyo. She was always friendly. No plates required for biscuits at her house, unlike at Mara's. And you didn't have to have a cigarette on the back porch.

'You two are going to miss each other, aren't you?'

She brought him over a creamy coffee – a drink he only ever had there. It was sweet and rich, made with evaporated milk.

'Don't know what I'm going to do without him.'

'He'll be back before you know it.' She took out a Benson and Hedges, offered Hal one. 'Have you got a job this summer?'

That was something he didn't really want to think about. It brought to mind the argument Hal had had with his father only that morning.

'Looking for one. I might have to do some temping,' he said, unconvincingly.

Mrs Adebeyo nodded. 'Well, it'll be a bit of money in your pocket.'

Hal sipped his coffee. Mrs Adebeyo took his hand.

'He won't say – but you've been friends for such a long time.' Mrs Adebeyo smiled at him, her face bright with approval. 'It's good that college hasn't stopped that for either of you.'

Hal went back to his house. His mum was out. He ran himself a bath and sat on the edge of the tub, watching it fill. He prepared his toiletries – Gillette Sensor razor and matching gel, Vidal Sassoon shampoo and separate conditioner – lining them up on the tiled portion behind the taps. He slid into the water, his clothes piled up on the floor in a little mound, his boxer shorts balanced on the top like a dollop of cream. He shaved in the bath, regarding his reflection, his high cheekbones, his deep-grey irises with their distinctive flecks of amber. More than one girl had commented on those amber flecks.

When he got back to Mara's, he wondered if her parents would still be there. They were going away for two nights to some do down in Bedfordshire – something to do with Terry's work.

'You smell nice.'
    'Do I?'
    'What is it?'
    'Shampoo?'
    'Smells like aftershave.'
    She had that thing of raising the pitch of her voice on the last word of a sentence, giving it an interrogative feel even if there was no question. An antipodean inflection. Hal theorised it had something to do with the number of young people who watched *Neighbours*.
    'You coming into the conservatory?'
    'Are your parents here?' he called to her as she walked ahead. The house was large and necessitated the raising of his voice, which he immediately regretted.

'Nah. They left about four.' She paused – turned her head slightly in Hal's direction. 'Just you and me.'

She sat on the big white rug in the middle of the conservatory floor, her legs folded up underneath her. She had a short skirt on, but with grey patterned tights underneath. He liked the shape of her calves.

'Shall we have something to drink?'

She was girlish, but he could see the kind of woman she might become. Perhaps like her own mother. Relentlessly middle-class. A whiff of sitcom about her. It didn't lessen her attractiveness.

'Coffee?'

'Beer.'

'I thought you only drank wine,' he said with mock incredulity.

'I like Guinness now. I like the can. The one with the thing in that gives it the head.'

'The widget?'

'The widget.'

During this exchange she had moved a little closer to him. He was on the floor, too, but cross-legged. He got some cigarettes out – waved them in the air, interrogatively.

'You don't have to go outside.'

'Won't your parents go mad?'

'We'll open the French windows. They're not back till Thursday. Can I have a puff?'

She got up to fetch him an ashtray. He watched her move as she walked away. She had a kind of grace to her. An assurance. She returned with a porcelain ashtray with a model of a skier in the middle of it. The back of the skis were designed to hold the end of the cigarette.

'How come your parents have ashtrays if they don't let your friends smoke in the house?'

'That's Terry and Jo for you. One law for them.'

Hal withdrew the cigarette – a Marlboro Light – from the box, tapped it three times for luck on his knuckles, took out his Zippo and flicked a confident flame. There was an element of showing off in this – he knew that – but that was part of smoking, wasn't it? Mara watched him without speaking. She was back on the floor, her feet folded under her bottom. She shuffled towards him, lining her left upper arm against his right. As she reached for the cigarette, she pressed her forearm against his. He smelt her perfume beneath the smoke. He liked it. It suited her. He liked the way it mingled with her sweat. She took the cigarette. Sucked it at. Looked him in the eye as the end reddened. She lowered it, exhaled the smoke to the side of his face. It made her seem older, more knowing. Which is why we all smoke, he thought. She put the cigarette back in his mouth, touching his cheek with her thumb as she did so.

He spent the night in her brother's room (he was away doing Camp America). Hal lay looking up at the ceiling, the pattern from the bedside light like two fleurs-de-lys on the cream-coloured emulsion. He remembered a holiday with Ridwan, four or five years ago. They'd gone to stay in Hunmanby and made friends with two local girls. Ridwan didn't seem to have any interest in either of them, and for the first time Hal had felt a natural superiority in this area. He'd enjoyed the novelty of it. Enjoyed standing above Ridwan, looking down. He found himself looking at the world with a new sense of possibility. The memory of the feeling warmed him as he faded into sleep.

They got the bus up to the Rauceby hospital; about a twenty-minute journey by the time it had got through the town centre. No one else got off at their stop, Hal noticed. There was a longish walk along a busy road not really intended for pedestrians.

A seemingly endless metal fence lined the left side of the road and they walked alongside it for a time, keeping close to it to create distance between them and the dangerously roaring traffic. Occasionally a glimpse came through the leaves of the hospital itself. It seemed huge. Hal only knew it by the elements that jutted over the treeline: the grey octagonal water-tower, the crucifix-tipped peaks of the chapel's pitched roof. Walking along its perimeter now, closer than he had ever been to the place before, he began to get a sense of its scale. Odd structures appeared between gaps in the foliage. Something like a summerhouse, though its roof was made of corrugated iron. A long rectangular building like a classroom, except the windows were barred.

'Do you know what we're going to be doing today?' he asked Mara. She was wearing jeans, tucked into boots. She looked older than her years.

'Whatever they tell us?'

'You sure they're going to be all right with me just turning up?' A sense of apprehension now as he saw a sign reading Concealed Entrance Ahead.

'Of course,' she laughed.

He was seized with a sudden desire to turn around, find the bus stop on the other side of the road.

She said something else, but it was obscured by the rumble of a passing lorry.

They turned up the drive. Hal wondered if there'd be some kind of high-security gates to get through. These gothic notions were offset when he saw the familiarity of the architecture, no longer concealed by the surrounding trees. The road was lined with the same blue and white NHS signage. It was just a hospital. They were just sick people, being helped.

'Hello, guys.'

This was Stuart. A friendly-looking man in his thirties with tight, silver curly hair; big-boned, expansive, with a warm sense of authority. He shook Hal's hand vigorously.

'I'm extra,' said Hal, apologising for his presence, perhaps still hoping he might be sent home for being *persona non grata*.

'Extra?'

'He means he's not from Kesteven and Sleaford's,' said Mara, as if faintly embarrassed by Hal's need to explain his presence. 'He's volunteered, as a friend of mine. He's a student.'

'Well, we won't hold that against him,' Stuart smiled broadly, clapping Hal on the back with a large hand. 'Great to have you here, Hal. I'll take you to meet the gang.'

'The gang', as it turned out, was a class of ten or twelve kids with Down's syndrome. 'Mongoloid' was the term Hal had grown up with, but of course nobody said that now.

'We're taking advantage of your presence to go on an away-day, if that's OK,' said Stuart as they walked down the seemingly endless central corridor that connected the various hospital buildings together. 'We thought we'd head off to Mablethorpe. To the boat park.'

'Hurray,' said Mara, clapping her hands as if it were a day out for her, too. She seemed completely unfazed by where they were – or what they were about to do.

As they walked, Hal tried to turn his mind from their environment. He didn't want to glance into any rooms. He didn't want to see any inmates. He didn't want to hear any snatches of conversation or speech, lest they contain fragments of insanity and that insanity might seep into him in some way. Even before they'd arrived at the dayroom, as Stuart called it, Hal heard distant shouting, felt his own apprehension at what he might be called upon to do. In truth, he'd never done anything like this before. He'd been to an old people's home to do some helping for a charity his mum was involved with. He'd visited his grandfather in hospital when he'd had his hip replacement. But he'd never spent time with anyone mentally handicapped. He looked for some similar apprehension on Mara's face, but it still carried the same bright, uncomplicated receptivity to whatever was going on. There was something in Hal that was vaguely troubled about the mentally handicapped being lumped in with the mad. He supposed that explained the sheer scale of the hospital: all aspects of mental dysfunction were housed there, and there were many facets to the defective mind.

As they approached the dayroom, the paintwork in the corridor lightened. There were shapes on the wall, amateurishly rendered, presumably by the members of staff. Hippos, monkeys, giraffes in primary colours – all peering out through fronds of jungle foliage. The doorway to the dayroom had been incorporated into the design, a large tree trunk wrapped in vines having been outlined around it. Stuart turned to them before opening the door. He smiled a broad, relaxed smile.

'Come in. Say hello.'

Hal's first impression was of a barely contained chaos. Chairs had been cleared to one side and a large grid had been chalked on the floor. A number of Down's syndrome kids – or maybe not kids – maybe they were older than him – were throwing a light-coloured plastic ball around, aiming towards the squares on the floor. There were incoherent shouts, cries, enthusiastic whoops. One of the boys turned languidly to regard Hal, but then saw Mara and immediately switched focus to her.

'Hiya,' he shouted. 'Hello.'

Mara smiled, waved.

'Hiya.' The boy had come over.

'This is Michael,' said Stuart. 'Although you like to be called Mick at the moment, don't you?'

'I am Mick.'

'Mick likes a bit of a laugh. You've got to watch out for him.'

Mick had slung his arm around Mara's shoulder. 'Are you here today?' he asked her. She was still smiling – *coping admirably* were the words that came into Hal's mind.

'We're going on a trip today, Mick,' said Stuart. 'Mara's come to help out. And Hal. This is Hal.'

Hal was pleased that Stuart had remembered his name.

'Hi, Hal,' said Mick.

'Hello.'

It didn't take too long to corral everyone into the minibus. And Hal found he was beginning to relax. He hadn't realised he was so nervous about what the day ahead held until he'd got to the hospital. But now parameters were in place: the unknown had become known, and whatever was required of him, he felt it would be in reach. Until Stuart gave him a job, that was.

'Hal, will you do me a favour? Could you go to the kitchen block and pick up the drinks? I didn't have time to get them.'

'The drinks?' Hal felt a little nervous snag.

'Kitchen have got us a coolbox with their juices. Only needs one person. And we can concentrate on getting the minibus loaded.' Stuart pulled a hopeful face.

'Sure.'

'Easy to find. Just head out of here, right all the way along to end of the corridor, take a left and then it's a second left, but you'll see a sign. Ask for Marlene.' This shouted after, as Stuart was already heading off. 'Bring 'em back here,' he indicated the room they were in, 'and one of us'll come back for you.'

And so Hal set off, turning right all the way along the corridor as instructed. He tried not to breathe in too deeply. There was a sickly smell in the air. It was a hospitally smell – mainly disinfectant Hal guessed, but with something else beneath it, something he recognised from a fairground. He couldn't think what it might be. And then he remembered. The dodgems. It was the smell of electricity – electrical discharge. The corridor seemed to narrow a little as he walked; narrow and darken. He kept his eyes ahead, not wanting to glimpse anything on either side. The one thing he did do was find something he could fix in his head for his return, so he would be sure of going in the right room: a smiling monkey face, painted on the anaglypta wallpaper. What did he think he was going to see?

There were no doors for a while, just blank wall; the children's pictures soon disappeared. There was a sound – off in the distance – a rhythmic repetitive noise, iron striking iron – like a machine, or perhaps a workshop. The corridor seemed to have developed a slight incline, as if it was heading downwards. Perhaps the hospital had a basement. Perhaps the volume of the mad and the mentally deficient was so enormous that ordinary people had no idea about the scale of building necessary to contain them all. He noticed some windows coming up on his left-hand side but there was no sign of any door accompanying them. There was light coming through them, but it wasn't daylight. It had the sickly white pinkness of too many fluorescent lights. He slowed as he approached the windows. He was naturally curious, couldn't help but speculate as to what lay behind them – what went on in there, what kind of room was it?

The windows were slightly higher than his natural eyeline. Idly, he paused in front of the nearest. The light beyond flickered slightly, as if there was movement within. Hal checked over his shoulder – there was no one in sight. He reached up with his fingers, pulled himself up, standing as high as he could on his tiptoes. The room on the other side was long and thin. He couldn't see a door, or much in it apart from three beds with grey hospital blankets. There were shapes in all three of them. He searched for faces at the pillow end. There was only hair. Was he imagining it, or were there bindings around the blankets? Straps to hold whoever was in there securely in place. He was imagining it, surely. Grasping hold of the wooden frame and the shallow sill, Hal pulled himself a little higher, lifting himself off the ground. His head touched the glass. Although this didn't create much noise, it was enough to make one of the heads in the beds move. It turned in his direction, revealing white skin and an eye. A man? The head looked at Hal. Jerked. Jerked again. A beckoning motion? Come in. Come on in.

Hal dropped to the floor and began to walk briskly, with purpose, following Stuart's directions – grateful that he could remember them as well as he could.

'They'll be all right. Once we're under way.'

'Are they going to be raucous? Singing?' Mara had a jolly lilt in her voice. She always seemed to be smiling.

'They're not a rugby team.'

In fact, Mick – or Michael – whom one might suspect to be the most raucous – already seemed to be asleep, lolling against Stuart, snoring.

'Is Mick all right?' said Hal, wanting to let Stuart know that he was concerned.

'He's fine. He's tired. Poor Mick.'

'Why poor Mick?' Again Mara's interest was genuine.

'He's still devastated about his tree.'

'His tree?'

Stuart rocked slightly with the motion of the minibus. He steadied himself as he talked.

'Michael's been here a long time. Pretty much all his life.' Stuart reached into his coat pocket, searched around, pulled out a tin of tobacco. He prised it open and began to roll himself a cigarette as he talked. 'When he was about, oohh, six or seven – seven, I'd say – his parents planted him an apple tree in the children's garden here. A gift. For his new home. Michael helped them plant it. And from then on, it was his tree. He looked after it. Went to see it when he could. Watered it. Talked to it. Collecting the leaves from around it in the autumn, so it was always tidy. No one could have cared for it more. It was his friend. On a rainy day he'd ask if he could go out and hold an umbrella over it, or put a coat on it. It was his friend and he loved it. He would have done anything for it.'

'I'm not going to like how this ends, am I?' said Mara, biting her lip.

'Three weeks ago, we had the storm.'

There had been a terrible storm – a weird summer thing – hot and muggy all day, followed by gale-force winds in the evening.

'One of the big trees at the edge of the children's garden copped it. Landed right on Michael's tree, flattening it. There was no way it could be saved. He was devastated. Actually – you can't imagine.'

With a practised hand, Stuart completed the cigarette he'd been rolling, slipped it into the tobacco tin and then began rolling himself another one.

'I was, too. When you saw how he loved his "friend".'

Stuart shook his head, smiled. Mara turned to look at Michael, who was still asleep on the other side of Stuart. Hal turned to look at Michael, too – his head moving gently with the motion of the minibus.

Stuart had said that the thing with these daytrips was always to avoid being ambitious. Although there were a number of things they could see and do in Mablethorpe, they would be spending all their time at the boating lake.

'And believe me,' he'd told them 'wherever we go, the meal is always the main event.' They'd brought drinks because they were premedicated, for those that needed medication, but it had been arranged for food to be provided there at the café. 'They know us well,' Stuart had said.

It was getting dark as Hal and Mara got on the bus to Sovereign Street that evening. They went to the back of the vehicle, and though it was almost empty and they could have stretched out if they'd wanted to, Mara and Hal sat next to each other. The bus turned a corner and the inertia rolled her into him. He felt her weight and her warmth against his side, caught a scent of tart sweat beneath her perfume, which he recognised – Calvin Klein, was it? Obsession? The sweat smell was not unpleasant. He waited for her to move away from him as the bus straightened up. She didn't.

When they got in, she opened the doors onto the patio and told Hal he could smoke while she went to put the kettle on. 'I fancy a coffee. Don't you? I can make a Boden.'

He pulled out the cigarettes, removed one, tapped it three times on the packet and lit it. He stepped out onto the patio, felt the pleasant warmth of a summer breeze coming towards him; a smell of cut grass from some lawn not so far away. He thought about the gale that had done for Mick's tree, shivered

– though that may have been a rush from the tobacco. A noise from behind. He turned. There was Mara, holding a tray with two cups of coffee and a plate of biscuits. She put them down onto a little stone table at the edge of the lawn. She came to stand next to him, nuzzled herself against him. She was about an inch shorter, maybe two – her eyes were about the level of his nose, and were big and dark, with long black lashes. There was no surprise in her proximity, not now. Their arms went around each other at the same time, and when she tilted her head back to receive a kiss he simultaneously lent forward to provide it. Part of him felt he was following her script; another part of him that he had created a script of his own. And what was his role? Jack-the-lad? The cheeky but irresistible chancer? And what about Ridwan? Had either of them written anything for him? Even a hint of something off-stage? Deep within him there was something vague, not articulated in words, but there, and with enough clarity to govern his actions. When it came to things like this, matters of . . . what? The heart . . . ? Lust . . . ? Women . . . ? When it came to things like that, he was above Ridwan. So far above him that, really – well, really, Ridwan didn't matter. Ridwan didn't come into it. Ridwan was not relevant. Ridwan was not anything to be concerned about. Whatever was happening there and then between him and Mara – well, Mara wanted him – of course, of course she wanted him. And that was that. That was just how things were. Who cares? It's a kiss. What does it matter? Did he even ask himself, 'What if Ridwan finds out?' Was that thought even present? No. Not in any substantial or meaningful way. He was concerned only with his story, the part he had been given that overlapped so well with the part he had written for himself in that moment. Of course that was all that mattered. He'd been hurt in the past. It was just stuff. They were just kids. Ridwan – what? Ridwan was less than him. When it came to stuff like this, Ridwan was less than him.

They'd overslept. They'd overslept and they were supposed to be at the hospital by nine o'clock. Stuart hadn't said what they were going to be doing. It probably wouldn't be another trip out, but there must be activities that took place in the grounds: there was a large playing field, there was a playground; also, Hal had observed what looked like an art room just past the children's murals. A day doing art and getting messy seemed quite fun. Much of yesterday's anxiety had diminished simply because the element of the unknown had disappeared.

They raced to the bus stop, with a KitKat and an apple each for breakfast.

'They'll have tea there, won't they?' Mara really didn't want to be late. And Hal didn't either, if he was being honest. He felt he had gained Stuart's good opinion yesterday and something about the man made you want to retain it.

He leaned against the bus stop, closed his eyes for a moment, tired. His groin hurt, the dull low grinding ache of blue balls. He wondered, on those occasions when he got in this situation, whether that was what period pain felt like.

'Ciggie?'

Mara had pulled out a packet of Silk Cut – the blue ones, the extra mild. She was the first person he'd seen to ever smoke them. There was barely any hit off them, you wondered what was the point? Nevertheless, he took one. She smiled at him; there seemed to be no reference in her behaviour to what had taken place the night before. They had slept in the same bed, but there'd been no penetrative sex. She had, however, stripped naked for him, let him feel her as they kissed. Finger her. As his own passion had mounted, he found himself lost in it and licking her, his nose pressed into her pungent pubic mound, his own crotch pressed against the end of her single bed. (There'd been no question of them occupying her parents' bed, it seemed. He didn't think the possibility had occurred to her.) She'd come – or given a good impression of coming. He'd assumed it had been genuine, simply because she cried out 'I love 'Dwan' at the peak of it, not something he imagined she'd have done for his benefit. Nevertheless, it had made him feel powerful. Up to something. She'd slept better than he had. He'd hardly slept at all. He'd felt cheated of his own climax. It didn't have to be penetrative, but he wanted to come in her presence. There'd be tonight as well, though – he was assuming.

They ran up the hospital drive, the huge edifice of the main admin block swelling towards them as they approached them. Hal ached, in his chest, in his loins. It was after nine-twenty – they were more than twenty minutes late. Stuart was waiting for them in the reception area, sitting on a grey plastic chair, his foot tapping up and down on the thin brown carpet tiles. He looked at his watch when he saw them.

'You're a little late.'

'Sorry,' they said together, overlapping each other. Mara smiled apologetically. Stuart didn't return the smile.

'We missed the bus.'

'We need to run a tight schedule, for all kinds of reasons, but mainly because of the people we're looking after.' He nodded his head. There was reproof in the movement. 'The others have gone on ahead.'

'Sorry,' said Mara again. Hal just focused on trying to appear co-operative.

'I'm going to split you up today. You had an easy day yesterday.' He turned to Hal. 'You should see the other side of things here.'

Hal swallowed. His belly lurched. He was also conscious of the area below, still burning from the night before.

'Mara, you'll be with me. Hal – you can go to the Special Care Ward.'

'The Special Care Ward?'

'OK?' The foot still tapping up and down.

'It's fine.'

'Good.' Stuart stood up. 'Go outside, round the outside of the hospital. Past the back of the kitchens, past the mortuary – you'll see signs for that. There are three low brick buildings, walk down the gravel path between the second and the third. At the end is another path, a paved path that runs between two walls. Walk down it until you get to the end. The Special Care Ward is there. Got that?'

Hal nodded.

'Staff Nurse Varden's waiting for you. Go on. Off you go. We'll see you back here for lunch.'

Hal left with such haste, he didn't even say goodbye to Mara.

He followed Stuart's instructions as best he could. Actually, he had no trouble remembering them. His keenness to please had led him to concentrate. It was cooler today. A group of catering staff huddled by the open door of the kitchen, from which a cloud of steam emerged, bloating into the air. Hal wished he'd brought a jacket. He looked for the sign that pointed to the mortuary. It was funny that they had their own mortuary; but it was a hospital and all large hospitals would have one. There must have been many who would spend their whole life here, from early childhood onwards. He was dimly aware of stories of other, less-enlightened times when women were incarcerated for falling pregnant outside of wedlock, or even for being sexually promiscuous – however that was defined. He thought of some pretty working-class girl – a whole life of experience ahead of her – robbed of it for following her natural impulses. And then what happened to her? He shook his head, to break the thought. He really didn't want to contemplate it.

He needn't have worried about missing the mortuary sign. It was mounted on a portion of the building that jutted out from the rest. It could hardly be avoided. He swerved round it, consciously holding his breath as he did so, not wanting to breathe in the scent of the dead, whatever that might be. Formaldehyde? Unspeakable decay? As he rounded the corner he saw the three low brick buildings. There was no signage on them. But something about them looked offputting. One of them at least was no longer in use. The front door was boarded with dirty plywood and there was a pile of equipment to one side. Hard to make out what. Gas canisters; an old operating-theatre light. He looked for the gravel path but there wasn't one, only scrubby overgrown wasteground clogged with dandelion leaves and broken bricks. Conscious he was late, and that there was a nurse waiting for him, Hal stepped over the detritus, towards the fence he could see at the end of the brick buildings. There was a gate made of iron, with a chain coiled around it, but nevertheless propped open. He walked towards it, crunching old glass as he did so. There were some thin trees and scrubby rhododendron bushes. He had to push between them. He thought about going back, to get clarification on the directions, but then was immediately relieved to see a gravel path just beyond, emerging from the mulch and mud. He stepped through the scratchy branches and onto the path. There was a building at the end of it, beyond the thin shrubbery. It was older than the rest of hospital. Probably Victorian, rather than Edwardian. Its stone was mostly black with soot, but there were pale patches where the masonry was crumbling. He jogged along the path towards the front door, where there was a sign. Again he felt relief when he read it. It said simply 'Ward 4'.

Inside looked rather dark. It reeked of disinfectant and damp. There were no lights whatsoever. Perhaps there'd been a power cut? He could see the remains of gas lamps visible on the wall. There were electric lights, too, with green metal shades, and a line of fluorescent strip lights imperfectly fitted to the high ceiling. Hal looked around for a member of staff.

'Hello?'

Sensing something behind him, he turned around sharply.

There was a figure: a black shape silhouetted against the light of the front door he had entered through. A woman. He couldn't see her face. He stood waiting, panting, expecting some response or instruction. None came. He felt he had to prompt. 'I'm Hal. From Stuart. I mean, Stuart sent me. I'm late. It was my fault. I'm sorry.'

'You're with us.'

'Yes.'

'Come upstairs.'

'Thanks.'

She'd stepped away from the door, moved towards him. She was about his height, with a smooth, ageless face. Forty? Fifty? Her hair was pulled back, pinned underneath a starched nurse's hat. Hal wanted to get a sense of whether she was irritated with him, too. Her coolness gave no indication of this, but nor did it refute the possibility. If he could get her talking, it would be easier to tell. Already he was fearful of what he was going to have to do today. He wanted to think there was some support to hand.

'We missed our bus. We left the house at eight-thirty. It must have come early. *Very* annoying.' He hoped this didn't sound too ingratiating. He'd been able to charm teachers at school when he needed to. The nurse didn't respond.

The staircase climbed round two walls of the entrance area. The black paint on its iron banister was peeling in places. Rust showed through.

'We're going to the ward,' was all she said.

They reached a small landing, with closed iron doors. This had to be the oldest part of the place. The doors were like those of cells: a little viewing eyehole embedded two-thirds of the way up. Hal doubted they'd keep patients in there now. Perhaps they used them for storage.

There were no lights, but there was enough illumination coming through the dirty skylight above to see where they were going. There was a noticeboard on the wall, tatty pieces of paper fixed to it with drawing pins. Hal tried to read what was on them, but the text was smeared by a dried-up streak of dampness. The disinfectant smell was stronger here, almost too strong. It reminded him of a school trip to the perfume factory at Grasse. He had felt sick for days afterwards. Perhaps he should prepare himself for what was ahead.

A few more steps in silence and Hal felt he had to speak again. The thought of what he was going to have to face was making him nervous. Better to put a bottom to it. 'Stuart said this was the Special Care Ward.' No answer from the nurse. He continued: 'What, um – what kind of . . . difficulties do – '

'Where we're going, there are only two of them.'

This woman was not going to help him at all. She reached down to her side, pulled at a large bunch of keys fixed to a spring-wound tension line. They'd come to a halt by a narrow, tiled alcove. There was another iron door, this one without the viewing hole. The nurse had located a single outsize iron key and inserted it into the lock. It took some effort for her to turn it, as if this was a lock that didn't get much use. Once it was unlocked, she let go of the keys and they were yanked back to her side by the sprung reel. She pushed at the iron door, which, like the lock, resisted her at first and then gave way.

There was a whistle of wind as air got sucked in. Beyond the door was not a room or hospital ward, as Hal had expected, but another corridor. It glowed a sickly yellow. Its left-hand wall was made of glass bricks of the kind you might see in the skylight of an underground public lavatory. The floor was tiled, but the tiles were dirty. It looked like it hadn't been cleaned for some time.

'Follow me,' said the nurse, 'and stick close behind' – as if there were any danger of Hal doing anything else.

They walked on. There were no more instructions forthcoming, no indication as to what to expect – until they paused by another door with a number fifteen painted on it. The nurse coughed, pulled another key from her holder and opened the door.

Inside, it looked like a nursery. Hal was relieved. He'd been fearing something more gothic. There was a cot bed in one corner, child-sized. The walls were a regulation hospital green, but there was a mural strip running around the centre of the room depicting circus elephants sitting astride balls. It had a 1940s sort of Dumbo feel. Over to one side, by the window, was a kind of pushchair, except it was bigger than a pushchair – more like a wheelchair. It was occupied. A child. From the curly dark hair, Hal could see it was a girl.

'She's all yours,' said the nurse. The girl was little. A toddler. At first Hal didn't want to look too closely. He could tell there was something 'off' about her. She looked like she was about four or five, from her height. 'Go on,' said the nurse. 'No need to be shy of her.'

Hal remained still, unable – it seemed – to move forward.

'She never speaks,' the nurse added. 'She won't say a word.'

Come on, he thought. *Marshal yourself*. An odd choice of words. Something his old swimming coach used to say to him before he began a race. He moved towards the girl.

'What's she called?' No answer. 'What's her name?'

'There's a pile of nappies on the trolley.' The nurse nodded at a chrome hospital trolley against the wall. 'She needs changing.' The nurse looked at Hal directly. 'You know how to change a nappy?'

A hint of accusation in this. There was something fearsome about it. Hal turned to look at the trolley. It contained a clean pile of terry nappies, a glass dish of safety pins. There was a bowl of water with cotton wool balls next to it.

'The water should still be warm. I'll be back in a few minutes, see how well you've done.'

Hal turned back to the little girl. When he glanced up again, the nurse was gone. There was nothing for it. He found he was caught in his duty. The air was heavy with a kind of seriousness. He had volunteered, and the volunteering came with an obligation. He was an adult after all. Twenty-one, nearly twenty-two.

The trolley was on wheels. He reached for one of the chrome bars that surrounded its upper surface and pulled it towards himself. Then he let the rolling movement take him closer the girl in the oversized pushchair. It was like a small deckchair on wheels, with a metal rather than a wooden frame, and a rubber rather than a fabric seat. The girl was sitting back, with her legs slightly splayed. At first she seemed oblivious to Hal, then, as he drew closer, she turned, looking up at him. Was there any awareness in her eyes? Or was she not really present at all?

'Hello.' She gazed at him, perhaps like a baby would. In size, she was a toddler. Her face was older. Her eyes were dark, black nearly. Long bovine lashes. She blinked slowly. His plan was to tell her what he was going to do – that is, change her. But standing over her, he thought better of it. He'd just get on with it. She had shorts on, grey shorts made of a sort of flannel. Hal had never changed a baby in his life. Best to break it down into achievable stages. Take off the shorts. Easy. They had an elasticated waistband. She accommodated him with lazy movements of her legs. Underneath were sort of rubber pants, pulled over the terry nappy. Next stage. Get them off. He reached up, again anticipating some resistance from her, but there was none. She made a noise, a sort of gurgle, but it didn't sound distressed. He placed the rubber pants on top of the grey flannel shorts, at the back of the trolley's surface. Trying to keep the pile neat. On the lower surface, there was a bucket with a lid. He lifted the lid, ready to receive the used nappy. Next stage, find the safety pins and unclip them. Easy. But before you unclip them, just get a sense of how they have been attached so you can repeat this with the clean nappy. He made a note of the arrangement, reached up, unfastened them and worked them out of the cloth. He swallowed, peeled the towelling back, away from the skin. The nappy was full. A brown liquid. He reached around, pulled it away, immediately bunching it up so he could use it to wipe. Just do it, don't think about it. As he wiped the skin beneath the child's belly, he flinched, noticing that despite her infantile stature she had a full complement of wispy dark pubic hair. Some of the shit was matted to it. Just wipe it. Reach for the cotton wool, dip it in the water. The water was warm. Squeeze it out. Don't think about it. Squeeze it out and wipe it clean. It's your job to look after it. Do your duty, Hal. Do what you've come here to do.

And he did. He managed to enact a version of putting a clean nappy on, relieved to have the girl covered up again. She struggled a little when he lifted her in order to place the cloth underneath her. He tried to think of her throughout the operation. Of making the experience comfortable for her. Of not frightening her, of not alarming her. He tried not to think – to keep away from himself – the thought of her life in here – the thought of her provenance – the thought of the life – what life – lay ahead of her. The thought of how old she might be and how much longer she might yet live. These were all questions it was impossible to imagine putting to the nurse. He turned, as he pulled the grey flannel shorts back on the girl. The thought of he nurse seemed to have brought her back into the room.

'All done?' No smile attended the question, no courtesy – a plain, clearly rhetorical question since it was based on observation. Hal nodded, a feeling of apprehension growing in his lower belly; an echo of the morning's blue balls.

'Yes.'

'Good.' The nurse held him in her steady, neutral gaze.

'We should go through into the next ward,' she said, after a moment.

'The next ward?'

'Ward Four Sixteen.'

Hal found his heart was beating fast, too fast. The sudden lurching drop of overwhelming terror.

'He's in there. Come on.' A gravity to the instruction. It was not to be disobeyed.

They left the girl in her chair. She gurgled as Hal departed.

'Is she all right?' The gurgling contained a sense of distress.

'Come on, please. Follow me.'

The Haunted Book

They left the room, back out into the corridor, walked for a few paces. Already the key on its sprung cable was in her hand. Hal struggled to quell the growing sense of dismay. 'Ward 4 16' painted in Victorian gothic letters and numbers, their swirls and curlicues now faded. She placed the key in the lock. She didn't turn back to look at Hal, she merely had an air of being about her business: this was the next thing on her list of things to do. He looked at the back of her head, the pale skin of her neck. He had a sense of how far he was from anybody else. What if she wasn't a nurse? What if she was an inmate dressed up as a nurse? And that was merely the most palatable of the ideas about her he was having. This was an old building. And he was in its oldest part. She turned to him. For the first time since he had been with her, she smiled. There was nothing pleasant about it.

The door groaned, as if it hadn't been opened for some time. There was a smell, a cold smell. Earth, dampness, decay – matter rotting. Unlike the room where the girl had been, this one was dark. There was a shaft of light coming through a high slitty window on the back wall, slicing down like a follow spot in a theatre.

'You have a visitor,' she said into the darkness. A snuffling sound, like an animal. Something unable to control itself. The nurse turned back to Hal.

'I'll leave you two to get to know each other.' And the door clanged shut.

Hal found himself fixed to the spot, despite his fear. It was a feeling that if he moved, he might somehow draw attention to himself – signal his presence there. And he didn't want to do that.

The snuffle had become a wheeze; whatever it was, secreted in the darkness, was becoming more agitated. Perhaps it was left alone most of the time. The merest hint of a visitor might be an

143

event of the most unbearable excitement. As if in confirmation, the sound of something liquid hitting the floor.

A sudden movement drew Hal's eye – a flicker in the patch of light, where it met the floor in a bright circle (surely that wasn't straw on the floor?). There was a hand. A pale, narrow dirty hand with long fingernails tapping the ground ahead of it, the nails clicking like a dog's claws. Following too close behind the hand was a bare foot and a thin hairy shin, pressed against a forearm which was in fact bent around the inner ankle. The hands were coming from behind the feet, like a circus contortionist's. The thing wasn't completely naked, but its back was bare, ribs pressed against its grimy flesh. It rested in the light for a moment, its head hanging down, messy hair matted like a mane, rattling breath catching in its throat. As Hal stood there staring, immobilised by terror, a thought worse than the sight in front of him snagged at his mind: he was reminded of something – by this scuttling animal and the dumb, overdeveloped little girl next door. Before this thought could complete itself, the thing before him lifted its head, shaking the hair away from its face and revealing a single eye. The eye glinted in the light, its distinctive grey iris flecked with tiny shards of amber, like Hal's own.

Hal ran, ran, ran, could remember little of his flight. He tore along the corridor, his descent down the stairs like a man running out of breath pulling himself up from the depths of a dive. Out into the fresh air, all his being screaming at him to exert every quantum of energy he had in fleeing that benighted place. Find another human being, find someone alive, find life, find light, find hope. He pulled himself through the branches of the thin, scrubby, scratching shrubbery, not caring that he wasn't near the path. He could see the redbrick of the mass of the hospital, and somehow its mundanity brought relief. He passed a small low modern building – a sign in the familiar NHS Helvetica – Special Care Unit.

He was still crying when Stuart found him. 'I got lost,' was all he could say as Stuart shushed and cradled him. 'I got lost.'

Whilst it didn't make much sense geographically to travel to Cornwall from Lincolnshire, I was certainly grateful that I'd arranged things that way. The promise of a trip to that sublimely beautiful county made a welcome antidote to the oppressive environs of the disused hospital and the uncomfortable experience I'd had wandering amongst its derelict buildings.

Of course, there was nothing spectral about what I'd glimpsed there. Surely it was just a local child, bunking off school. Maybe they'd seen me skulking around the grounds and were curious as to who I was, so they'd taken up a position on the pile of bricks in order to try and ascertain my identity.

In truth, they were the vulnerable one, not me – given that they knew nothing about me. It's children, after all, who are vulnerable in the presence of adults, not the other way round.

Why I should be so afraid of this figure, I don't know. What was I scared of? What did I think would happen? What was the precise nature of the peril I imagined? What did this 'phantom' child mean to me? I had no answers to these questions. There were only feelings. But it was another reminder of the private nature of fear, invoked not by perception but rather by the interpretation of perception.

Personally, I'm not comfortable owning up to the experience of fear. My own relationship with it has been too charged, too bound with value judgments about my character; words like 'cowardice' and 'weakness' come to mind. The idea that the vulnerabilities *of childhood are still present in the fullness of adulthood is not something that I'm keen to acknowledge. This book began, so I thought, from a 'fun' place – without wishing to trivialise my own endeavours. Perhaps 'playful' is a better word than fun, but it was in a playful spirit that I'd set out. So I was surprised to find a certain heaviness setting in so quickly. And if I'm being honest, 'heaviness' isn't the right word either. Choice of words is, of course, everything. Maybe this isn't imprecision, but rather denial. 'Heaviness' is not the word I should be using. 'Dread' would be closer.*

The Liskeard and Looe Union Canal is one of many abandoned British waterways. Opened in 1828, it survived for more than eighty years before finally closing in 1910, to be replaced by the railway, which followed its course. Its main purpose was to carry lime and sand inland from the coastal town of Looe, but as mining in the area prospered it began to traffic copper, tin and lead as well. Ultimately, the canal became a victim of the industry's success: the growth of what was produced outstripped the canal's capacity. Whereas other canals have enjoyed new life, thanks to the Inland Waterways Association (the IWA) – the L&LUC has yet to be restored. There is a walking guide available and, at under ten miles, it makes for a pleasant expedition on a fine afternoon.

The best way to approach the canal is to head along the A38 towards Liskeard and follow signs for the Liskeard and Looe Railway. There is a public footpath from Coombe that will take you alongside the first stretch of the waterway, too.

The account I'd found in Aiden Fox's files is centred around a lock-keeper's cottage near Lamellion Mill Bridge, and that was where I headed. In that version the cottage is derelict, so I was surprised to see grey smoke coiling upwards from its chimney as

I made my approach. It was the chimney that was visible first above a bank of overgrown reeds. The cottage wasn't served by a road, so it didn't seem to be a practical place to live. Maybe it was rented out to holidaymakers. I was aware that the National Trust has a scheme whereby it leases a number of its more characterful properties as holiday homes. Perhaps this was something similar administered by the IWA. In fact, as I was about to discover, this wasn't the case at all.

The man outside was sat on a small wooden stool. He had a pipe, from which smoke coiled like a miniature version of the cottage's chimney. There was evidence that he was living there (a bottle of washing-up liquid in the window and, hanging in the open doorway, a dead hare). He had something in his hands, I couldn't quite see what, but he was engaged in some form of idle activity – whittling or net-mending. He gave the impression he was waiting for somebody – and maybe he was. He had cropped grey hair, a tanned and weathered face, an air of health and vigour about him enhanced by the white tennis shorts he was wearing. He glanced up at me as I approached along the uneven footpath, mildly interested in who I was, but no more. Feeling I should make an effort to be polite, I slowed my pace. Some people, notably my mother, have the facility of beginning conversations with those unknown to them. I, myself, will go as far as avoiding even people I know, should I spot them coming.

'Hello!' I said, smiling.

'Afternoon to you.' He looked up, but kept most of his attention on whatever the craft-based task was in his hands.

'Lovely house.'

'Hmmm?' He looked up. If there was irritation, it didn't show on his face. I pointed towards the cottage. 'That it is,' he said, smiling warmly. The crow's feet that crinkled around his eyes as he did so added to his appeal.

'S'pose you get bothered by passing walkers a lot, this time of year?'

'It's no bother.' There was still no indication that he wanted me to walk on, even if there was no open invitation to continue the conversation.

'I wonder . . .' I was surprising myself with my own willingness to make conversation. 'You don't know anything about any of the stories relating to this area, do you?'

His smile shifted subtly – from one of neutral geniality to something more knowing.

'You're about the book, aren't you?'

'Sorry.'

'This is about the book. The haunted book thing.'

It was me who was smiling now, if a bit incredulously. How did he know about it? Had someone called ahead? But who knew? Aiden Fox? No. I'd only just decided that was going to be my title. I hadn't even written it down yet.

'Hang on.'

He got up from the stool. His legs were strong and tanned. He disappeared into the cottage. I stood there, feeling the sun on my bare arms, wondering what he'd was going to get. A copy of the story I'd found in Aiden's files that had brought me here? But that story wasn't from a book, or for that matter from one of Aiden's columns. It was a letter from one of his readers who said he was telling it for the first time. After about five minutes, maybe a little longer, an amount of time that suggested he'd had to dig around for a bit, the man appeared with a book in his hand – an outsized hardback with a battered-looking dustjacket. He waved it with an air of mild triumph and handed it to me. He had an apple, which he took a bite from. The dustjacket carried an illustration – a white and purple watercolour sketch of a spirit appearing from a reed bed. Despite the warmth, I'd gone cold, a light, nauseous feeling in my stomach. It wasn't the picture, mildly *unsettling as it was. It was the title written in a dark green font.* This Book Is Haunted, *it said. I felt my mind working, trying to make sense of the situation. Had I seen this book before and forgotten it? Was it one of the many that I'd consumed in my childhood? But there was none of the charge that usually accompanies the viewing of a long-forgotten item. What I was feeling, looking at it, was nothing as pleasant as nostalgia. I opened the cover, flicking through to the title page – aware the man was studying me as I did so.*

THIS BOOK IS HAUNTED

by

H. Den Fawkes

Hamlyn
London
1978

'It's about a third of the way in. Page is folded down.' The man was smiling, still pleasant, a hint of mischief perhaps, or enjoyment at whatever confusion was playing on my face. 'Want an apple?' he said. I looked up, not expecting this. He pulled one from the pocket of his shorts, threw it at me. My right hand let go of the book and I managed to catch the fruit. 'Sit down,' he added. 'Have a bite to eat.' He gestured towards a small rock about four feet from where he sat, jutting out of the overgrown grass like a memorial stone. Feeling a little dazed, I did. My fingers felt their way into the pages, finding the break of the folded corner. I opened it up. What I read chilled me further, despite the warmth of the day and the absence of a breeze.

Chapter 4
Water Ghosts

There are almost as many stories about spirits and legends connected to water as there are to the castles and stately homes of antiquity. The Celtic traditions give us varieties of waterhorses – *Aughiskies*, *Kelpies*, *Nuggles*, *Shoopiltees*; German mythology has the *Ondine* and the *Nix* – the latter being shapeshifting water spirits who can take any human form they choose. They have a relative in the Slavic *Vodyanoy*. The Slavs also believe in a *Rusalka* – a water nymph or succubus that dwells alongside waterways waiting to snare passing travellers. Similar legends occur on other continents, too. Japan has its *Kawako*, or river child. Africa gives us the *Miengu* and *Mami Wata*.

Inevitably on our journey round the British Isles we are going to encounter spirits related to water. This is, after all, an island nation and many legends and traditions have accumulated over the centuries. Some of the most beguiling stories are to be found in the beautiful county of Cornwall. By turns lush and pastoral and bleak and forbidding, its landscapes are amongst the most evocative in all of the United Kingdom. (It's worth recounting that we, ourselves, had a mysterious encounter whilst researching the background of the following story. As we walked the isolated footpath that took us to its setting, we were overcome with a very strong sense of being followed. We turned on several occasions and saw nothing untoward. It was only on the last occasion, before we reached the abandoned lock-keeper's cottage at the heart of the following encounter, that we caught a glimpse of something – a small figure wearing a light-coloured coat, long brown hair falling forward over its face. Something about its countenance and posture made us shiver. Naturally keen to record this in case it was there was anything significant about it, we reached for our camera. When we turned again, the figure was gone. Of course, it could have been entirely material in origin, nothing more than one of the local children playing truant. However, we consider it worthy of reporting because of the otherworldly feeling that accompanied the sighting, and its proximity to a location already associated with a paranormal encounter.)

The story that follows was recounted by a local man who had left the area about eighteen years previously, returning occasionally for holidays on his own. He had family in the area, but most of them had died. Nevertheless, he retained a sentimental attachment to the locale and it was enough to draw him back there, to go walking the footpaths and coastal ways of his youth. The place in particular of most interest to him was an abandoned canal built in the early part of the nineteenth century but unused since the beginning of our own. It was now overgrown, unnavigable – yet the towpath, or at least a good portion of it, remained walkable. It was not a popular destination, un-signposted and generally unknown to tourists. Locals, too, were not overly familiar with it, and it had a reputation for being treacherous in places, its banks crumbling and its locks a potential snare for children. It was the latter fact that may have contributed to the unwholesome reputation the canal had acquired. Whether or not there had been any actual accidental deaths associated with it was unclear, but the stories may have grown up around these abandoned locks in order to dissuade the local youth from going anywhere near them. None of this was of concern to the teller of this particular tale, however, since he was man in early middle age without family of his own. Nor was he a fearful or superstitious individual, being a surgeon by trade, a sober individual quite unaccustomed to believing the more colourful tales that emanated from the county of his birth. All this is worth holding in mind as you read the account transcribed below. The gentlemen concerned may have believed his scepticism protected him from such an encounter. It seems his opinions were of no relevance to that which visited him.

THE MEANING OF WATER

Water is an ancient and universal symbol of life, purity and renewal. Many creation stories begin with life emerging from the primordial waters. Water inevitably stands for birth, regeneration, fluidity and dissolution. There are many Jewish rituals involving water, specifically the Mikveh – or cleansing bath – which finds its analogue in the Christian ritual of baptism, symbolising the washing-away of sin, the effacing of an old life, giving ground to a new one. Water can also represent spiritual nourishment and replenishment. There are many traditions where water rejects evil – not least the witch-ducking of medieval times. In the Orient, water is equated with wisdom as well as impermanence. In our own century, Jung defined water as representing the deepest regions of the unconscious. In Greek mythology, water divides the world of the living from the dead via five rivers. In Celtic traditions, water spirits are prophetic and providential – as evinced in the ongoing beliefs in wishing wells and pools.

An Encounter by Water

'I am not a superstitious man. Not a religious man. Not a particularly fearful man. And yet I had an experience I find it hard to account for by my own reckoning of the world, at least up until now. I'm a neurosurgeon by profession, and have been involved with medicine and a medical view of things as long as I can remember. My grandfather and father were both surgeons, although of the orthopaedic variety. Maybe it's inevitable I would end up with a sense of life as plumbing. Perhaps my own attraction towards the brain and its function was a response to this. After all, my forebears were all about preserving structure, repairing breaks, and I often baulked at the way they talked about cases as an engineer would a troublesome bridge or building. The brain is the opposite of this. It is very difficult to think about it disconnected from the personality that springs from it, not least surgically, because subtle changes in that personality are an invaluable component of diagnosis and pathology. The other fact about the human brain I found gripping from an early age was its startling complexity – the most complex structure in the entirety of the known universe. As a structure, it has only just begun to yield the tiniest proportion of its secrets. I am not one of these blithe characters you come across in the medical world who see it as only being a matter of time before science peels back all the veils. One does not have to subscribe to anything supernatural to have the humility to admit that there are some things we may never know. It is quite plausible that we have limitation built into our perceiving mechanisms and it is ultimately impossible for us to step outside the structures of our own cognition. Just as human hearing is limited to a broad band of frequencies between twenty hertz and twenty-thousand hertz, so human understanding may be bounded by the very way our brains are wired up. I say all this as a preamble to the experience I am about to recount. It allows me some kind of 'out' that does not contradict the model of the world I must adhere to and reside within.

For many years I have been holidaying in the southern part of Cornwall. I was born near Looe, and spent the beginning of my life there. Maybe because I was sent to a private school in Monmouth (another family tradition), I acquired a particularly romantic view of this part of my childhood and its environs. The already idyllic landscape, which contains both rolling hills and coastal drama, takes on an added glow of nostalgia from a time when all was one and I was part of it, before I was wrested away aged eight and a half. My family, or at least my immediate family, is no longer living, so it wasn't those ties that kept pulling me back. If anything, their absence increases the pull, and the romance I attach to the place. I've often wondered if I'd live there, were there a suitable hospital in the vicinity. The fact that there isn't means I don't really have to give the issue serious consideration, but it's an internal game that's played with some regularity on boring car journeys or waiting in post-office queues.

The encounter that follows took place after a difficult time at work. Let me be as clear as possible about what (I think) happened.

It was June, the week after Whitsuntide. I do not have children of my own, but I knew when the holidays were and planned around them. More than ever, I found it was solitude I sought and I didn't want it punctured with the cries of children. I took a cottage in Polperro, right on the western edge of the harbour. I'd been doing this for several years. I worked hard and tried to take three holidays annually – if not for me, then for my patients. Though even as I write it I'm aware of a dishonesty in that statement, and one thing this encounter has shown me is the importance of being honest. 'One man speaking the truth can save the world,' said Solzhenitsyn – or something to that effect. Yes, I took these holidays for my patients' benefit, but my motivation was not entirely altruistic. The truth is I was ambitious, and what really drove me was the thought of my position. The more effective my results, the more my reputation was boosted. Rest and recuperation, as it's known in military circles, was an essential prerequisite for this. In my personal life I was edging towards the status of confirmed bachelor, not in the euphemistic sense but rather in the temperamental one. *Not everyone is born to have children* was a thought that kept finding itself in my head. And because of the intense nature of my work, I had started to guard my pleasures jealously. One of these pleasures was hi-fi. High-fidelity sound. I had become what is known as 'an audiophile', buying publications, auditioning equipment, regularly upgrading it – constantly seeking to maximise the pleasure I could yield from it. A friend came round to listen to my latest set-up and commented on the experience of listening to Glenn Gould playing a Bach partita, that it was like – and I quote – 'receiving fellatio'. Other interests developed in accord with this. Fine wines, which I had never particularly had a taste for earlier in life, began to yield more appeal. Similarly I discovered the delights of French cheeses, noting that, as with the wine, and indeed the audio equipment, the more money one spent, the more pleasure these interests gave up – providing one was prepared to spend enough. Of course, they had one thing in common and that was that they were all solitary pursuits. Not even the communal joy of grand opera or the Royal Ballet for me, which I knew other unmarried colleagues both took part in. My 'hobbies', as I ironically referred to them, were all enjoyed solo, upon returning from work or at a weekend. Occasionally I would catch a whiff of guilt when balancing chequebook stubs, which I would quickly counter with a thought about what I *might* be spending my money on. There were other colleagues who belonged to private clubs that kept books of young ladies on the door. Or worse, would frequent Shepherd's Market (one older gentleman even kept rooms in Mayfair in support of this more unsavoury pastime). No. My interests, while perhaps putting me into the category of connoisseur, were entirely ethical and no more sinister than a rewards system to promote my continuing commitment and hard work.

I think I had come to the point where a choice was going to be made. Because the other thing about this lifestyle was that things which had started as luxuries had drifted, almost without consciousness, into becoming necessities. And I knew that if I was ever to share my life with anybody, I would to some extent have to give them up. Of course, children would be out of the question. I did enjoy the company of women, and there had been affairs that had lasted – though they had taken on a disappointing pattern of dissolving and fading out when my lack of interest in matrimony became apparent. There had been a couple of recent liaisons with married women, but this did not sit easily with me and I'd vowed not to give in to that urge again. It was a vow I'd taken seriously and meant. So, having passed my forty-second birthday, I was beginning to reach an accommodation with myself. It might be that I was going to remain a single man. I'm avoiding writing about the specific why of this. So let me get to it now.

I had recently been involved with a case which had not had a satisfactory outcome. Still the euphemism. What I mean to say is that the patient had died. Yes, patients die. One does not become a surgeon – particularly one working in my area – without learning that bitter fact early on. But something about the circumstances of this one had wriggled its way within and wouldn't leave me alone. It was a child that had died, and I think she could have been saved. She was eleven. Had fallen off a playground slide. She'd developed a subdural haematoma that, had it had been diagnosed in a more timely manner, could have been easily dealt with, giving her every chance of survival. There was an uncomfortable irony in that I wasn't available to make the diagnosis because I was operating on another patient with a similar condition. Except she had been in her late seventies. But afterwards, I couldn't stop thinking of the girl, and worse, her parents. The looks on their faces. And though I had been in similar situations before, this one affected me intravenously, as it were. And now I was in Cornwall, the land of my childhood, thinking, *I am better without children*. It was almost a decision.

I have to say that this thought, this conclusion, was like the final pin of a lock's mechanism sliding into place. There was sadness attending the thought, the sadness of grief, but I thought this a healthy thing. Grief was a process, not a final state. I would move beyond it, into a different, but ultimately stable place.

It was with these thoughts in my head that I set out on my morning walk, my favourite walk – the length of the old Liskeard and Looe Union Canal. It was a perfect length, being about ten miles, give or take. One could almost do it as a round trip, if one set off early enough; not that I had ever done this, though I occasionally toyed with the idea. My usual routine was to walk to Liskeard and get the train back to Looe, taking the coastal path round to Polperro if the weather was fine. This particular morning, it was dry but cool. A light mist had rolled in from the sea and, rather than evaporating after the dawn, it continued to hang between the trees, concealing what was only a few hundred yards ahead. The canal was reached by a narrow footpath that ran alongside the railway line. The hedgerows were overgrown. This was not a managed landscape and in places one had to duck to pass an aggressive limb of hawthorn. The pathway was uneven, and it rose a few feet above the field it edged in places. One had to concentrate to keep one's footing. After a while it began to descend and one could smell the brackish water of the canal. Unused for several decades, not one of the waterways that had been reclaimed in the rush for rescue that had begun in the fifties, there was something otherworldly about stepping onto the towpath, which was reached by climbing over a stile and stumbling down some rough steps cut into the grassy bank beyond. The sharpness of the incline on both sides of the water was such that the surrounding landscape disappeared and one felt like one had disappeared from it. It was quiet, but not silent. Too much nature for silence. One didn't do this walk expecting to see other people, which was part of its appeal.

The air was still. The mist hung suspended over the canal. Great clumps of reeds emerged from it in places. I'm saying they were reeds, but I use the word generically as I'm no botanist. The stone slabs that lined the water were covered in moss and pearly lichen so that they lost their sense of having been fashioned by a human hand, merging back with the natural world around them. Somewhere above, a seabird cried and I pulled my coat around myself, though I hadn't felt cold when I'd left the cottage that morning. The path ran straight for a good few hundred yards before dropping down a little. There was no lock but the towpath was built-up for a section and fell through a natural hollow in the bank. I could see no one ahead through the mist and was content in the knowledge that, for a while at least, there was no other place where walkers could join. I was alone with my thoughts and with my feelings.

A heaviness had settled about me that was simultaneously a hollowness, an emptiness in the base of my stomach, such as one might feel in an aeroplane if it drops suddenly. It was at that point I was aware of hearing something, like a soft echo, in time with my own footfall. Footsteps, just a slight beat out. I couldn't help but turn around. But there was nothing, or no one, behind me. At least no one visible. I walked on, straining to hear. Still the slight slap of my footsteps coming back at me, except they were louder. I tensed, without knowing why. So there was another walker after all. Not a habitually nervous person, I was assailed with a thought. What if I were to encounter someone violent? Some youth. Some vagrant. No one knew where I was. No one would come for me. The water at my right suddenly looked very black, viscous like oil. A movement made me turn. Something was forming in the mist ahead, coagulating. A figure walking towards me, in time with my own step. I tensed up, preparing to defend myself. Almost immediately I smiled, inwardly at least, shaking my head at my own stupidity; noting how easily panic and fear could take hold, symptoms of mood and unrestricted emotion. This walker was a few inches shorter than me, with a neat white beard, close-cut white hair, very thin on top. Liver spots dotted his smooth pink pate. He had a stick but he moved with a steady stride, giving the impression he carried it for reasons of company rather than necessity. Although it didn't come naturally to me, I nodded and smiled slightly as he approached. (Odd that in my professional life I would happily greet strangers – be they patients or staff – with a firm handshake and a confident holding of their eye. Divested of that authority, a different, more diffident personality was revealed – keen to avoid any contact whatsoever, if it could. And yet I felt no less myself when I was in the professional context. I suppose the story I was embedded in changed, and with it the character I played.) I walked on then, having smiled and avoided the gentlemen's eye, though I had been struck by his stylish suit and bright orange waistcoat. An unpleasant thump made me turn.

It seemed the gentleman was not as sure-footed as he'd appeared. He was now sitting on the ground, one leg at an unpleasant angle. Without thinking, I was at his side.

'Are you all right?'

'Stupid. Stupid. Stupid. Stupid.'

He rubbed at his thigh. He was old. He could have broken a hip. I began to make mental calculations – where was the nearest A&E? How quickly could they be here? How close could they get an ambulance?

'Anything hurting?'

'I'm stupid.' he said again, trying to haul himself to his feet.

'Just be careful,' I said.

But before I could finish speaking, he was upright. He rubbed the side of his leg again, but he was moving quite easily and evidently was in no great pain. His cane had fallen in the canal. It was drifting languorously away, like a pooh stick. I stretched out across the towpath to reach for it. The water was cold, with a thick scum running across its surface. It gathered around my hand as I pulled the stick out. I shook it, smearing its wet part across the grass to dry it a little. The cane was nicely carved from a piece of hazel, polished, with a horn handle. I handed it back to him and he took it, smiling ruefully. How old was he? Late seventies? Older? Maybe even a well-preserved eighty.

'Thank you,' he said, wiping the handle of his cane with a handkerchief. 'At my age you can't afford to be so careless.' I suppose he knew what I'd been thinking. His voice was cultivated, but there was the soft hint of a West Country burr beneath.

'Are you sure you're OK?' I asked, still concerned. I didn't want him walking off, covering any injury or pain out of pride. 'I am a doctor.' I winced as I said it, but his need overrode mine in that moment.

'Doctor?' He eyed me, perhaps assessing whether I was being truthful or not, though why I would lie about it I don't know. 'What kind of doctor? Sawbones?'

I laughed.

'Funny?'

'It's what my father used to call my grandfather – "a proper sawbones".'

The old man stared at me for a moment. He nodded.

'I am a surgeon, yes. Not orthopaedic.' I held back, not wanting to give myself away so easily. 'General surgery.' In truth, 'general surgeon' actually means one who specialises in the abdominal regions. But most lay people assume it's like a general practitioner – a little bit of everything. His eyes narrowed as if he could tell I was lying.

'Well,' he said after a moment. 'No bones broken. Pretty sure of it.'

'Good,' I said, before adding, 'I'm on holiday.' This was meant lightly but it sounded mean-spirited.

'I'll tell you how you *can* help me,' he said, tapping his stick on the ground. 'I think I might be lost.'

'What were you looking for?'

'Old lock-keeper's cottage. Abandoned.'

I knew the building he referred to. It was about two miles north of where we were, alongside a stepped line of locks.

'You're heading in the wrong direction.' If I felt a drag of dismay at the thought he might accompany me, there was another part of me that was pleased. It was an opportunity to make reparation for my lie – to help him on his way. 'It's about an hour's walk from here – that way.'

'Really.'

'I can . . . um. I can show you the way.'

He took in my evident reluctance. 'Oh, I wouldn't want to inconvenience a young man like you. You'll want to be striding off at your own pace, not crawling along with an old snail.' I liked that he'd called me young. At forty-two, I felt nothing of the kind. But there's nothing more relative than the perception of age.

'There's no inconvenience, I can assure you. I never walk at anything but the most leisurely of paces.' A moment in which he scrutinised me. 'I'd be glad of the company.'

He nodded again. 'Well. You're very kind, sir. Thank you.'

We walked in silence for some time and I inwardly did a volte face, now regretting my act of altruism. I would be stuck with him for at least an hour, more like two given the sluggishness of his pace. His stick tapped against the rubble of the towpath, his breath audible, if not laboured. I felt a responsibility to make some kind of conversation.

'Are you holidaying here?'

He didn't reply at first, so I let it go. After an odd pause, he did speak up.

'Not exactly.'

I felt a shadow behind this so I didn't press him on it.

'I – er . . . I like to come here to recuperate. R&R, as they call it. I come more than once a year.'

'Exacting work.'

'It can be.'

His brow creased, as if he was trying to remember something. Another pause, and I felt that I should be trying harder to make conversation. I was not, after all, a sulky teenager. I was a mature man, and if this was a professional situation I would be trying harder.

'I am curious. What brings you to this particular . . . footpath? This walk? Forgive me. I'm not being nosy. It's just . . . silly, really. I pride myself on . . . I think . . . I always think . . .'

I was trying to be sensitive, but it was making me inarticulate. I thought of the neural pathways involved in speech. The nerve impulses flying across synaptic clefts on their way to the motor-neurones that controlled the larynx.

'It's just I think of this being a private walkway – not mine, of course – but not one that's well known. Even some of the people who live here aren't aware of the old canal in their midst.'

'I've known of it for a long time,' he said. 'I used to come here when I was a boy.' I wondered if he was old enough to remember it in use.

'Do you live hereabouts?'

'I've a cottage up at Lansallos. It was my wife's, actually . . . She left it to me.'

I sensed the heaviness again. As if speaking these facts in that way was something unfamiliar to him.

'Was she from around here?'

'No – no.' A moment of silence. It was obvious now he was in the thick of his grief. He must have just lost his wife. I couldn't begin to conceive of that pain. To have shared your whole life with somebody and to have them disappear from you. He swallowed. 'She bought it for me. The cottage . . .' He lifted his spectacles, wiped an eye. 'She saved for years, without telling me. It was a gift. A wonderful surprise.'

The sun clouded over momentarily. Without its warmth, there was a definite chill in the air. The reeds – or rushes, or whatever they were – shook in the winds, a wave of motion spreading towards us through them.

'Are you married?' he asked.

I felt he already knew the answer to this. I didn't look like a married man. And, of course, I wore no ring.

'No.' He made no comment, nor demonstrated any emotion. It's possible I was projecting all kinds of paternal qualities onto his somewhat noble face – that air might only have been a function of his facial hair, and advanced years, combined with the sense of grief. 'I fear I'm not the marrying kind.'

'Wedded to your job,' he said. Or it might have been a question.

'Yes,' I said, in a somewhat circumspect manner. 'I've got used to my freedoms.'

'Freedoms! Oh, dear. That's no good. No good at all.'

'Why no good?'

'There's little freedom in anything that feels like freedom. Quite the reverse.' He laughed a little as he said it. It sounded rather Confucian to me. Not to mention presumptive. 'Take children. The opposite of freedom. The very opposite. But . . .' He exhaled; a sound of deep satisfaction. Now I felt he was being insensitive. But he was old. And grieving. And doubtless prone to sentimentality.

'I've seen much unhappiness in friends. In family.' There was a bite to my tone; hard to keep it hidden. 'I've no desire to pair for the sake of it.'

'I favour Abraham Lincoln on happiness: "Most folks are about as happy as they make their minds up to be."'

This would teach me for trying to be good. The old canal path was now a road to hell. I felt irritated, angry even. And once anger descended, it clamped me round the middle like a band of rubber. I wasn't in control of it. Maybe there was a point – a single moment in time where it was possible to avert it via an act of will – but I was so rarely able to catch it. Another reason why I couldn't be married. I could not face the thought of a lifetime of such incidents; or what was left of my life. How ridiculous that this stupid old man had brought this out in me after only a few minutes in his company. We walked on together, the rustle of the reeds, the regular beat of his stick.

'I'm sorry,' he said after a moment. 'Forgive me.'

'Forgive you for what?'

'I'm not myself. I'm – ' He paused to steady himself against the remains of a wall. And, quite unexpectedly he seemed to fold up, physically. He released a great wracking cry, almost a scream. It was something he clearly couldn't control. I was embarrassed. I looked away, not knowing what to do. *Don't turn away*, some quiet voice said within. *Just let him be.* The old man looked frail, hollow. Very old. He steadied himself, pressed his hand to his face.

'I'm so sorry,' he said after a moment.

'It's quite all right.'

'I haven't done this walk for many years. Many years. My wife died.' A pause in which the air around us felt like a heavy blanket. 'It's so long since I did this walk. I thought it was something I'd dreamed. But losing her reminded me.'

'Do you want to go on?' I asked. 'We could turn back.'

'No. I'm meeting my daughter.'

'You have a daughter?'

He smiled at my mention of her.

'I do. Normally she would not let me do a walk like this unaccompanied. On this occasion, she was wise enough to let me, and trust to providence.' He searched for a handkerchief in his jacket pocket. 'Please,' he said. 'You can go on. I will be fine.' But I was concerned for him now. I didn't want to leave him. We both stood there, momentarily frozen. Slowly, almost imperceptibly, we began to walk on.

'You know – I would often have the conversation with my wife – we could never decide. Is life a happy sadness? Or a sad happiness?' He put his handkerchief back in his pocket, pulled his jacket straight. The sun had come out again, and in the brighter light his suit was revealed to be cut from a fine and expensive linen. Not that I was an expert on such things, but I didn't have to be one to see it.

'How long were you married?'

'I'd say all my life. But it wasn't all my life. It was less than half of it. We married late. We wanted children and she worried she was too old, that she'd miscarry. But when the pregnancy came, all went well. Our daughter was healthy.'

Again, a moment where the emotion overtook him. The scale of it was the thing I couldn't process. So pure. So raw. The dissembling of courtesy couldn't cover it. It was life undisguised and as it was. One normally felt it only obliquely. Perhaps just as well. Who could function in the truth of its terrible glare? He looked up at me, through his tears, gathered himself again. A light breeze blew, carrying the sweetness of cut grass from somewhere not too far away. It kept me in the moment whilst simultaneously pulling me back to childhood – at least the feeling of it. He rubbed at his cheeks with the palms of his hands.

'You know,' he said, picking up his pace, 'a patient once said to me that if people could see what was ahead of them, the rivers would be full. And I used to fear that was the case, too. But I don't feel that now.'

'Do you have a photograph of your wife?'

Now it felt like the right thing to say. He'd softened. And it was an authentic question. I wanted to see her. Maybe I thought it was a kindness to ask to see her, too. Maybe that was uppermost.

'Many.' He reached into his pocket, pulled out a slender oblong of glass. Odd, I thought, to carry a framed picture. But it wasn't framed. It was clear glass. He touched it and the glass darkened, immediately. It was now covered with brightly coloured little squares. He pressed one of them and a photo appeared. A handsome woman with short hair, in her seventies. I wanted to ask about the glass, but he was showing me the photo. She had bright, large blue eyes, one of the pupils flecked with brown. He touched the glass again, flicking it like the pages of a book, and another photo appeared. The same woman, but younger, in her late thirties, handsome, smiling, vivacious. Her hair longer, a deep chocolatey brown. He looked down at her, shook his head. Pocketed the glass.

'Don't look back when you've your hand to the plough,' he said. I could hear the emptiness of his pain in the words once again, so while I desperately wanted to ask more about the glass with the photos, I restrained the selfishness of my curiosity.

We had reached a long straight section of the canal. The water was clearer here, less overgrown. It almost looked navigable. In the distance, through the clearing mist, I could just make out the darker shape of the lock-keeper's cottage.

'There's the cottage,' I said, pointing. We were nearer than I'd thought.

'Would you like to meet my daughter?' said the old man, simply. He had looked calmer, but abruptly his face darkened, his eyes widening behind his spectacles. The shock of sudden recognition or remembering. In that moment, I experienced a sudden shock, too – the kind of thing one feels in those rare moments when one is awake but suddenly thinks one might be dreaming. Looking at him, it felt as if I was staring into a mirror, angled slightly upwards, and that beneath the deep lines, the glasses, the facial hair, I was looking at myself. I swallowed.

'I won't. Thank you. Actually . . .' I had noticed a stile about thirty yards in front of us. 'Actually, I may take my leave of you here, if that's all right? The day's turned out finer than I thought. I might head out to the coast.' I was aware how fast my heart was beating, how dry my mouth. We didn't shake hands. I glanced at the lock-keeper's cottage ahead, that little bit nearer now. I didn't look back, almost falling over the stile.

I met my wife not long after this experience, at a fund-raising event at University College, London. She was a poet, unpublished at that time. In her late thirties, she was fearful she couldn't conceive. I knew her the minute I saw her, the distinctive fleck of brown in the lower part of her left pupil. I knew also she would bear me a daughter.

And so she did.
    And she was beautiful.

Chapter 5
Mysterious Disappearances,
Inexplicable Occurrences

BOTTOMLESS

Mrs J. Tinsley, Garston Park, Abbots Langley, Herts, writes:

I wonder if you or your readers can solve a creepy problem. My husband is fond of curries and makes them quite often. About five years ago he bought a tin of turmeric powder and each time he makes a curry he puts one heaped teaspoon of turmeric in it. Yet the next time he gets the tin out, it is packed tight under the lid. In other words, although he has been using the turmeric for five years the tin is still full! We can't understand it.

In our review of supernatural encounters from around the country it feels right to cast the net as wide as possible when it comes to the kind of phenomenon reported on. As the newspaper cutting above reminds us, the strange and the inexplicable can occur in the most mundane of settings. And indeed this suggests a way of approaching the world that differs from the everyday rational frame we customarily place around it. The father of this approach – dubbed 'phenomenalism' – was Charles Fort (1874–1932). In summary, the viewpoint he championed goes something like this: accept everything; believe nothing absolutely; do not explain. Any theories offered are tentative and temporary. The study should be of the content of human experience: things that happen, or are believed to happen, or are said to happen. Most interesting to the phenomenalist is that enigmatic range that lies somewhere between the 'hard' reality of nuts and bolts, bricks and mortar, and the 'psychological' reality of dreams and the 'inner' world.

Indeed the experience we ourselves had in Cornwall, with the small figure that appeared then just as abruptly disappeared, fits neatly into a Fortean view of phenomena. As does the repeated sense of glimpsing this figure that has accompanied us since then – an inner sense that it may actually be behind us as we write this.

Phenomenalists recognise no certainties. Yet, all around, the rest of the world contrives them: the certainties of dictators, doctors, high priests of science and religion, eccentrics and zealots, each one consisting of different selections from the common source material, the sometimes unreliable world of sensory perception – and each one a rival to the others. Phenomenalists think these certainties are best avoided, considering them to be maintained by studied ignorance and selective blindness.

The anomalies phenomenalists deal in are interesting on two levels, partly for the colour and fascination they evoke in themselves, but also for what they reveal about the flexible and subjective nature of scientific reality – a way of looking at the world that, we should remind ourselves, is less than three hundred years old. Phenomenalists are concerned with symptoms rather than causes: with rains of animals pouring from the sky; with impossible coincidences; with inexplicable sightings of creatures or objects. The conclusion these observations lead to is that there are, in fact, three modes of reality, 'hard', 'psychological' and, between the two, 'phenomenal', and all of these are active, all blur into one, when truthfully described, without the need to immediately leap in with rational explanation. Charles Fort himself described that urge as the 'Worcester Fishmonger'. In 1881 there was a storm over Worcester that deposited tons of winkles and mussels and miscellaneous crustaceans all over the streets, backyards and gardens of the great cathedral city. Because there was no science (and still isn't) that could explain this happening, very quickly an explanation emerged: a local fishmonger with a surplus of unsaleable stock had simply dumped them about the place. This became emblematic for Fort of all the inadequate, hopelessly overstretched explanations that rationalism sometimes has to make do with.

Most interesting is the light that phenomenalism throws on consciousness itself and its elastic relationship with reality. It is an inconvenient truth that the experience of every single human being that has ever lived is ultimately entirely subjective. The convenient fiction of an independent reality to which our language and our science refers is just that. For there are no chairs and tables and bricks outside our mechanisms of perception – things that remain there quietly when we leave the room, waiting patiently for our return. They are seen and made in the brain of the perceiver, that brain filtering down and organising an impossibly massive amount of sensory data provoked by the constant bombardment of information in the form of waveforms caused by particles in motion that, looked at in a certain way, can become what we label, for our own utility, 'chairs' and 'tables' and 'bricks'. But those things are not there if we are not. This is the only thing that is ultimately indisputable. In the light of this, is it so unreasonable to suppose that there are indeed anomalous flickers in this process that can present themselves to us in the most unusual of ways? The more interesting question than whether such things exist is surely 'What do they mean?'

The Fortean Classification of Phenomena

Charles Fort was the first to categorise anomalous events and conclude that there were numerous recurrences and similarities between them. Broadly these categories include: unexplained falls from the sky; mysterious lights in the sky or atmosphere; spontaneous human combustion; stigmata and bodily distortions; animal mutilations; inexplicable footprints; mysterious and monstrous creatures; levitations; teleportations; and phantom cities, buildings or other places. It is interesting to observe how adaptable and resilient these original classifications are and how phenomena from our own century still align with them – UFOs, for example, being mysterious lights in the sky; and the Sasquatch or Surrey Puma belonging to the mysterious or monstrous creatures category.

We feel that Fort would have cherished the following tales – one culled from a newspaper, and one donated by the Merseyside writer and broadcaster Norman Thomas, who is himself a keen phenomenalist.

The Pleasure Park

The two stories below are reproduced by kind permission of the
Bridgewater Times. *The first of these ran in June 1973. The second
just over two years later.*

Dennis Swain, his wife Barbara and their son, Alex, will drive 100
miles next weekend – in search of a phantom fairground.

The trip will be roughly their 250th in a quest that has gone on
for seventeen years. The mysterious, mist-shrouded amusement
park the Swains are seeking has a lake in its middle and many
abandoned but well-preserved rides and attractions. It is
surrounded by forest and seemingly unconnected to any nearby
habitation.

Mr Swain, a 52-year-old manufacturing co-ordinator, his
wife and their son Alexander, 24, know the mystery park exists.
They've seen it.

They were on holiday when they came across it near Beaulieu
Abbey in Hampshire's New Forest. Alex was ten at the time.

Mrs Swain explained what happened: 'We were driving down some little off-beat lanes on a picnic trip when we saw the fence. It was very ornate, wrought-iron, though completely overgrown – wrapped in ivy with vegetation and bushes all around it. My husband suggested stopping the car because it looked so unusual. He thought we might want to see what it was.'

Mr Swain picks up the story: 'It didn't really look English – more like something you might see on the continent, in France or the Low Countries. We drove for a while, to see if there was a way in, thinking it was part of a stately home or a park. We didn't know the area so it seemed like a possibility. It was only afterwards that we discovered that there was nothing like that for miles around.

'We found a spot where the fence was open to the road – though with hindsight it may have just collapsed. We made our way inside, with our picnic things. There wasn't really a path, but the trees were sparse and they opened out onto a kind of glade, which was very attractive. It was my son, Alex, who saw the first of the rides.'

Alex, a tall, softly-spoken young man, picks up the story. His memories of the day, like his parents', seem remarkably vivid.

'I remember looking up through these very tall old trees, and among the leaves seeing what looked like a cable car. It was just hanging there, very high up. Right above the leaves. I shouted to my dad – we both loved engineering and Meccano – and it looked really interesting. At first I couldn't see what it was hanging from. It looked like it was floating there. Then I realised it was suspended from cables. They were held by a series of beautiful iron poles. We followed the line of them and it took us further into the forest. It was then that we stumbled across what looked like a switchback ride. It was built out of wood, and raised above the forest floor – not as high as the cable car, only about ten feet, and it wound its way through the trees. Well, that was it. I said to Dad, we had to have a ride on it – it looked quite amazing. We walked on for a bit, trying to find where the start of it was, or whether there was a booth where you paid to go in it, but there was no sign of anyone else around.'

Mrs Swain picks up the story.

'It's funny – we all remember different things about it. The thing I still have in my mind's eye is the map-board. I think it was because I used to do marquetry when I was younger, and this was the finest and largest piece of marquetry I'd ever seen. It must have been about ten foot along the bottom and five or even six feet high. It was mounted on two posts carved from oak and it was a map of the park. There were the rides on it, including ones we didn't find: a labyrinth with sliding doors; some kind of chute that ran underground; what looked like a menagerie. Each thing was really well detailed in different wood veneers. It was an amazing piece of work, and if I close my eyes I can still see it all now, all these years later.'

'It's the feeling I remember,' says Mr Swain, 'walking around – the four of us – all not believing what it was we were seeing. All of us amazed – like kids on Christmas Day, even though we were the parents – we felt the same. There was a wooden carousel on a raised area in a circle of rhododendrons. I'd say it was about forty years old or more, but in terrific condition. We didn't get to ride anything or see more because it started to get dark. We didn't have torches, and though we could see lights strung in the trees they weren't turned on. We felt we had to get back to the car or else we risked getting lost.'

'There was a light, but I was the only one who saw it,' added Alex. 'Well, me and Phil? I think Phil saw it – but we didn't really talk about it.' Who was Phil? I asked. 'Phil, my brother – '

'Phil moved away,' Mrs Swain explained, unsmiling.

Alex continued. 'There was a light – a single light. We saw it through the trees. And there was a sort of rippled reflection underneath it, so it appeared to be on an island over a lake. Phil gave me a leg-up onto a branch. Because everything else was sort of misty, I couldn't see whether it was a house or some other kind of building.'

'None of it seemed such a big deal at the time,' said Mr Swain. 'We thought "We'll find out more about it and spend a day here on the way back." Well, we asked around when we got to where we were staying, which was about fifteen miles from there, but nobody knew what we were talking about. Still, it didn't seem like anything because we thought "We'll just stop on the way back." And that was when it began. Because we couldn't find it. It wasn't marked on any map. Nobody knew what it was. We drove around in a bit of a frenzy, not believing we couldn't find the place.'

'I felt sad, really sad,' said Mrs Swain.

'So I vowed that we'd come back – in a few weeks – armed with a better map,' explained Mr Swain.

And that was how their regular trips began. 'After four or five of them, I thought, were we going mad? But we all saw it, so we knew we weren't. There had to be a solution. We did lots of research – in the libraries – writing to people – though, to date, nothing has come up that explains what we saw that day.'

Nor have the Swains ever come close to finding the park again, despite having searched the New Forest meticulously in the years since they sighted it. Is it possible that what they witnessed was a travelling fairground of some kind? They all shake their heads. 'The structures were too substantial,' says Dennis Swain.

Could it have been demolished?

'Who would demolish such a beautiful thing?' says Mrs Swain, incredulously.

'Besides, there would still be evidence on the ground. Remains to be found,' Alex protests.

Alex then shows the book of drawings, very elaborate and skilfully done: the switchback ride; the cable cars; the wooden carousel.

'Even then, engineering was my thing, so I knew about drawing things,' he tells me. 'Aircraft engines, in particular – my real love. I'd go with Dad and do them. All I've ever dreamed about is working with aircraft. It's why I'm going to do the job in Chicago.'

It turns out this week's visit is the last one Alex is going to make with the family.

'I've got the offer of this job, at Lockheed. Working in the department that designs the engine systems. It's quite a thing. To be going to America, doing what I've always wanted.'

'Which is why this is the weekend that we are going to find the park,' says Mrs Swain, 'to see it again before Alex goes. All of us together.'

I ask the Swains: what is it about this place that has meant they never gave up their search for it when many others would have abandoned it?

'It was something we all experienced together,' says Mrs Swain, 'and all of us wanted to see it again. And we know we saw it – we weren't going mad – and we all need to see it again, together.'

Mr Swain smiles. 'Other people do not understand – it's a Swain family thing, all of us together,' he says, repeating his wife.

And what if they don't find it this weekend?

'I think we will,' says Mrs Swain.

Two years later, in August 1975, the newspaper published a follow-up article.

Several years ago this paper ran a story about a local family, the Swains, and their ongoing search for an amusement park they saw once on a drive through the New Forest and were never able to find again, despite regular searches. There have been a number of letters enquiring whether the Swains located the park, and this prompted us to follow up the story, which appears below.

Much has happened for the Swain family since I last met them in September 1973 – unfortunately, not all of it good. Mr Swain passed away, unexpectedly, in 1974 after a short illness. Mrs Swain was not left alone, however. Youngest son Alex, it transpired, never took up his job at Lockheed Industries in Chicago.

'It wasn't such a difficult decision in the end. I enjoyed being with the family so much I think it would have been too far to go. And I realised I could be just as happy working on my models at home. Dad helped get me a job at Marshall's, where he worked, and it's still connected with engineering – administering the stores – so I guess it's the best of all worlds.'

There are two questions I'm impatient to put to the Swains: did they ever find the park and, if not, did they continue their search in spite of their recent bereavement?

'It's funny. The week before my father got ill,' Alex explains, 'we thought we'd had a breakthrough. There was a narrow little road that ran off one of the B roads and we'd never seen it before. It looked like a hedge had grown over the entrance and someone had trimmed it back, revealing the road beyond. Well, we could just about get the car down it so we set off, and we all got increasingly excited when we saw a rusted wrought-iron fence along the left-hand side of the road over a ditch. It looked very familiar. We pulled the car over where we could and got out to explore. Mum's not as nimble as she used to be, but she managed to get over, too.'

He smiles to show he's being good-natured, although Mrs Swain doesn't seem to share the joke.

'We stepped into this wooded area – and it was all overgrown – much more than we remembered the park to be – but we took that as an encouraging sign. Anything could have been hidden in there . . .' Alex's voice tails off. Eventually he picks up the story again. 'Dad got ill. So we didn't get back.'

Have you not been back since? I ask.

'We are going to resume – not next week. The week after.'

'For Dennis,' says Mrs Swain. 'In his memory.'

While Mrs Swain makes us some tea, Alex asks me if I would like to see some more of his drawings. He remembers that I'd appreciated them the last time we'd met. The drawings are kept neatly filed in his small study. 'It used to be Phil's room. My brother. I don't like to mention his name in front of Mum.'

He says no more about it. There are model aeroplanes everywhere, exquisitely detailed. Models of aircraft engines, immaculately painted, mounted on wooden blocks. Alex shows me maps he has drawn of the areas they have explored over the years.

'The New Forest is such a large area, and the available mapping is surprisingly incomplete,' he explains. There are photographs, too. 'This is the fence,' he says, showing me a series of snaps of a rusted section of wrought iron.

When we go downstairs, I ask them if it would be possible for me to accompany them on their forthcoming trip? Given the interest we've had from readers over the years, I think they would find it fascinating. At first they are uncertain.

'The car is very small – an Austin Wolseley,' says Alex.

How about if I followed in my own vehicle and we met up together? Eventually they agree.

We drive for about two hours without stopping. The sky begins to darken. This is not likely to deter Alex and Mrs Swain. They are prepared for all weathers. They stop and I make to pull up behind them – but almost straight away they begin to drive again. Eventually they come to a halt. Alex gets out of the car and clears some vegetation and foliage away from what I take to be a gate. It reveals itself to be a very narrow road, almost a dirt-track. I wonder whether it is wide enough to take my own estate car, but before I can get out to question them about this, the Swains have turned into the lane and driven off. The branches flick at my windscreen. I have my headlights on. Eventually their car pulls up again. I see a glimpse of the fence they've talked about, the one from the photographs. The road is so narrow that even parking our cars against the very edge of the road leaves it impassable. I get out and consult with Alex and Mrs Swain. Alex says the road is clearly so little used that they will be all right. Besides, if anything does come it will doubtless honk its horn to gain our attention.

The three of us climb over the fence and into thick woodland.

There are no signs of any paths, structures, or evidence of anything but trees, bracken, foliage. The ground is thick with leaf mould. What do the Swains think? Might this finally be the place? Alex seems excited. 'There is something about it,' he tells me. We walk for what seems like half an hour or more. I worry about our cars on the road. The wooded landscape doesn't alter. Suddenly Alex grows excited.

'What's that?' he cries out. I can't see anything, but he points and shows me. 'A pole,' he says. Mrs Swain remains silent. 'It's a pole. It's carved.'

We press on towards it. I can feel his excitement. He starts to run, moving away from me. I race to keep up, pushing thick bracken out of my way. I find him stood, staring up. It is not a pole. It is the remains of a tree – a tall silver birch – dead, most of its bark peeled away. Alex stands, gazing up at the remains of its bare limbs. His mother comes to stand at his side. The ground around him is thick with undergrowth; tangled life that will not be stopped. Alex bends, finds a dead branch on the ground and pulls at its twigs, shaping it into a club. He starts beating at the greenery around him. Without looking back, he vows out loud: 'We will find it, Mum. We will find it.' After another twenty minutes we turn back in the direction of the cars and the narrow distant road.

Tetherdown Lock

We are grateful to the broadcaster and raconteur Norman Thomas for supplying us with the account below, which makes for an interesting companion piece to the preceding items. Norman tells the story in his own words.

'The following was told to me by a young man who worked for a brief time as an engineer at Radio City in Liverpool. We'd got talking about these kinds of things because I'd brought in a copy of *The Fortean News*, which was a self-produced affair that had just started up. This man – whom we'll call Charlie – was a recent graduate; a clever chap; no-nonsense, I would say, and not the kind to want to draw attention to himself with overly colourful stories. He'd picked up and read the Fortean thing one lunchtime and quite freely began to talk about an experience he'd had that would fit right into that publication – one he'd never been able to satisfactorily explain.

Charlie had studied Electronics and Electrical Engineering at UMIST in Manchester, as an undergraduate and then as a post-graduate. A couple of years earlier he had taken some summer work with the Manpower Services Commission. He hadn't known what it would involve but he was working on his research project at the same time and guessing that whatever it was, it would be fairly mindless and physical. He thought it would fit nicely around his studies. The fellow from the MSC had been quite vague in his instructions but had told Charlie to turn up at the railway station in Ince-in-Makerfield (a little place a mile or so south-east of Wigan) very early on the Monday morning, and everything would be made clear to him then.

He'd had to get the first train from Piccadilly at some god-awful hour, but the weather was mild and although not a sociable creature he was quite looking forward to a week away from the university library. Also, the work was quite well paid and it seemed preferable to cleaning or being a Redcoat or some of the other dreadful things university students occupy themselves with over their summer holidays.

When he arrived there was already a small group of similar-looking individuals gathered. In fact, he was the last of them and it transpired they'd been waiting for him. They were about six or seven, plus the group leader – an irritable-looking man in his forties with a military-moustache, who didn't seem best-pleased with his billeting. He told them they were going to what he called a 'government storage facility' a few miles west of were they were and that they'd be making the journey in a minibus. Well, this was the first thing that was strange about the day: when the minibus arrived, it was more like a Black Maria. Charlie said it was white – not a Transit van, a bus-type vehicle – but the windows were blacked-out or, rather, where the windows should be there was sheet metal instead. Inside, it had conventional coach seats, but it was designed so that the passenger couldn't be seen – at least that's what he thought at the time. It was only later that he realised it was actually about the passengers not being able to see out – that is, to see where they were going.

The others were mostly, though not exclusively, students. Charlie found himself sitting next to someone a little younger than him with thick, long, black hair and striking looks – 'Like a pop-star', he said – and was immediately struck by the guy's 'charisma'. At first he was nervous of talking to him, but the young man himself spoke.

'Perhaps they are taking us to be executed.' Not quite a joke, but it immediately made Charlie laugh.

'I guess it would get the unemployment figures down,' he responded.

'And cheaper than the dole, too,' said the other. They immediately warmed to each other. The guy was called Ardel. Ardel Wray.

After not too long, the minibus pulled up. The last part of the journey had been over bumpy ground, and there'd been a pause while someone had got out to open a gate. They emerged to discover they were in sparse woodland, high up on a hill. Charlie said he could hear the roar of a motorway nearby, but there were no other clues as to the specifics of their location. In front of them was a small circular brick-built structure without windows, like a Second World War bunker. There was a steel door in one side – very secure-looking. Ardel looked at Charlie and Charlie looked at Ardel. They had both got the same sense that this was something to do with the military. They smiled at each other, a knowing smile. There's few things more enticing than the thought you are going to get to see what's on the other side of a heavily barred door.

Charlie expected there to be stairs, but instead there was an iron lift – like a miners' cage, but sturdier. Charlie said they were told to stand away from the sides, huddle together in the middle while it descended, which it did at great speed. When they got to the bottom they were standing in a concrete tunnel. There were boxes of cleaning equipment, mainly brushes and industrial

Hoovers, the kind they have in hospitals or schools. The concrete tunnel was lit all the way down with fluorescent lights. Charlie said it went as far as the eye could see, receding to a point in the distance; it must have been half a mile long or more. There were cables and pipes running along the ceiling and the walls were broken at regular intervals, doors and rooms running off its length. Charlie also said there was a strong steady breeze. The air smelt fresh, not musty in any way, and there was a low electrical hum, probably from the lights.

'Right. If you'd listen to your instructions, please,' the group leader said. 'You're here to clean, inspect – low-level maintenance. This is a government storage facility, intermittently used. Some of you are going to inspect, some of you are going to maintain, which will involve vacuuming, sweeping, dusting.'

'Always knew my degree would come in handy,' said Charlie. He was cut off by the group leader.

'You need to listen to these instructions. Pay attention. Or you'll find yourself dismissed.' When the group leader had turned away, Ardel had held two fingers under his own nose in Hitler fashion – stupid, but enough to make Charlie laugh, warm to him more. Everyone else seemed a bit stuffy or dull; not interested. Ardel had some life, some colour, to him.

So Charlie and Ardel paired up. They were assigned a large room not too far from the lift shaft. There was a corridor that branched off the main one. Charlie noted that there were two sets of doors to go through, both steel and lined with concrete, both with submarine-type sealing wheels in the centre. The doors were folded back into the walls, but it was obvious they were designed to keep the area as secure as it could be. The room had thick shelves on both sides and there were some loose papers on the floor, which needed tidying, and they'd been asked to dust and sweep. The papers were coded.

'We could spend our time cracking these,' Ardel had said. 'A mathematician and an engineer should be up to it, don't you think?'

'Doubt it would be worth our while.'

'How so?'

'They wouldn't have left anything valuable lying around like this.'

'That is where you make your first mistake, my friend. That which is freely abandoned often tells the whole story. So it was with the Nazis. When it came to prosecuting them, what they thought of no consequence told everything.'

'What do you think this room is? What do they store here?' said Charlie, a bit intimidated by Ardel's worldliness.

'This isn't storage,' Ardel laughed.

'What, then?'

Ardel gestured to the shelves, as if they were self-explanatory.

'The shelves.'

'Look again.'

Charlie shrugged.

'They are made for mattresses. These are cots.'

And so they were – although without their bedding.

'A barracks?' Charlie asked.

'Or a bunker.'

'How far do you think that tunnel goes, outside?' said Charlie, cottoning on.

'Why don't we see?'

'Won't we get done, if he finds out? Colonel Blimp?'

'Are you such a bourgeois?' said Ardel, grinning.

Charlie wondered how they'd remember which room they were in, given the length of the tunnel, and the fact that everything looked the same.

In answer, Ardel took off his jacket and tied it loosely by the arms from one of the pipes that ran along the ceiling, so it hung down like a banner.

They knew that they had two hours or so before the group leader's return. He'd gone off with the inspection party in the other direction.

'We'll say we've been looking for the loos.'

They'd been walking for about fifteen minutes when it became apparent that there was still no end in sight to the tunnel. It continued to recede to a point without any indication it was going to terminate, or even turn a corner.

'How far can you walk in half an hour?' asked Ardel.

'Why?'

'I want to know how long this thing is.'

'A mile, mile and a half.'

'So if we get to the end in half an hour, we can safely say the thing is at least a mile long?'

'Sure.'

And so they continued. The tunnel didn't seem to change. Charlie said it was like being in a cheap cartoon where they just keep moving the same three doors past the characters as they walk. There was something hypnotic about it. They actually walked for about three-quarters of an hour, and Charlie told Ardel he was getting a little freaked out.

'Just a little, huh?'

'Can we turn around now?'

'I want to keep going.'

'I can't see the jacket any more.' Charlie said, looking hopefully over his shoulder.

'I lost sight of it about five minutes ago,' said Ardel. 'We must have walked a mile and a half. I bet there's at least as much in front of us.'

'So?'

'I get the feeling, my friend, that this goes all the way to the coast.'

'It's more than thirty miles to the coast.'

'That's where it's going.'

'What makes you say that?'

'Isn't it obvious? This is a supply tunnel.'

'Supply tunnel?'

'In a time of war. This would be a means of getting goods in directly from the coast, whatever was happening up top.'

Charlie stared ahead at the dark point where the tunnel floor and ceiling converged, the light breeze still blowing against his face.

'Let's go back,' he said.

They turned around, setting off in search of the hanging jacket – which had completely disappeared from view. Charlie had an irrational fear that the thing would have gone; that they would never be able to locate their passageway; that they would be lost down there, out of reach of the rest of the party, who might conclude that they had gone back to the service. That they would die down there.

As if responding to all this, Ardel said: 'You can smell the fear, can't you?'

'What do you mean?'

'This place. Reeks of it. Fear of what the other side's going to do to you.'

'Well – that's rational, isn't it?' said Charlie.

'Fear's self-fulfilling. It brings about its own conclusion. That's the most frightening thing about it. One side is frightened. So it gets angry. It lashes out. Protects itself with its anger. The other does the same. And ultimately, everyone ends up crawling their way down, back into the mud.' Ardel gestured around him.

A moment's silence filled only with the hum of the strip lights, the gentle whoosh of the air. Then Ardel began to speak again.

'My family . . . We fled from Ongania. La Revoluçion Argentina. La Noche de los Bastones Largos. My father was a Catholic. An intellectual. Driven away from the country he loved by men he knew personally because they feared his ideas. For that, they tore a country apart. Because of what they feared. They were frightened of him. Of what he had to say.'

Charlie wanted to question him more about these experiences. He knew little of the political situation in Argentina. But he sensed it was too raw to talk about. Instead he turned the conversation to domestic politics – to Northern Ireland and the IRA. The Tower of London had been bombed only a few days earlier.

'It makes me sad,' said Charlie. This was a softer approach than he might normally have taken. Something about being with Ardel put him in a different place. Being young and a bit of a firebrand, he usually found himself siding with the Provos, at least politically. But now he thought about the woman he'd read of; visiting the Tower as a tourist with her two kids.

'What else could you feel? What else is the right response?' said Ardel, shrugging.

'Sometimes we have to fight – don't we?'

'Sometimes we like to fight,' said Ardel, correcting him.

That night they returned on the train together to Manchester. The rest of the day had been uneventful. They'd made it back in time to the 'storage' room without the group leader knowing they'd been away, though without finding any indication of the tunnel's end either. They decided to go for a quick drink and ended up in the Lass o' Gowrie, round the back of Oxford Road. Ardel talked more about his memories of Argentina, growing up near Cordoba; his father's idiosyncratic brand of Catholic intellectualism. Charlie spoke about his youth in Winchester, looking for small ways to break the boredom of school; his escape into electronics, mastering circuitry. He told Ardel how he built a working radio when he was thirteen.

'I'd sit tuning it in to anything I could find. Voices from all round the world.'

It was a short hop from there to discussing their day underground. Perhaps the ale got them talking at an intemperate volume, despite having been cautioned to avoid doing so by the group leader. And it wasn't long before the discussion of the tunnel and its length drew the attention of an older Irishman at the next table.

'Tetherdown Lock,' he said, pulling his stool towards their table. He had a look of amazement on his face. 'You've been in Tetherdown Lock?'

'Sorry?' said Charlie, wanting to play dumb.

'Shhh,' said Ardel, to Charlie, not the Irishman.

'Tetherdown Lock,' the Irishman repeated. 'I worked there. Building the hideous thing. 1962. I'm guessing you boys won't remember Cuba?'

'A scary time,' said Ardel.

The Irishman laughed. 'That tunnel.' He shook his head. He gestured with his glass to the barman. 'What you been doing down there?'

Ardel told him about the MSC, their summer detail.

'You don't want to spend time down there, boys,' he said, draining his glass.

'Why not?' said Ardel.

'Bad air?' asked Charlie.

The man laughed again, but bitterly.

'That tunnel. Built round caves. Go all the way back to Pendle,' he said. Charlie and Ardel looked at him blankly. 'Pendle. Now, ain't you heard of Pendle?'

They shook their head.

'Pendle Hill? The Pendle Witches?' They hadn't. He looked at them, incredulous. 'They used to hide down there in those caves. And some people – still – when they go down there . . .' He shook his head. 'When they come out again, they've been changed.' He looked into his glass; swirled the whiskey round. 'Not bad air. Bad magic, in that place.'

Later, back home, Charlie said he found himself lying awake, unable to sleep despite his tiredness. He'd been up for nearly twenty hours, and he'd have to be up again in another five or so. He was reflecting on Ardel – and on the day – and on the tunnel, the length of which still perturbed him. But there was pleasure, too – a kind of excitement, even – at having made a new friend, having 'clicked' so decisively. In truth, he was normally conservative in his affections. It was rare that he met people he actually liked.

The next day began at the same ungodly hour. It was cold and raining, so Charlie was grateful for the minibus and even the prospect of the tunnel, for the dryness and steady temperature it promised. Today the others – or at least some of the others – were more communicative, and while waiting for the bus they began to talk (in lowered voices, not wanting the group leader to hear) about what they had seen the day before.

'We are in some kind of commissary, I think,' said the youngest of them, a Geography undergraduate f om the polytechnic. 'There were chairs and tables all piled to one side. We had to count sets of plastic cutlery.'

'We were just sweeping,' said a coloured boy, a medical student in his final year. 'I dreamt about sweeping last night.'

The minibus seemed to be travelling in a different direction this time. No rolling over uneven ground, no pause to open a gate. When they came to a halt and climbed out of the back, they were in what appeared to be a large garage. The group leader made no comment about the different location. He led them over to a metal door embedded in a white-tiled wall. This time there was a staircase behind it: a large circular one of the kind you might find in a London Underground station.

They arrived at the bottom (Charlie tried to count the steps, but gave up when they passed two hundred) and immediately sensed the environment was different. The room they stood in was a kind of lobby, brick-built and with a vaulted ceiling. The group leader – who'd been even more taciturn – addressed them for the first time.

'There are certain areas in this part of the facility which are unsafe.'

'What kind of unsafe?' asked Ardel.

'In a state of disrepair,' he said, without adding any more. 'Therefore it is vital that you stick to the parts of the site that are detailed in the map I'm going to hand out. You do not stray from the thoroughfares indicated, and you remain in groups of three or more, which I will designate.'

'What are we going to be doing today?' asked Charlie.

'Maintenance again,' said the group leader, not hiding his irritation.

'What *is* this place?'

'A storage facility – as I've explained.' His manner made it clear he wasn't going to be answering any of their questions.

The group leader handed out maps on purple mimeographs. Charlie remembers them as looking more like a maze in a puzzle book.

'How are we supposed to find our way around?' he asked.

'Stick to the illuminated areas,' said the group leader. 'That's all you need to know. There are numbers marked at the junction points of these plans. They mirror those you'll find on the wall of each actual junction. I shall be handing round torches, too. In case of any lighting failure.'

'I thought this was a government facility. How *could* anything fail?' said Ardel. A ripple of laughter from the others.

'You listen to me,' shouted the group leader, drawing on a vein of authority he had not yet tapped. 'I will say this once and once only. You will not venture beyond the designated areas. For your own safety. Do you understand? Do you understand what I'm saying to you?' Such was his authority, Charlie recalled that he elicited a few 'Yes, sir's from the assembled workers.

Charlie and Ardel were paired with the coloured medical student and assigned to a smaller corridor that seemed to circle the vaulted area. There were electrical junction boxes fixed at regular points along the walls. Their job was to test the circuits with a current meter and make sure they were unbroken, a task that sounds more complex than it was. Even without Charlie there, they would have mastered it quickly. They weren't required to fix anything, merely to mark any of the boxes that were malfunctioning with a piece of red insulation tape. The work soon became boring and they got to talking, about where they were and theories of what it was really for. It was hard not to be affected by the dark archways they passed every so often, and the blackness that lay beyond.

'It's a bunker, isn't it?' said Charlie. It was obvious now.

'Is it all one place? Does this place join up with the supply tunnel, then?' asked the coloured medical student.

Collectively, they shrugged.

'Big as a city,' said Charlie, half to the darkness around him. The unlit passageways were presumably the very thing that the group leader had been referring to; the places they weren't to go.

They'd brought packed lunches again, as they'd been instructed to do. Clearly there was no cafeteria or anything in the vicinity, up top, particularly since it had been kept from them exactly what the vicinity was. Instead they found a room off the circular corridor. It wasn't lit, but their torches revealed it to be self-contained, with no doors or passageways visible anywhere, and if they left the door propped open there was enough light to be able to see. Crucially, there were seats – the first seats they'd come across in their time down there. They were fashioned from concrete. Charlie was drawn to examine the back wall with his torch. Not only were there pews, but there was a hollow cross embedded in the concrete.

'It's a chapel.'

They shone their torches together onto the concrete, revealing the grains and lines in its rendering.

'Why a chapel, down here?' said Charlie, almost with distaste.

'There's chapels everywhere, isn't there?' said the coloured boy. 'Railway stations. Cross-channel ferries. Maybe they use this for troops.'

'Why is it such a surprise that there should be a chapel?' said Ardel.

'It's not a surprise, I suppose,' said Charlie. He found Ardel's tone irritating. Maybe because he was tired. Or was it because he sensed a challenge in Ardel's question? If he was being honest, a kind of heaviness had descended on him. He wasn't sure if it was atmospheric, or just a change in his own mood.

'In a way, it's comforting,' said Ardel, running his fingers along the edge of the cross.

'How is it comforting?' said Charlie.

'That there are values present. Even in the midst of this.'

Charlie wandered round the plain box of a room, shining his torch idly into its corners. He found a bookshelf, presumably to take prayer books or bibles, but there were no books there. He swung the torch round, taking in the lines of spartan pews.

'What values?'

'Spiritual values,' said Ardel.

'Is the Church of England a spiritual organisation?' asked the coloured medical student, without irony.

'It's not about the organisation,' said Ardel with a touch of passion. 'It's the aspiration behind it.'

And now Charlie could feel his irritation swelling into anger. As far as he was concerned, the words 'church' and 'value' were mutually exclusive.

'Churches are about nothing but power. Same as this place.'

'You're an intelligent man. You can do better than that,' said Ardel.

The anger was turning to heat in Charlie.

'What are you saying? You believe in fairy stories?'

'Now you are being stupid,' said Ardel. 'It is not even worth talking with you.'

Charlie felt something tip. He was shining the torch straight at Ardel – like an interrogation lamp.

'There's nothing spiritual about the church. Any church. Churches are about controlling people.'

'Is that what they're about?'

'It's all sick. The fact this is even down here shows you how sick it is.'

'The churches are human. But what about the direction they point in?'

'Oh, yes. And what direction's that?'

'To God,' said Ardel – his face not moving.

'God?' said Charlie, aware the coloured medical student was looking at them both. 'You should grow up a little, don't you think? This is 1974.'

'And?' said Ardel. Charlie was aware of his calm, which only made him feel his own anger more acutely.

'Where's God been for the past sixty years? Where was he in Dachau? Huh? With the gassed kids?'

'Maybe,' said Ardel, nodding his head slightly. 'Maybe that's exactly where he was.'

'Oh, fuck off.' Charlie screaming now; all attempts at self-control gone. It felt good to give in to the purity of his anger. His words echoed off the concrete and the vaulted ceilings beyond.

And now it was Ardel who looked angry.

'You think I'm an idiot?'

'Only an idiot would swallow that kind of bullshit.'

'You think I'm weak-minded? Huh? What gives you the right to condemn what I think so cheaply?'

'The rubbish you're talking?'

'You think my position isn't considered?'

'What does it matter, if it's indefensible?'

'It isn't.'

'It's a child's view.'

'My father became a refugee for his beliefs. You think *he* didn't "think them through?"

'Well, obviously not very well.'

They stared each other. A dreadful silence settled over them. Eventually Charlie lowered the torch and walked away.

They ate the rest of their lunch without speaking then returned to their junction-box testing. It took half an hour before they noticed that Ardel was missing. This was easily accounted for by the gloom in their environment and the sense that, even though he wasn't next to either of them, he was probably just sat off to the side somewhere, a few feet away. Charlie assumed he was sulking. And Charlie was still stinging from the heat of their exchange. In his head he rehearsed the argument, reminding himself that he was right – by his own logic and values – and that it was an unavoidable aspect of human relations that people would have differing views and would express them with passion. The medical student was the first to recognise that Ardel had gone truly AWOL.

'You think we better look for him?' he said.

A quick search of the circular corridor revealed he wasn't there. The rooms whose doors were open yielded nothing. Thinking that Ardel would still show up (and Charlie was confident that he would), they returned to the last part of their circuit-testing task. When five o'clock had passed – only half an hour before they were supposed to reassemble by the spiral staircase – Charlie had to start thinking about what he'd been avoiding thinking about: the map the group leader had given them, and the chilly warning about the dangers of straying beyond their designated areas.

Five-ten came. Five-fifteen and still no sign of Ardel.

'I really think we need to search for him properly.'

At five twenty-five, which was five minutes later than the time
they'd all agreed to set off back to the rendezvous point, Charlie
agreed that they should go and confess to the group leader
that Ardel had gone missing. As they walked off, he ranged his
torch around the vaulted brick area, hoping to catch a view of
Ardel running towards them. There was nothing but brick and
shadow.

They were walking along the concrete-lined tunnel that led from
where they'd been to the staircase, when a distant noise brought
Charlie to a halt.

'Shhh!' he said, the sound ricocheting around him. When the
echoes had died down they revealed another sound beneath,
distant, quieter. Animal. A sort of panting. There were footsteps,
too. Running at speed.

'Shhh!' Charlie said again, though the medical student was
stock-still and silent. The footsteps and panting grew in volume,
fading up from some immense distance. They pointed their
torches in the direction it was coming from, though it was difficult
to be precise about that, given the mess of echoes all around
them. The relief was palpable when Ardel's face appeared out of
the darkness, caught in Charlie's quivering torch beam.

Nothing was said upon Ardel's return. He didn't talk about where
he'd been or what had kept him. And beyond the 'Are you all
right?'s, the others didn't press him on it, for the man was clearly
shaken. It was only too apparent when they reached the surface
and they saw how pale he was.

The next morning, Ardel didn't show. They were back on sweeping
duty, entering the place via the lift they had used on the first day,
though working on a different section of the tunnel. In Ardel's
absence, Charlie was paired with the coloured student again. It
was he who raised the subject of Ardel's disappearance the day

before. Sharing a bus back with him from Piccadilly, it seems that Ardel had confided what had occurred the previous afternoon. Charlie couldn't help but feel a little put out that Ardel hadn't confided in him. But then Charlie hadn't asked, sitting in self-righteous silence in the minibus back.

According to the medical student, this is what had happened.

Smarting from the disagreement – upset by it – Ardel had gone walking down one of the smaller corridors without taking a map, not intending to go far. He had just wanted to get away from the group. He wandered aimlessly for a while, keeping the light of where he'd come from behind him as a guide. Trusting his own sense of direction, something must have gone awry because when he turned back to check he found he couldn't get his bearings. He must have taken a turning into a different network of corridors and he was unable to find his way back. He tried shouting, but there was no response. There was a breeze travelling through these tunnels, which there hadn't been where the others were, and this must have carried his voice away in the opposite direction. Vowing not to panic, Ardel attempted to retrace his steps as methodically as possible; but, if anything, he seemed to be moving further away from where he'd set off, as the walls seemed unrecognisable – a lighter shade of concrete, with no sign of any brick whatsoever. After an hour or two of this walking, he was gripped by a rising sense of terror. The environment was almost pitch-black and his torch was failing. He was having to ration its use. He had resorted to running his finger against the side of the wall – just to get a sense of which direction to move. Surely they would search for him. But what if they didn't? It was so hard to see. When he saw a rising glow of light ahead, his spirits rose, and he ran in its direction. The light grew as he moved towards it, the tunnel curving off to his left. The odd thing was that the ground was sloping down, at an increasing incline.

He rounded a corner and there was an arch off to his left – quite high – about twelve or fifteen feet. The ceiling was noticeably higher, too. He passed under, and what lay ahead left him reeling. He said he had to grip onto the wall behind to steady himself. He was standing in a roadway – a wide underground roadway – well-lit – like a regular tunnel with sodium strip lights at regular intervals along its roof. It headed down, deep into the earth, at a very sharp incline. Parked all along the left-hand side, with their drivers' doors open and keys visible hanging in the ignition, was a long line of Mercedes sedan cars. They receded down the incline as far as Ardel could see.

Staying only a moment to take it in, Ardel turned and fled back the way he had come – praying for guidance. The relief when he found the others was unspeakable.

Charlie pondered this account, and it stayed with him long after his week for the Manpower Services Commission had been completed. He thought a lot about Ardel, about their initial meeting, and as the summer vacation drew to its close he vowed that he would find him and see him again. In truth, he felt guilty about the brief argument they'd had, and the fact he had allowed himself to lose his temper in that moment – given in to the temptation of its heat.

Once term had recommenced, Charlie took to hanging around the UMIST common rooms, going so far as to find the Mathematics department and wait around there at lunchtimes. After a short while, his patience was rewarded. He saw Ardel heading out of a tutorial room, a squash racquet slung over his shoulder. Charlie followed him outside and ran up to him, feeling warmth for the man swelling within. But he was shocked when he saw the expression in the other man's eyes. At first he had the weirdest feeling that he, himself, wasn't actually there, as the other man was looking straight through him. Charlie reached out to grab him, searching the other man's eyes for an anticipated flicker of recognition. But none was forthcoming; he merely looked puzzled.

'It's me,' said Charlie. 'I came to find you.' Charlie smiled broadly. Still nothing. 'Ardel?' said Charlie, patting the other man's arm as warmly as he could.

'Lyall,' said the man, slightly irritated.

'You're Ardel Wray,' said Charlie, clarifying. 'From the MSC.'

'Lyall Brooks, mate, from St Helens.' The strong Merseyside accent immediately confirmed this identity.

'Ardel, it's me. It's Charlie. From the bunker,' said Charlie, now feeling a little panicked.

'Yeah, all right, mate. You've got the wrong person.'

Charlie stood there, staring, felt a flash of desperation, remembered his love for the man who was, it seemed now, someone else.

They remained in front of each other for a moment, Charlie trying to comprehend what he was in the midst of. Eventually the man shrugged and turned, walking off across the concourse. Charlie watched him as he disappeared into the crowd.

He did not know what had happened, or by what bad magic it had come about, but he was never to see or hear of Ardel Wray again.'

Chapter 6
A Ghost Among the Bookshelves

THE HAUNTED INSTITUTION

Alongside the more established history of haunted houses – most usually houses with history attached, such as ancestral homes – there are many paranormal events recorded connected to non-domicile buildings, particularly institutions. Hospitals and hotels are both commonly associated with ghosts. The old Langham Hotel in London (now part of the BBC) was famously haunted by Victorian and Edwardian apparitions, particular stories being associated with Room 333. Residents of Bedford are familiar with the story of the Gliding Girl, when in 1972 two nurses at the Bedford Hospital watched an attractive girl in a long dress and a coat glide into a toilet on the South Wing of the building. They followed her, only to find the room empty. The Shand Ward in the same building has a number of reports of shuffling footsteps with no visible source. Stories of haunted theatres are common; Drury Lane and the Duke of York's in London's West End have well-known ghosts. Perhaps less familiar are stories of the Grey Lady of the Bath Theatre Royal, last seen in 1975. More charmingly, the same theatre reports a ghostly butterfly said to appear on the same day once a year. Stories of ghosts in schools are uncommon, but they exist on record. The author Dennis Wheatley tells of a spirit with a white bloated face who appeared to him while he was boarding at his school in Broadstairs. Even prisons have their stories. Dartmoor Jail is reputed to be haunted by French PoWs from the Napoleonic wars. And inmates have a legend that the jackdaws that frequent the area contain the spirits of dead prison officers.

Most of us are, of course, familiar with the notion of the haunted house – and inevitably we shall be examining that very phenomenon in a subsequent part of this book. But there are many more unusual accounts of ghosts and hauntings relating to a non-domestic building, such as the striking story detailed below. The following tale was brought to our attention by a spiritualist acquaintance. She, herself, had been told it by a medium she had taken instruction from in the early part of her psychic career. The anecdote – as she referred to it – has some extraordinary features. Unfortunately for us, there was another aspect that was a little offputting: wherever possible, we were committed to actually visiting the various locations we were reporting on. However, in the case of this particular account, certain information came to light that made this an unappealing prospect.

In addition, during unrelated research we came across a book we hadn't seen before. The very first case in it was a detailed account of our own library-based tale. There were two notably peculiar things about it. One was the author's description of his own supernatural encounter in his introduction, which bore uncanny similarities to the one we ourselves had at the Liskeard and Looe Canal. It wasn't just the fact that this involved the figure of a child, but also that the figure was described in the same posture and wearing a light-coloured coat! The other peculiarity was the title page of the book (reproduced below), complete with staining on its lower portion, whose shape seems to be an exact simulacrum of the silhouette of that very apparition. Of course, this may well be pure coincidence – but, allied to the description that follows, it begins to take on an anomalous air that Charles Fort himself would have found more than intriguing.

A BOOK OF HAUNTINGS

A Survey of Evidence

by

SIR EDEN VACHS

Late Fellow of Hertford College, Oxford

with an afterword by

The Very Rev.
The Dean of St Paul's

FABER AND FABER LIMITED
24 Russell Square
London

First published in June Mcmxxxviii
By Faber and Faber Limited
24 Russell Square, London, W.C.1
Printed in Great Britain by
Western Printing Services Ltd., Bristol

To
the memory of
U. REEDER

CONTENTS

PREFACE

ON HAUNTINGS
Précis of a broadcast made 14th May 1933

All down the years, in all places, civilized and uncivilized alike, tales of spirits, phantoms and apparitions persist and in our current age, too. Even amid the ever-greater developments in science, men and women of reason and full faculty report seeing phantasms of both the living and the dead, under circumstances which absolutely preclude deception or illusion.

It is not my intention here to elaborate on the phantasms of the living – though an audit of available evidence seems to suggest that they are more numerous than those of the dead. Nor have I any wish to lead you into the doubtful environment of the drawing-room séance and all its discredited productions of partial and complete figures (though I can state categorically that I have experienced some extraordinary events in the company of genuine mediums such as Alexandra Cook and Eusapia Pangrazio). My focus here is with the ghost in the ordinary sense of the word – the apparition of a dead person. These abnormal experiences occur more frequently than is generally supposed. In 1889 the Society for Psychical Research organized a Census of Hallucinations that took in Great Britain, the United States, France, Germany and Italy. Replies were invited to the following enquiry: Have you ever, when believing yourself to be completely awake, had a vivid impression of seeing or being touched by a living entity, or of perceiving a voice, which, so far as you could discover, was not due to an external physical cause? Of the nearly seventeen thousand answers received, almost ten percent were in the affirmative.

The society has over the years accumulated a very large number of narratives. The first-hand evidence has been analyzed and every possible channel of corroboration has been explored. We deduce from this comprehensive study of selected narratives that apparitions are seen in any light from dawn to daylight, sometimes at night with a luminosity of their own; they appear in any house, be it old or new, and are perceived by persons of every type, independently of temperament, health or intellectual character. In addition, it is apparent that apparitions are seen not only by individuals at odd moments and places, but, unless one's mind is closed entirely to the testimony of other human beings, ghosts of a more persistent type are associated with certain localities and houses.

If it is attested fact that apparitions of the dead are seen, then how are we to explain these manifestations? One line – the popular line – is that these are the spirits of the dead men existing in space externally to ourselves; things that are always there, but only occasionally perceived when, through some as yet unexplained cause, our eyes are opened to behold these essences from another plane of existence.

There is another line – more popular in this scientific age – that what we are seeing is in fact an hallucination; that all such experiences are in fact subjective, perhaps due to some momentary dysfunction of the mechanisms of perception itself. Of course, this fails to account for the simultaneous perception of a phenomenon by a number of parties, as detailed in multiple accounts that follow.

A third theory, which appeals to this author, is that there is no one explanation that covers all anomalous encounters but rather a myriad spectrum of explanations. Sometimes what appears to be one haunting may in fact be covered by two or more of these explanations. For example, scientists such as M. Chardoux in France have suggested that what is being encountered is akin to a wire recording, and that those that perceive the instance are more developed in evolutionary terms and have the requisite 'machinery' to replay the record. This seems to apply in some of the cases detailed here. Other, more esoteric, explanations abound governed by the prevailing spiritual and religious faiths of the territories in which the ghosts are observed. The Orientals profess beliefs relating to whole categories of spirits, suggesting that some who cleave to our plane are spirits addicted to the narrow stratum of physical sensation associated with this, the heaviest and thickest of the ethers. They refuse to believe they are dead because they still crave material feeling and hence incarnation. Consequently, they 'hang about' in our world and are occasionally perceived so doing.

(It is worth noting that the author himself had had his own experience when researching an aspect of this very book. Whilst traversing a disused railway yard in Norfolk, he perceived a figure watching him. This apprehension came before any visual stimulus to provoke it. Upon turning, it was discovered there was indeed a small figure, in a pale-coloured cloak or smock, perched on a wall, staring straight towards the author. The figure had long hair hanging across its face, making it hard to discern its age. By its stature, one presumed it to be a child. To approach the figure it was necessary to move behind a large cistern. Upon emerging, the figure had disappeared. There was no sign of it behind the wall.)

Ultimately, given the current state of science in this area, there can yet be no single satisfactory answer to explain these occurrences. All one can say is that one knows when one has been affected by the presence of spirit, because one feels a particular sensation. It is akin to entering a dream. The normal rules of perception are bent as if through a prism and a certain chill is experienced – a raising of the hackles, in the vernacular. I prefer to use the word awe, for ultimately we are in the presence of something we cannot understand, and that it is not an experience that we should deny. We are all of us, everyone, swimming in mystery and an infinite unknown and that is the truth we so rarely open ourselves to. It is hoped that by studying accounts where that mystery becomes explicit, we may open to it a little more.

Whether 'tis ampler day, divinelier lit,
Or homeless night without.

I.
APPARITIONS OF DARKNESS

CASE ONE

The following account came from a gentlemen (known to U. Reeder) who, for understandable reasons, preferred that his name should not be given. He, in turn, had been passed this narrative in a will by an old friend, the teller of the tale (now deceased).

Readers of a delicate disposition should be aware that there are distasteful elements to this case (and indeed the next), and may wish to move on to the second section of the book. These elements are included for reasons of scientific interest, as they are essential to understanding the phenomenon herein described.

'In 1911 I succeeded a Mr Q. as Chief Librarian of the X. Library in L— , a prosperous city in the north of Great Britain. I had never met Mr Q. personally and only knew of him by reputation. The Library was a private one and housed a number of valuable collections that had been bequeathed to it over the years, both by its original benefactor and others. It was established in 1768 as a subscription-based establishment owned and run by its members at a time when such institutions were springing up in all the major cities of the realm; not just libraries but cloth halls, assembly rooms and canal companies. Books in particular were being published in ever-greater numbers, but they were expensive and the aim was to acquire new volumes that the Library's members would wish to read and thus keep increasing their collections in size and value. By the time I came into the institute's employ, the Public Libraries Act had been in effect for more than sixty years, and naturally this had eroded a good amount of the membership that such establishments formerly enjoyed. Consequently, the place was not in a state of perfect repair, and though it had electrical light in its main reading room, the rest of the building retained gas illumination. It is worth noting that, unlike similar libraries I knew of in Exeter and Plymouth (I was born in the West Country), the X. Library had a reputation for being in possession of a – shall we say – esoteric aspect, not least because it had been bequeathed the entire collection of Lord F— , a notorious collector of rare and exotic manuscripts with a particular interest in the Orient. Mr Q., the librarian, had to some extent gained a national reputation because of his role as curator of this, in part unspeakable, portfolio and requests to consult it had to be made by personal application, making it necessary for Mr Q. to be convinced that one's interest was genuinely scholarly, rather than merely prurient.

In order to similarly convince my employers (and perhaps myself) of my own scholastic interest in the material, I suggested that I undertake a thorough and dispassionate audit in order to prepare a new catalogue more appropriate for twentieth-century academia than the understandably euphemistic (though consequently opaque) existing version. This I was prepared to do in my own time, in addition to my scheduled daily tasks. Given I was a bachelor in a new town, this was not such an onerous undertaking. In truth, I was looking for something to occupy my evening hours. Not being possessed of a gregarious nature, I had yet to find friends or even acquaintances with whom I could pass time outside my working environs.

I must admit that, at least to begin with, I found the building itself to have a certain appeal. I began my work there in early October. The leaves were beginning to fall, the nights darken, and the Library was warm and comfortable, with its worn oak shelving and panelling, and overstuffed armchairs. I should perhaps give some description of the place to aid the reader in picturing what follows.

The Library was housed in handsome premises built in 1808. (The shops incorporated beneath the first floor provided an income in addition to the subscriptions.) Prior to that it had more modest accommodation above a bookseller's shop described as 'a dark and incommodious garret in a back yard'. But the current location was designed by architect Thomas Johnson and was added to over the course of the nineteenth century. (It is worth noting that Johnson was an associate of Lord F— 's and shared his beliefs in esoteric knowledge and practices. Apparently these fed in to the design: the six pillars over five alcoves on the Library's front are rooted in secret descriptions circulated amongst cognoscenti concerning the construction of the Temple of Solomon.)

By the time of my arrival the building was a veritable labyrinth, albeit of the pocket variety, and it took some time to discover the best way of navigating from room to room. Doors were often where one least expected them to be, leading to other areas that were not the areas one anticipated them to open upon. There was the Main Room, the East Room, the North Room, the New Room, the Smoking Room, the Meeting Room, the Nelson Room and the Long Room. The last four were accessed from the upper floor. And there was also the basement, which was not open to members. Many of these rooms were cheerful enough once the fires were lit, and it was the only the Smoking Room that I tended to keep out of when I was alone after closing.

Our hours varied through the week. We opened from nine to five o'clock Monday to Friday, remaining so until seven on the last Thursday in every month. Saturdays we opened from nine-thirty until one.

During my evening sessions, I tended to spend my time in the Main Room, as we kept the fire lit there, the others having been left to die out after we shut. The Main Room was also the brightest, benefiting from the then-new electrical lights. However, once I'd begun work on Lord F— 's collection I had to go to the Meeting Room on the upper level, which was accessed by a spiral staircase at the far end of the Main Room. The Meeting Room was ironically named, given it was where the private collection was mainly housed, and meetings were never held there. I assumed the name was a remnant of some long-forgotten arrangement from days-gone-by. It was gloomy, with two small transom windows in the outer wall, and the gas lights lending it an orange hue.

I had come across a box of Japanese prints, exquisite depictions of the act of love, rendered in quite shocking detail. I myself was not repelled by them, being of a more libertarian sensibility (a position held in theory rather than practice, I should add). At that time I was a passionate follower of H. G. Wells, who held notoriously forward-thinking views in this area. Nevertheless, these etchings were the closest I had come to the actuality, and once glimpsed it was hard to remove the images from my mind's eye. It was while searching for another box referred to by the original catalogue that I made the first of my strange discoveries. The Meeting Room was lined with shelves from floor to ceiling along all four of its walls, even around the doorway. Because of its height, there were neat library ladders, wheeled in their bases, attached to rails at the top of each shelf. It was whilst up one of these ladders, quite near the ceiling (near enough to be experiencing vertigo), that I found a set of fake books. What looked like an edition of Gibbon's *Mémoires Littéraires de la Grande-Bretagne* was in fact the spines of the three volumes glued to a small wooden box. Even from a close distance the illusion was perfect. Given its height off the ground, and the room it was in, I could well imagine that mine were the first hands to have touched this item for fifty years. When I pulled the box away from the shelf I nearly dropped it, so surprised was I to discover what lay behind. It was pair of field glasses, embedded in the wall. They were held there by a kind of pivot, so that they could move on two axes: left to right and up and down. Without thinking, I placed my eyes against the eyepieces. I strained to view something in the darkness. Was that a shape in the murk? I wiggled the mechanism up and down. In truth, I could make nothing out. I shivered, feeling suddenly cold, and placed the box back, covering up my discovery and once again reinstating the illusion that there was nothing there but learned volumes. I resolved to mention this unusual find to my deputy in the morning.

The next day was a Thursday, the last in October as it happened, and therefore a day for late opening. The Library was quite busy. A cool but clear evening had encouraged our clientele to stay late and with the fires blazing and crackling the building took on a peaceful and cheerful air. I found my own spirits were high – and, if I'm being honest, this was in part at the prospect of another evening in the Meeting Room, spending more time alone investigating Lord F— 's collection. Maybe it was these good spirits that kept me from mentioning my peculiar find of the previous night to Mr L., the deputy librarian. Once the Library was locked, and I was sure the building was clear, I found myself dashing up to the Meeting Room. I noticed, perhaps with a touch of discomfort, that my heart was racing, presumably with excitement, as I unlocked the cabinet doors. Certainly, there was a tremor in my hands as I found a box full of rolled up etchings – simple nude studies of adolescents made by a skilled but unnamed artist. The part of me that remained sober enough to analyze and assess did have the thought that there was an unpalatable irony in play; that with all the combined learning of the world at my fingertips – all that knowledge, insight, wisdom and experience – the thing I was most compelled to look at was so oppositely placed. Nor did I choose to go and examine the mysterious field glasses again. I was too engrossed in the material I was in the process of uncovering to engage with their slightly troubling mystery.

Perhaps about nine p.m. I paused for a light supper of ale and cold meats that I'd purchased that afternoon and then I made my way back to the Meeting Room to carry on with my audit, which I continued for the next hour or so. Taking another break from this – feeling slightly ill-at-ease – I now found the discovery from the previous night to be on my mind. I mounted the burnished steps of the rear wall-ladder in search of the disguised little casket. Removing it, I gave closer examination to the portion of the field glasses jutting from the wall. There was a crude feel to the way they had been mounted there – the work of an amateur attempting to get a job done, rather than a professional installation. The same could be said of the concealing box, too. It was fashioned from ply and nails, a purely functional item. I leaned forward, pressing my face against the glasses. Were those shapes now visible through them? My fingers searched for, and found, a focusing mechanism. It was definitely possible to discern some kind of space beyond. There were boxy items covered in cloth and bare wooden floors. There must have been a skylight in the room and the clearer night gave more illumination. Once again, I found I was shivering. I looked at my watch. It was ten forty-five. If I did not make haste, I should miss the last train to H— , which left at eleven-five. I picked up the lamp, which I'd balanced on a step of the ladder, and prepared to leave the Meeting Room. And then I heard a noise – a bang – from somewhere outside, but definitely in the main part of the building itself.

There was someone in the Library.

Quickly and quietly I left the Meeting Room and made my way to the Librarian's Office, opening the safe, where I knew there to be a revolver kept for just such an eventuality. I made my way back along the narrow passage that led to the Main Room, holding the lamp before me, and as soon as I was there turned on the electric lights which I'd extinguished earlier. Peering around each of the dividing rows of bookcases in turn, I could see no-one. My heart beating fast again, I mounted the spiral staircase at the west end of the Main Room, calling out loudly for the intruder to show himself but more with the hope of attracting a passing policeman. From this vantage point I could see the whole room spread out, the narrow lines of bookcases and the heavy oak desks. I watched carefully for any movement or shadow. All was still.

I turned my attention to the upper rooms. Ahead of me was the Smoking Room – the place I instinctively avoided even during the day. Nevertheless, it was an obvious hiding place and I had an obligation to investigate.

Pushing open the baize door – which I'm confident I had closed earlier – I saw a face peering round at me from one of the bookcases. I say peering round, but it had an odd appearance, as if the body were actually *in* the bookcase. It was pallid and hairless, and the orbits of the eyes were very deep. I advanced towards it, though my belly was cold with fear, and as I did I saw a man with high shoulders seem to rotate out of the end of the bookcase and, with his back towards me, walk rather quickly from the bookcase to the door of a small lavatory, which opened on to the back of the Smoking Room and had no other access. I followed the man at once, brandishing my revolver, determined to face down any fear I was feeling. Steeling myself, I pulled at the door handle. To my extreme surprise, I found no-one in there. I stepped inside, examined the window (which was about fourteen inches by twelve) and found it closed and fastened. I pushed it open and looked out. Beyond was a well, the bottom of which – a good twelve feet below – was a skylight, while the top above was open to the scudding clouds. It was in the middle of the building, so no-one could have dropped into it without smashing the glass, nor climbed out without a ladder. Nevertheless, there was no-one there. Mystified, I opened the little cupboard under the fixed basin in the lavatory, but even a child couldn't have hid in there. I confess I began to experience for the first time what novelists describe as an 'eerie' feeling. The distress of all this was compounded when I finally left the Library a short while later and found I had missed my train.

Now, I felt had no choice but to discuss this with Mr L., my deputy. He was an older man, perhaps in his mid-fifties, circumspect, diligent, with a crippled foot, which meant he preferred to avoid the more physical tasks around the Library. It was this – or so I assumed – that kept him from applying for the position I myself now occupied. I only had to register the look upon his face when I recounted a (slightly redacted) version of my story to realise he knew immediately to what I was referring. 'Why, it's old Burness. Burness has come back.' He had gone quite pale. Who was Burness?, I naturally enough wanted to know.

'Burness was a murderer, sir.'

Mr L. showed me the newspaper cuttings. Burness was hanged at W— Prison back in '92. His crime, the murder of a number of prostitutes and other derelicts for which he offered no mitigation save only the following, chilling statement: 'Lion-hearted I've lived in pursuit of my pleasure, and when my time comes, lion-hearted I'll die.'

'Old Q. knew him – even said he liked him. It was perhaps fortunate for the old gent that he did not live to see Burness hanged,' said Mr L. 'They were chums, you see. Burness used to come in here a lot. After hours, too. He'd sit and smoke – up there.' He pointed with shaking hand to the Smoking Room, its door ajar, as I had left it the previous night.

It transpired that Burness owned a rooming house which backed on to our building, though it was no longer there, the premises having been converted into separate shops. The prostitutes he dispatched used his rooms to accommodate their clients, the same rooms presumably that backed on to the Meeting Room upstairs. Had anyone, I asked, somewhat tentatively, seen his ghost before?

'Some have spoken of a cold or uncomfortable feeling in that room,' said Mr L., pointing towards it. 'This is an odd building, with an unchristian air', he continued, 'and there are times when I do not like to be in it.'

Later that day Mr L. came to find me, in the Librarian's Office, in an excitable state. He said he had a friend, a woman from his church, who practised as a medium. 'Under the auspices of Christ, you understand,' he added, a little awkwardly. It occurred to him that his friend might come and perform a cleansing ceremony, if I was willing to permit such an enterprise. 'She has done it before with great success,' he told me. After a little coaxing he confessed that he had long wanted to bring her into the building. 'But I never thought, until now, that I would get a sympathetic hearing from my superiors.' I must confess that in these matters I had never considered myself to be what one might call 'a believer' and, indeed, had never had any kind of supernatural experience until the encounter I have just described. But the events of that night had left me under a cloud of what I could only describe as 'dread' – not a word I had had cause to invoke in regard to any aspect of my life up until this point. There was something about the countenance of Burness's spirit as I had witnessed it (ridiculous to be talking so definitely about it, but I seemed to be so doing without any doubt attached) that had pierced me. So, although I didn't assent in that moment, later the same day I took old L. aside and, without placing too much emphasis on it, asked him if he could investigate the possibility of his friend coming in to the Library, one evening, after hours. Naturally, I thought it best if discretion were applied all round, and that this matter should be kept purely between the three of us. It was all too easy for this kind of thing to slip out, and before you knew it the story would be all over the town – fodder for the newspapers and the magazines. Mr L. agreed, and there was a sense of relief about him that I had given him this permission.

The 'sitting' (as Mr L. referred to it) was arranged with surprising speed, and this I was grateful for. Indeed, since my sighting I had curtailed my evening sessions of cataloguing. Partly I wanted to avoid any chance of seeing the apparition again, whatever it was (and, naturally, being a rational man, I had been trying to find rational explanations alongside the spectral ones). In addition, there was the sense that my enjoyment of Lord F— 's collection might have somehow triggered the whole thing. Of course, this was superstitious and nonsensical, but the enterprise seemed tinged with danger now that was enough to keep me from indulging.

It was a cold, clear night when Mr L.'s 'medium' friend came to perform her ceremony. A stout woman in her middle years, with what I took to be an Edinburgh accent, she bustled in with a carpetbag and a leather-bound pocket bible in her left hand, which she brandished like a torch in a darkened room. I, myself, not being a religious man, was normally made uncomfortable by fervency in any form. As a schoolboy, my housemaster had been a covert atheist and I think he might have made quite an impression on me. I never went the whole distance with it, being more minded to take Pascal's bet, but I couldn't help but be suspicious of others' certainty. Nevertheless, Mr L.'s friend's assuredness in this matter was somehow welcome. If one employed an electrical engineer to install wiring, one wanted them to be confident about the forces they marshalled. This was no different. We made for the New Room, which was directly beneath the Smoking Room. 'These things are better approached obliquely,' she informed me, gripping my arm with surprising firmness. 'We don't want to let him see us coming.' I nodded, as if I understood what she was talking about, and it was routine for me to be exorcising spirits – if that was indeed what we were doing.

The New Room was perhaps the most elegant of the Library's quarters. It had long Georgian windows that stretched from floor to ceiling, and a generally stately and pleasing aspect. There was a large table that contained various periodicals arranged in fans along its centre. Mr L.'s acquaintance asked that we remove them, and she spread in their place a white cloth. 'Silk,' she told us, 'sanctified and blessed with Holy Water.' Once this was done, she asked that we recite the Lord's Prayer with her, omitting the last stanza, which she explained was a later addition and not part of the original benediction. Then she sang a hymn – 'A Balm In Gilead' – to which I can remember all the words because of the extraordinary events that followed. She popped in a mint, began humming the tune, and then reached out for my hand, and for L.'s hand, too.

'There is balm in Gilead,
To make the wounded whole;
There's power enough in heaven,
To cure a sin-sick soul.
How lost was my condition
Till Jesus made me whole!
There is but one Physician
Can cure a sin-sick soul.'

As she reached this last line, there was a terrible commotion from above – as if books were being thrown off the shelves. I jumped in my chair as it began. The Library doors were locked. There was no way anybody could have made their way in, as I'd established the other night. Mr L. looked to the ceiling but seemed more composed than me. The one thing I did not want was to see that pallid face again, with its black-rimmed eyes. She gripped my hand. The gas lights, which she had dimmed before the ceremony had begun, flickered as if there were a breeze though the air was quite still.

'Come,' she called out. 'Come.'

I wanted to stop her there.

'Come, that we may know you and send you on your way, in the name of the Lord, in the name of the Christ. Your story has ended here. You have no place amongst us. Your story is over. It is time for you to leave us.'

Thump. Thump. Thump. The sound of books being pushed singly off the shelves above.

'Oh, he's a feisty one,' she said, squeezing my hand. 'You've let a feisty one in.' She squeezed even harder, as if to lend me new resolve. 'We must stand,' she said. 'Maintaining our link with one another, we must stand and pray together – Lord, have mercy.'

We repeated. 'Christ have mercy.' We repeated again.

Now the sound of a whole bookcase being tipped.

'Lord, have mercy.' Wood splintering.

'Christ, hear us.' Glass breaking.

[12]

'Christ, graciously hear us.' Stone grinding.

'God, the Father in heaven have mercy on us.' Metal twisting, as if in a forge.

'The Son of God, Redeemer of the world. God, the Holy Ghost – cast this one – for his time has come and come – he should not be here – he forgets where he should be – collect him – take him – you – you – you – this means you – we are talking to you.'

The protest of every material thing, ripping, tearing, breaking. It did not want to leave.

She continued. 'In the name of St. Michael, St. Gabriel, St. Raphael, St. John the Baptist, St. Joseph, St. Peter, St. Paul, St. Andrew, St. James, St. John, St. Thomas, St. James, St. Philip, St. Bartholomew, St. Matthew, St. Simon, St. Thaddeus, St. Matthias, St. Barnabas, St. Luke, St. Mark. All holy apostles and evangelists. All holy disciples of the Lord, All holy Innocents . . .'

A pause in the battery of sound. I feared the whole Library would have been upended by the time she was through. Another thump, closer this time, just beyond the closed door at the rear of the room.

She continued. 'St. Stephen, St. Lawrence, St. Vincent, Saints Fabian and Sebastian, John and Paul, Cosmas and Damian, Gervase and Protase, St. Sylvester, St. Gregory, St. Ambrose, St. Augustine, St. Jerome, St. Martin, St. Nicholas, St. Anthony, St. Benedict, St. Bernard, St. Dominic, St. Francis. All holy priests and Levites, all holy monks and hermits, St. Mary Magdalene, St. Agatha, St. Lucy, St. Agnes, St. Cecilia, St. Catherine, St. Anastasia, all holy virgins and widows, all holy saints of God in their name and ours – be gone, be gone, be gone, be gone, be gone.'

She collapsed forward, exhausted, having barely paused in her litany to take a breath. There was silence filled only with her heavy breathing. Eventually, she spoke.

'It is finished,' she said. 'He is done.'

I hardly dared to venture out from the room for fear of what destruction we would find. Nothing prepared me for what we did find. Which was nothing. Not a single book was out of place, not a single window open, not a single pane broken.

As Mr L.'s acquaintance took her leave from us, she clasped my hand once more. 'You know, I am glad he is gone. I thought it most strange he was here at all.' And with this she was gone, taking L. with her; and I was left in the dimness of the entrance lobby, wondering once again if I had dreamt the whole thing.

Over the next few weeks the affair faded from my mind, to the extent that I queried in retrospect how much I had imagined the whole thing, perhaps fired by own rather childish guilt in the face of having been so enjoying my work with Lord F— 's collection. My imaginings were the further fuelled by old L.'s superstitions, culminating in the parlour theatre of his acquaintance's séance. It was not hard to reconstruct a version of the evening's events that was more rational in provenance. I was tired, the light was dim, I was a little drunk from the ale. I'd caught sight of my own reflection in one of the glass-covered bookcases in the Smoking Room and misinterpreted it. This was all certainly possible.

Inevitably, I found my thoughts returning to the continuation of my cataloguing of Lord F— 's collection. There was a good amount of extraordinary stuff in there, and perhaps I had a responsibility to make it accessible to those in positions of learning who might be interested in it. It was, after all, possible to see beyond the surface carnality of the material to the considerable matters of cultural interest beneath. And there was a whole amount I hadn't even started to look at. Owing to its fragility (and apparent singularity), it was kept in a locked room in the basement. And so, on a particularly dark day in mid November, I decided that I would begin work again. I'd spent a little time in the cellars when I first arrived. Mr L. had taken me round and shown me exactly what was down there. They were accessed via a spiral staircase from the New Room, which passed through a channel in the wall bypassing the ground floor completely. This subterranean space covered the area of the whole building, but was divided into a number of different rooms, each with different purposes. There were some rare and delicate books kept boxed in two oak-lined areas, under lock and key. There were other storage areas, some for damaged books and some for additional items used for repair: card, leather, paste and the other machinery of bookbinding. It was no surprise that the electrical lighting had yet to make it down there. I was dismayed to discover that the gas lights hadn't either, but then these were not rooms that one was meant to spend any length of time in.

At first it was not entirely clear what it was about this adjunct of Lord F— 's collection that had made Q. decide it should be kept separately from what I had already seen. Even in the rudimentary catalogue that existed, it was described in the vaguest of details. References to French and Italian texts and illustrations of Russian and Turkish origin were about all I could discern from what was written. So, armed with a large oil lamp, its reservoir fully filled, and a pair of fingerless gloves, I descended.

It was more of a cage than a room, and there were two locks: one in the iron-work itself and one a chain and padlock that wound around the grid-work. The wrought iron cast crawling shadows over the shelving beyond as I lifted the oil lamp on to a nearby shelf in order to find the right keys. Perhaps ordinarily these surroundings would have made me nervous. One doesn't have to be cursed with a vivid imagination to be fearful of a dark, enclosed place. It is a part of our animal natures to feel apprehensive in such environments. However, any such feelings seemed to be overridden by the keenness of my anticipation to discover what was in this part of the collection. The first box contained a set of handwritten texts in French. My French was functional, and some of the language seemed to be esoteric in nature, but as far as I could tell these were works by De Sade – private letters and journals. They were accompanied by a set of drawings which can perhaps best be described as being rigorously, almost surgically, anatomical in nature. At first I thought perhaps they were drawings made from corpses, like Leonardo's; but a number of them made it apparent that the subjects were living at the time of record. The next box contained more handwritten journals, this time in German, of which I knew nothing. The drawings that accompanied these made me glad I could not comprehend what was written down. Perhaps I should have stopped there, but the sense of dread these things had activated in me was mixed with a particular kind of stimulation that compelled me to continue. What was it I hoped to see? I don't know. I didn't want to think too much. I just wanted to look. To keep on looking. There was a hunger, now stimulated, that wanted satisfying. I carried on rifling through the boxes. I pulled another from the shelf, this one made of leather, which suggested whatever it contained had been owned by someone wealthy. Inside, a journal of some kind, also bound in leather. This was written in Latin, a language I could read fluently. The book seemed to contain accounts of liaisons between its author, a wealthy Italian count, and various consorts. One story detailed how he would discreetly offer a generous dowry to peasants in his vicinity upon the day of their weddings if they forfeited their brides to him on their honeymoon night.

After he was sated, he would then tattoo his monogram upon the young bride's pubis. These stories were accompanied by a series of sketches of each of his conquests, bound hand and foot to the count's bed.

Thinking I'd spotted another, equivalent, leather box on the highest shelf in the corner of the back of the room, I found something to stand on – a set of small library steps – and reached up for it. The box was empty, and I nearly lost my balance pulling too hard at it. Behind it was a tattered flap of canvas fixed to the wall, oddly – like a small curtain. I retrieved the oil lamp and raised it to obtain a better view of what was there. Lifting the flap a tad gingerly, I was surprised to discover a version of what I'd found in the Meeting Room upstairs: a pair of doctored field glasses fixed into the wall in a crude, pivoted housing. I fiddled with them again, peered through them as before. There was only darkness beyond. Leaning next to these field glasses was a plain-looking notebook. Not antiquated, it looked like one you might buy at W. H. Smith. I picked it up, flicked through it. Lines written in ink, hurriedly in places, judging by the smudges; also in Latin. I flicked through the first few pages and saw this:

'I write this – these entries – I think by way of confession.'

I searched more for some indication of whether this was part of the collection. I flicked to the middle.

'He came again today. Even though I now know what he is. And I still allow it. He smiles at me and I fear him.'

It was a riddle. And I have always had a taste for riddles. I made to step down, and noticed that the shelves I was at were reinforced around their middle. Two of them had flaps in the centres which could be let down by adjusting the hinged brace beneath. It was designed to be stood upon. The flaps in the central shelves could be let down to better accommodate a person's chest. One could stand on the centre shelf to more comfortably and better look through the field glasses. I stepped down again, clutching the notebook. My mouth was suddenly dry and I did not want to be down there. And then a glimpse of the other items I'd been looking at reminded me that I did. Clutching my lamp, I peered out into the main thoroughfare of the basement. Of course, there was no one there. It was instinctive to check. I looked at my watch. It was only nine. I had another two hours before my last train.

Returning into the caged room, I sat at the small wooden desk and set the lamp near the book so I could read more from the journal. Better to read it in order. I turned to one of the earlier entries:

'I find Burness charming, if roguish. His appreciation of old F— 's collection is equivalent to my own. As he says, there is no wrong in looking, no more wrong than a farmer appreciating the stock in a market. I took the five guineas he offered me as a courtesy.'
    Flicking forward:

'It is an admirable arrangement – and no harm in it. I commit no crime, pay no harlot's fee. To peer into his bedrooms and watch what occurs – unnoticed – as if I were invisible. She was a young one, too, tonight. Barely more than a girl. Watching her being undressed – it was as if it were my own fingers unbuttoning her chemise.'
I shut it. Then opened it again. This whole clutch of pages referred

to the chamber upstairs, the one behind the Meeting Room. Was it Q., then, who put in the field glasses? To judge by the volume of pages referring to what he saw there, this was a favourite pastime: to watch what went on in the room behind.

I read on. More accounts of standing in the Meeting Room – up the ladder – watching Burness and his clientele at their pleasure. But what occurred down here? What did his gaze find in the room behind this wall?

'Are you coming downstairs again, tonight?' he asked me.
I did.
I did not know what he was going to do to her. Dear God – what heard I through the wall. How many have seen such things?'

I shut the book. There was someone in the cage with me. This was no phantom. Or an image of the imagination. This was a physical presence. Someone in the same space as me. They were between me and the iron door. I feared it was going to slam shut and I would be caught in there with them. I did not want to call out. I did not want to draw attention to myself. I just wished to get out of there as quickly as I could. I picked up my lantern and swung it towards the door, feeling for the key in my pocket. I found the keys as my lamp showed me the door. But not before it had caught the glimpse of an oval face, pockmarked, pallid – with wild, desperate, black-rimmed eyes. I knew who it was without doubt. Not Burness, whose face I had seen in L.'s newspaper cuttings. It was Q. As tangible and there with me as if he had been alive. He touched me. His hand cold, like meat. He pressed my flesh. I ran, somehow locking the door behind me, though leaving it unchained.

The next day I was shaken. I thought I should go into the basement, take Mr L. down with me – check what was there. But I could not face it. For worse than the memory of his touch – was the sense of yearning I felt – which must have been his. L., being meek in temperament, did not question me about my state of mind. It was apparent to him that I was perturbed, agitated. I caught him looking at me as I attempted to carry out my duties. I found it hard to concentrate on the job I was doing. I felt hollow, almost like an ache – an ache of emptiness. An awful sense of regret. It was unpleasant and I willed it to pass; but it would not pass. It was accompanied, too, by fear, lurking behind it. A sense of foreboding. A real feeling that something awful was going to happen; as if some kind of hex or nemesis had attached itself to me. This, too, played on my mind. Oddly, it was accompanied by a solution presenting itself as an image whenever I closed my eyes. A woman's face, resolute – firm. L.'s acquaintance: the medium.

Fearfully – perhaps I was ashamed to even be asking – I cornered Mr L. at the end of the day. Would it be possible to speak to his friend again? There was a matter – a spiritual matter – I wished to discuss with her. His face seemed to darken. 'What is it?' I asked, registering the change immediately.

'She asked me the same of you, only last night,' he said.

A handwritten note came the next day. She requested that I visit her as a matter of some urgency. She regretted that she would be unable to come to the Library. There was no explanation as to why this was the case. I took the electric tram to the area south of the city, passing through lines of terrace houses, all colour drained from them by the thick smog beyond the glass. The view became more phantasmagoric as the tram progressed; figures barely visible in the grey haze. I thought the sense of occluded reality would pass as I stepped off the vehicle upon my arrival but, if anything, it grew. Sound was deadened and the still, cold air numbed my fingers.

I hoped there would be relief upon arriving at her house. It looked comfortable enough, but there was no comfort in her face. She took me into her parlour, a warm-looking place, but neither the fire nor the red drapes seemed to lift my chill. I thought she might offer me tea, but she offered me nothing. She did not, it seemed, want me to stay any longer than I had to.

'You are in trouble,' she told me plainly. 'It has been communicated to me.'

I wanted to know how she knew this.

'My Guide has instructed me. The one you have found seeks enfleshment, possession. He does not know what he is or quite where he is. He is only hunger.'

I began to speak, but she silenced me before I could ask anything more.

'He is not the one we thought. A man who has hanged for his crime rarely haunts. His spirit has been laid by the act of reparation. But this one – this kind,' she continued, 'normally it is found in families, in domestic situations, clinging to that which it loved. It is pathetic. It will not pass because it cannot let go of its yearnings. These spirits normally yearn for their spouses, or their children – and when those persons pass, the spirit will pass, too, and the spiritual problem is solved. This . . . thing, however,' she spat out the words with distaste, 'is different. What it yearns for, it could never have had in the first place. It craves sensation. But on the Other Side you cannot imagine how that craving burns – because it was not sated in life, because it never could be. It is pure animal want, disconnected from any means or hope of gratification. It will not accept it cannot have it. And so it lingers.'

She shook her head, sucked at her teeth. The fire burned low in the grate and I pulled my jacket around me. She carried on.

'Now . . . now, it has found someone alive it resonates with.'

She picked up something from the top of her piano and struck it hard, holding it against the lid. It hummed as if it were suddenly alive. A tuning fork.

'It thinks it has a chance to bind with you. And it does.' She looked grave.

'What?' For a moment I was speechless. I utilized all my reserves to frame the question. 'What can be done?'

'You must strike now. You must be resolute – before this thing destroys you. And it is capable of so doing. It will suck the life out of you and lead you to ruin. This may sound like melodrama, but I promise you it is true. It will grind every ounce of life, of hope, of potential, out of you. It will eat away at everything you could and should be.' She handed me an envelope. As she did so, she spat on the ground.

I had to prepare in secret. To say I had no appetite to do what I would have to do, would be to understate matters violently. But – and here was the thing – I knew that everything I had been told was true.

It would have to be done at night; that was made clear in the charges. It had to be after midnight, which meant I would have to spend the whole night in the Library. The task would have to be completed by dawn, which would only give me six or seven hours. And I would have but one chance at it. It seemed the metaphysics in these circumstances were unforgiving. I made the arrangements the week before. The bricks were to be delivered early, before the other staff arrived. I knew how to mix mortar. My father had taught me when we built a wall together in our garden. The rest I would have to do as I could.

The first task was to draw him out again. Where he resided in the interim was not clear; in the thick darkness, in the dust, in the damp; lurking between the very molecules that made them. I pulled a collection of French lithographs from the 1830s by the artist Achille Devéria, depicting a variety of unspeakable acts. I leafed through them, alarmed to discover that even in these circumstances my animal side could not help but be provoked. As I turned the loosely bound leaves in their binder, I braced myself: the sense of dread was beginning to rise, even as the arousal did. It was all I could do not to turn, but I waited. He had to take enough from me for what was to follow to succeed. I made a pact with myself. I was not to run. I was to see this through. My resolve was unbreakable. I would get to the end of the collection. The last drawing – which involved two grotesquely large phalluses and a courtesan – was my cue. I raised my lamp and swivelled around through 180 degrees.

He was sitting in the corner, against the back wall, squat like a beast. He seemed more corporeal than before. His face looked up at me – hollow, eyes black. He reached for me. Quickly, placing the lamp on a shelf above me, I pulled the razor blade from my pocket and sliced carefully the tip of my thumb. The blade stung. I took the phial of vinegar from my pocket and poured it over the wound, grimacing as I did so. Then I allowed the blood to drip in a row of dots about two feet in front of where he crouched. He would not be able to cross that line, or so the medium assured me. I turned back to the door and reached for the bucket which contained the mortar I had mixed. Squeezing my thumb hard, I dripped another thirteen droplets therein – one for each apostle and one for Judas. Then I bound my thumb with a handkerchief, holding it tight until the flow ceased. I could sense him watching me. He did not breathe, but there was a low moaning in the air, which I assumed emanated from him.

The bricks were on a trolley meant for books. I wheeled it in. The ceiling was low enough that it meant the job was possible in the time available. Thankfully, because of where he was, it would be easy enough to make the wall around him. I began to build, working as quickly as I could. The wall did not have to be perfect, so I could go fast. He did not have the corporality to affect it in any way. He could touch me, but he could not impact upon the physical world – or so I had been informed. I hoped and trusted that this was the case. He would be sealed behind this wall and gradually starved of his compulsion; his addiction. It would take time – perhaps decades – but the medium assured he would finally realize his hopeless state and this would release his need to linger in this, the heaviest of the ethers. Sealed behind this wall, there was no danger of him infecting and ensnaring another. And the collection he curated would not be able to, either. I would see to that.

He stared at me, seemingly querulous, as I worked. He could not speak, of course, but he did begin to vocalize. I tried to avoid the black smears of his eyes, concentrating on lining brick upon brick. The moaning seemed to be growing in volume. It had an air of complaint. He was looking at me, I knew. He was reaching for me. He stood up, in tattered remnants of ragged cloth, or so it appeared. The line of bricks grew. It was already above my stomach. The thing was trying to form words; or else I was hearing them in my imagination. It was my job to build the wall – to not listen to him.

He was begging. Pleading. Weeping. I want I want I want I want I want I want. It was want without hope. I shook my head. The pleas came harder. Pay it no attention.

The pleas became begs.

I placed brick upon brick.

As the wall rose, I reached the level of his face. The pain therein was inescapable. Grunts. Guttural caws. A hand rose, filthy palm towards me. On went the next brick. When it was the eyes alone, staring out at me, I was nearly overcome with a wrenching sense of horror and panic. As if it were me who was being walled up in there, alive with want, with need, with appetite.

It is a phantom. It is a shade. I slid the final brick in place.

This part of the job was done. I was sweaty. Filthy. But there was still another part to the commission.

I gathered everything in wooden crates, and carried them upstairs. And then I lit a fire in the Meeting Room and locked the door.

It all went in, everything from Lord F— 's collection. I spared nothing. I was still burning things when L. arrived at eight the following morning.

My letter of explanation to the Library's board said that my religion was the cause, that I was obeying a divine edict. It's ironic that this was more plausible than the truth of the matter. Of course, I lost my job, and only narrowly avoided prosecution. In the end it was only because the Library feared what I would say about the collection at any trial and what would be reported in the newspapers.

In the long term, it was no matter. I had a small private income that allowed me to travel to Italy, where I studied bookbinding. I write this now, by way of confession, sitting in the beauty of the library at the Pontifical Gregorian University in Rome, where I have worked for the last five years. There is a fenestra above me and it lets in much light.

CASE TWO

Like a castle of olden time
Ben Rhydding proudly stands,
And a watery welcome gives
To comers from every land.

Ben Rhydding Ballad

The following account dates from some twenty years ago and was recorded by U. Reeder on behalf of the Society for Psychical Research. It was recounted to him by a friend with connections to the constabulary. U. Reeder's acquaintance was a sceptic by nature; however, the earnestness of his colleague when recounting the events that led to his downfall was enough to at least give the other pause.

The Ben Rhydding Hydropathic Institute – or Hydro, as it was often shortened to – is no a longer a functioning establishment, having gone out of business when such places fell from favour at the end of the last century. The premises were, until recently, a golf hotel but are now closed to the visiting public. The little village in the valley beneath the old Hydro retains the institution's name.

'It has been said that there is little worse than a policeman turned bad, which might have explained why Mr. Christopher Metcalfe's visit to his fellow officer Mr. Harold Baird in Armley Jail was a source of some trepidation. Metcalfe was not sure what state his former colleague would be in, not having spoken to the man since his arrest for murder, or during the events leading up to that arrest. It was a shock to discover, therefore, his acquaintance seemingly unchanged from the calm, intelligent, somewhat stoical figure Metcalfe had known for nearly five years.

[26]

Baird was escorted from his cell to a specially designated visiting area (visits for the condemned at the jail had to be conducted away from those allowed to other prisoners). Metcalfe stood, finding he did not quite know how to comport himself. He was grateful, and perhaps surprised, to find that it was Baird who made an effort to put him at his ease rather than the other way round.

'The worst thing about being here is simply that I know too much. As a policeman, I mean.'

Metcalfe swallowed, unsure what the other man was going to say.

'This place has the longest walk of any jail from condemned cell to noose. A journey of some forty yards. Just my luck.' Baird gave a bitter smile. 'Because of my profession, I know that the last man hanged here was Joe Brumfit. I know he struggled so much that it took fifteen minutes to get him from the cell to the gallows.'

Metcalfe nodded, for he had heard the same story. He was shocked when Baird took his hands and held them, staring into the other man's eyes.

'Thank you, Metcalfe, for coming to see me.' Baird paused before adding, 'You are the only one.'

'It was my duty to do so. I felt I must . . .' said Metcalfe, earnestly.

'I have accepted everything,' said Baird. There was a flatness to his voice. He had a fine-featured, pale face and thoughtful blue eyes. He was as far from the usual denizen of that hateful place as one could imagine. 'I am unmarried, without living siblings. My parents are dead. I am grateful for all of this.'

Metcalfe nodded again. There was little to add. A silence ensued, which Metcalfe wanted to break, without knowing how. He had no sense of what to say.

'I am guilty of the crime,' said Baird. 'I had no choice about the plea. What I could not do at the trial – felt unable to do – was reveal the true nature of my mitigation. I committed the murder. It was a deliberate act. But I am still certain it was the right thing to do.'

There was more silence. Metcalfe broke it with a question.

'It was self-defence?'

Baird considered.

'Not in the sense you mean, no.'

Somewhere, a clock struck, and Baird's face clouded. 'Christopher . . .' he said.

Metcalfe started at the use of his Christian name.

'I need to tell someone what actually took place. Someone who may at least stand a chance of understanding. I need to have my story witnessed, before it is too late. Forgive me for laying this yoke on your shoulders. But you were the only person who came to mind.' Baird paused. 'I could have spoken to the pastor, but I am not a religious man. And I want what happened to be understood.' He paused again for a moment before adding. 'I think there is a chance you will understand.'

After a moment's consideration, Metcalfe nodded his assent.

'I will be as brief and succinct as I can, but you will need to concentrate. For there are things I will speak of that I know you will find hard to grasp. Hard to believe. I think I can only tell my story once. Will you hear it?'

'I will . . . Harold.'

Baird did not smile as such, but there was a moment of light in his eyes.

What follows is Metcalfe's record of the extraordinary story he was told.

The community of Ben Rhydding is a peaceful village in lower Wharfedale. It had been untroubled by crime of any notable kind – at least recorded crime – for a century or more. Certainly there would have been disagreements, domestic disputes, theft; but these matters would not have required the intervention of the offices of the law. As for violent crime – well, it was pretty much unheard of. Leeds, Bradford, Manchester: these places on occasions paid host to the worst aspects of humanity, but in every respect Ben Rhydding was the archetypal rural idyll. Therefore the community for some distance around was thrown into turmoil by the disappearance of a young girl, one Martha Bowen, on the evening of the 15th of June in 1907. That was the last time she had been seen alive. She was fourteen years of age and had been seen walking from her home in Upper Wheatley to Westwood House on the far side of the moor, where she was delivering a basket of eggs, a journey of no more than a mile and a half. It was not necessary for her to travel that way, but it was the quickest and shortest route, and it was a fine evening. She hadn't returned by nightfall, but her mother was at first unconcerned, assuming that the girl was dallying with friends. However, as the hour approached midnight, she became more distressed and raised the alarm.

The girl's father, together with her uncle, went up on the moor with lanterns, following what they thought must have been her likely route. Although the paths were generally safe, there were sheer drops into the two quarries, one small and one large. The latter in particular was effectively a crater, with falls of twenty feet, thirty in places. It was possible the girl was injured, unconscious, unable to seek help. This was what they were hoping for with all their hearts. No body was found that night, and it was decided that the search should continue in daylight. Come the dawn, it resumed and the family's worst fears were fulfilled. Poor Martha's body was found, badly mutilated, in the vicinity of the Woodhouse Crag on the northern edge of the moor.

Because of the nature of the injuries, it was assumed that she'd been attacked by an animal, though there had been no reports of any livestock mauled in the area. Farmers and locals were put on alert that there was a wild dog in the vicinity and to be ready to shoot it on sight. It was rare, though not unheard of, for such a thing to occur. Even a large fox – if rabid – might be vicious and the girl was slight in build.

Then, less than three months later, the second attack came and it put paid to any thoughts of an animal cause. This time the victim was a little older, but the tragedy was just as acute. Alice Manassero – a young Italian girl of no more than twenty-one and who was in service in the nearby town of Ilkley – had gone missing one afternoon. At first, it was assumed that she had perhaps travelled to Bradford or Skipton, as she was wont to do, particularly as her nuptials were impending and she was looking to be making her dress. With no direct family to be concerned about her, it took a little longer for the alarm to be raised. But once again, and with memories of poor Martha Bowen's death still fresh, a search party was organized and a corpse was found, this time in the bleak and lonely vicinity of the Twelve Apostles, an ancient stone circle that stood about a mile and a half above the village, on the highest part of the moor. It was an examination of her body that led to Baird being brought in from Bradford to investigate the case.

Baird was a bright and dedicated member of the constabulary, having served as a sergeant for four years. He had only recently been appointed to the post of Inspector, but had already impressed his superiors with his ardour and ability, successfully breaking a group of ruthless armed robbers who were operating from Ainley Top. It was with some relief that the local constabulary received him, as they were genuinely fearful of what was happening in their vicinity.

When Baird arrived at the small police station in Ilkley, he was greeted by one Sergeant Randall: a bluff and burly Yorkshireman who had been in charge of the investigations up until that point. Baird's first questions, having read the notes associated with Martha Bowen's death, were about what was being done to hunt down any wild dogs or foxes in the area.

'Well, since this latest one, sir, we've given up on that line,' said Randall, grim.

'And why is that?' asked Baird.

'I think you need to see the girl's body.'

The body was being kept in the mortuary at Middleton Hospital, on the other side of the valley. Although relatively young for his position, Baird thought of himself as being of robust constitution; but he was not prepared for the nature of the injuries he encountered. The girl had been mauled, as before, but it was clear from her remains and the nature of her injuries that she had also been subjected to the most brutal kind of rape.

'Could you take me to the site where she was found?' asked Baird.

'Well, it's getting dark now, sir. It might be best to go in the morning,' said Sergeant Randall, avoiding his eye.

Baird looked at his watch. 'It's not yet six, we've another hour of light.'

'Yes, sir.' The other man was clearly still reluctant. 'But darkness can fall fast, and if the clouds are low it can be very dim up there at twilight. There'll be more to take in at daybreak.'

'Draw me a map, man,' said Baird, not bothering to conceal his impatience. 'I'll go by myself.'

And so Baird found himself walking the unfamiliar moor in the half-hour before twilight. He took a lantern at the request of Sergeant Randall, though he did not anticipate needing it. Baird was following his instincts. He wanted to look at the place of Alice Manassero's death while it was still fresh with the memory of her. Whether it would directly yield any information as to who or what lay behind the attack was not really part of his thinking. Baird knew from experience that the act of spending time at the scene of a crime – close to the committal of that crime – could influence his thinking to the better. It may have been an instinctive process, but it was as if the ether itself gave something up from merely standing in its presence.

The stone circle was on the highest part of the moor. It wasn't hard to find, being at the crossing of two paths: one leading from Ben Rhydding, and one traversing it laterally, heading towards the small settlement of Burley Woodhead about three miles away to the east. The view was extraordinary, taking in the expanse of the Wharfe Valley, but a chill wind blew and the darkening sky was thick with scudding clouds. The track from the main path to the stones themselves was muddy, puddled in places from recent rainfall, and Baird had to go carefully, not wishing to risk turning his ankle (or worse). He walked towards the stones, which were laid out in a large circle some fifty feet in diameter. He had read of such places, Stonehenge and Avebury springing to mind, and he had some recollection of seeing engravings. This place was not on that scale. The rocks which formed the structure were uneven, differing in size, giving the arrangement here a more brutal, antediluvian air. The recent rainfall had been significant enough that it had washed the ground clean of any evidence of butchery, and for this Baird was grateful, even as he regretted the opportunity of studying it for any evidence it might yield. In truth, he had been deeply shocked by the injuries he had seen – the savagery, the brutality, the cruelty of them – and he wanted to focus on something else, some other approach that might allow him to discover who lay behind them. (He was still tempted to add 'or what', but he avoided that mental trap.)

Baird went to stand in the centre of the circle, which was where the body had been found. Despite this being early September, the wind had taken on a winter bite, partly because the area was so exposed. The heather shook around him like a whipped-up ocean, but it was not this that made him want to turn and flee. There was something so forbidding about the emptiness of the landscape around him that it entered him like a pain. He gazed at it, wondering to what dark purpose the arrangements of stones had been created. Again his knowledge in this area was minimal. He knew a little, enough to make the connection to ancient religions and pagan practices, but he had not much more of a sense than that. As he turned and walked briskly away, willing his descent to be as speedy as it could be without actually picking up his heels and running, there was one word that flitted through his mind to describe the sense he had been overcome with, standing there at the centre of those ancient stones: that word was evil.

Baird had a disturbed night's sleep and woke unrefreshed. He arrived at the station in Ilkley at 8.00 a.m. to find Sergeant Randall waiting for him, perhaps ashamed about his reluctance the previous night to take Baird to the scene of the crime. The first thing Baird asked of him was to make a check, if he had not already done so, as to whether any lunatic had escaped from the nearby asylum at Menston. And then he asked for Randall to take him to the scene of the first murder, near Woodhouse Crag.

Baird was grateful for the morning light and the cheerier air as they walked briskly along the path from the town. He quizzed Randall about anything and everything that he knew of the deaths, both what he had seen with his own eyes and what he had heard locally, no matter how outrageous, but the man remained disappointingly taciturn. He recounted what the Inspector already knew: the theories about wild animals, the certain knowledge that there could be nobody in the town capable of such atrocities. This would get them nowhere.

'Do you have any theories, Sergeant, about what kind of man could be behind such a thing?'

'A madman, sir. What else?'

'Has there been anyone new in the vicinity? Has anyone observed . . . a vagrant, perhaps, who has taken up in these parts?'

'Nothing like that, no, sir.'

'Where could this madman have come from? Why his sudden activity?' Baird spoke this question without really expecting an answer. To some extent, he was thinking out loud.

'No accounting for it. All you can say is . . .' And Randall trailed off, not wanting to complete the sentence.

'All you can say is what?' asked Baird.

Randall remained quiet for a moment before speaking.

'I didn't want to say it, sir – so I stopped myself. But what I was going to say was . . . whoever he is, he's got a taste for it now.'

Woodhouse Crag was a collection of boulders on the crest of one of the gentler slopes of Rombalds Moor. It looked over to Langbar, on the north side of the valley, and consequently was a touch less forbidding than the stone circle. Nevertheless, the sky opposite had darkened and the way the clouds were smearing towards the crowd suggested sheets of rain would soon be coming their way.

'Can you show me exactly where the Bowen girl was found? Hard to remember for sure, I suppose?' asked Baird

'Oh, no, sir. Not hard. Not hard at all,' said Randall, and he walked over to a rock at the centre of the outcrop, right at its edge. Immediately he was over it, Baird could see why Randall would have remembered it. For there was a carving made into that filled all of its flattened surface. At first Baird wondered if it was graffiti; it was not uncommon to see names etched into the hard rocks of crags and outcrops like this. But peering closer, he saw the design was abstract, and had been incised deeply. The erosion around the edges of its lines spoke of its antiquity.

'What is that?' Baird asked.

'The Swastika Stone. Least that's what they call it. Old. Ancient, they reckon. Old as the Apostles . . .' Randall trailed off. It was as if he realized for the first time what it was he was saying.

'Swastika.' Baird rolled the word around his mouth. 'What's that mean?'

'Dunno, sir. It's been in a book. More than one book.'

Baird studied the design. It was hard to say what it looked like. A sort of windmill, though it had an organic air to it, like something unnameable washed up from a deep sea. The shape was simply drawn, decorated with button-like dots. And though it had four bent limbs, there was a smaller member projected from its eastern one (if one likened it to the points of compass). This additional limb was curled, like a scythe. Something about its antiquity chilled him, as if it were older than human.

'The Bowen girl was found on it?' asked Baird.

'Her arms and legs all crooked, like the thing itself.'

'Had she been . . . arranged like that? Why wasn't this in the notes?'

'Didn't occur to anyone at the time, sir. They thought it was . . . an animal'd done it.' Randall swallowed. 'You think it might . . . pertain?'

'It might just,' said Baird, bitterly.

He squatted down, extending his forefinger, inserting into the groove of the design.

'That's north, isn't it?' said Baird, pointing in the direction of the uppermost limb.

'Aye. And that one,' said Randall, indicating the one with the sickle-like thing protruding from it, 'that one points direct at Almscliffe Crag, over to the east.' He gestured towards a sinister-looking rock that broke the line of the horizon over towards Blubberhouses.

'And where does this one point?' asked Baird, his extended finger having wound its way down to the bottom-most limb.

'To the stones. The Apostles,' said Randall, swallowing.

Having found nothing concrete on his reconnoiters, Baird thought his only option was to resort to trusted methods: diligence, perseverance and plain old-fashioned effort. He set about re-interviewing all the original witnesses and suspects, and for good measure he also conducted a series of additional house-by-house enquiries. He was not expecting these to yield any direct breakthroughs, but in his experience there were occasions when a single fragment or thread, casually found, could later transform itself into a key that might unlock the door to the whole case. The difficulty was that it was never apparent at the time of the questioning what that thread might be. The effort necessitated maintaining a heightened level of attention against the inevitable ennui the task itself generated. He tried to remind himself of this, on the third day of this operation, listening to an elderly butcher spend twenty-five minutes complaining about the endless traffic to and from the Hydropathic Institute.

Exhausted by this process, even if it was only temporarily, Baird concluded he should try another approach – if only to freshen his senses. His imagination kept being drawn back to the moor, and the strange carved stone in particular. Remembering that Sergeant Randall had spoken of books that referred to its heritage, he made his way to the small library in Ilkley.

The librarian was a helpful, bright-eyed chap in his sixties perhaps. White-haired but with an enthusiastic and spritely nature; perhaps keen to be given a task to fulfil.

'Oh, yes. I know the books you're speaking of,' he said, his eyes gleaming with pleasure.

'Would it be possible to see them?'

'Ordinarily, yes,' he said. There was an awkward pause.

'And . . .?' said Baird, feeling the need to prompt.

'Both books are missing.'

'Missing?'

'Occasionally things are stolen. It is a peril of running a public library. The books are of local interest . . .' Again, his voice trailed off as if this alone were explanation enough.

'Is it possible to . . . obtain replacements?'

'It is,' said the man, brightening again. 'But it will take several weeks, I'm afraid.'

'I see.' Baird stood there, mentally examining his options, the librarian still smiling at him. 'Well. Perhaps we should set those wheels in motion,' Baird added after a moment, having concluded it would do no harm even if he had to wait a while. With that, Baird touched his hat and turned toward the exit.

'There is a chance, sir . . .' said the librarian, calling after him.

'Yes?' Baird turned, standing near the doorway.

'There is a gentlemen in the town – an academic kind of gentleman – he teaches at the university, in Bradford.'

'Please, go on.'

'Professor Vincent. He is a friendly kind of chap. He comes in here quite often. I think he has copies of both of these books in his personal collection. I'm sure he would not object to me passing on his address. Perhaps you could write to him and he may give you access to his volumes? While you are waiting for us to acquire ours.'

'That would be most generous, thank you.'

Frustrated in these initial attempts to find out more about the locations of the victims' bodies, and what significance, if any, they had to the deaths, Baird thought perhaps he should revisit the sites. In truth, he had been putting this off. Not for any rational reason, but simply because of a deep aversion he felt within to both places. Calling on his logical side, normally a powerful ally, he reminded himself of his duties and responsibilities and concluded that one thing he could do would be to take a rubbing of the design on the so-called Swastika Stone.

Having obtained a large sheet of white wrapping paper from Furniss the butcher's, together with a large wax crayon borrowed from the Post Office, Baird made his way back up to Wharfedale Crag. It was a dry day but cold, more like November, and there was no escaping the bitter wind. The sky was dark with ugly clouds which threatened rain. Baird thought he had better work fast. He looked around for some loose rocks to weigh the paper down over the Swastika Stone. As he spread the paper out, he thought about the person who would have made this carving. What was its function? Was it merely mindless ornament? Or did it have some practical application? Presumably it was not done for idle amusement. His first attempt at rubbing tore the paper. Fortunately, he had brought more than one piece with him. He went gentler this time, allowing the shape to form gradually beneath the thick black crayon, order resolving itself in the chaos of black lines, a ghost lurking in the darkness. He shivered, feeling something standing close behind him. He turned. But the moor was empty. Nothing but clumps of grass and gorse. He could see in all directions. He was above the world, demonstrably alone. And yet there was something thick in the air. Something he knew intimately, closer to himself than the pulse beating in his neck. Something elemental.

It was on his return to the police station that the idea hit him. Visible across the moor, halfway between its peak and the base of the valley below, was the enormous edifice of the Hydropathic Institute. Here was a place that played host to people from all over the Empire, some of them returning for treatments over a period of months. Might it not be possible that there was somebody who had arrived in time for the first murder, gone away again, and then returned in time for the second – or indeed been present for both?

'Did anyone check the records of the Hydro's guests at the time of Martha's death?'

'No, sir,' said Randall, immediately taking on a shifty air.

The Hydro was approached from the north. The gloom of the day had not lifted and many of the windows were lit. The points of its many spires stood out against the sky, its castellations giving it the air of a building from a fairy tale or a romance. It was huge, imposing; its stone surface, once pale, was now black with soot carried up from the chimneys of Bradford and Shipley.

The enormous front door was made of oak and, unusually for such an institution, closed. Baird pulled the bell and heard an answering peel within. He looked around, and while waiting for a reply he stepped back, taking a good look at the considerable building before him. Its two wings formed a kind of courtyard. The ground was laid with gravel, and each step that Baird took made a crunch which reverberated off the stone walls that enclosed him. A face peered down at him from one of the windows to the side of the central column of the front entrance. A noise in front made him start. It was the creak of the huge oak door. A large man in nurse's whites looked out at him.

'Good afternoon, my name is Inspector Baird, from the Bradford Constabulary. Would it be possible to speak with Mr Gurdeyman?'

Frederick Gurdeyman was the Hydro's manager. He was on record as being in charge of the building and its estate.

'Please, come in sir,' said the nurse. 'I will see if he is available.'

Baird didn't like the surly attitude behind his voice. 'I would ask that he makes himself available. This is a matter of the gravest importance.'

The nurse nodded solemnly. 'Yes sir,' he said.

There was a sizeable fireplace in the entrance area, with a leather-covered seat built into its surround on either side. The hallway was panelled in dark, polished wood. It smelled faintly of damp and dust. Gas lights in ornate glass globes hissed faintly. An occasional gust of wind whistled under the front door. On the wall opposite, behind a heavy unmanned desk, were a number of framed photographs with names beneath them on little brass plaques. Baird moved towards them to examine them closer. These were pictures of the current staff. They all looked rather severe and tutorial, he thought, apart from the last picture, a friendly-looking face topped with rather wild, curly hair. The name beneath read 'Dr J. Deitch'.

'Inspector Baird?'

Baird turned suddenly, to be faced with a tall, lugubrious-looking man. He had mutton-chops and wore a funereal suit and an old-fashioned square bow-tie.

'I am Frederick Gurdeyman. You wanted to see me.'

'I did, yes.'

'How can I serve?'

Perhaps not wanting a man in a policeman's cape to be so visible on his premises, he steered Baird into his office.

Behind the closed door, beneath a large ticking oak-cased clock, Baird explained that he was there in connection with two serious crimes which Mr. Gurdeyman was no doubt aware of. Mr. Gurdeyman immediately took umbrage.

'And what possible connection could there be, Inspector, between these monstrous occurrences and this institution?'

'None, I'm sure, sir,' said Baird, in as soothing a manner as possible. Part of his swift rise to the position he held lay in his abilities as a diplomat. 'In fact, I am only truly here to eliminate you from our inquiries so that I can leave you – and your guests – untroubled from here on in.'

'They are patients, Inspector. Not guests,' said Mr. Gurdeyman, still bristling.

'Of course. I would be grateful if you could let me see the register of patients, for the last year.'

'That information is confidential.'

'Of course. It will go no further than me, Mr. Gurdeyman. But I'm sure you understand the requirements of the law.'

Gurdeyman said nothing, and then stood sharply. 'You will wait here, please.'

Gurdeyman returned with the register, a large leather-bound tome, and stood over Baird's shoulder while the policeman began to leaf through it. Baird searched for any residents whose stay straddled the two murders – any names that returned, indicating they were there at the time of both murders – but the register yielded nothing. He did not allow himself to be put off by Gurdeyman's baleful presence. Without giving in to the temptation to be deliberately inflammatory, Baird did comb the names and dates with his customary rigour, undeterred by the figure at his shoulder. Eventually, though, Baird had to concede he could find no connection between any pattern of attendance therein and the dates of the two murders.

'As I, of course, expected, there is nothing to tie any of your guests to the crimes under investigation. I'd like to thank you for your co-operation, Mr. Gurdeyman.'

Baird got to his feet, and very casually asked, 'Your most recent member of staff, Mr. Deitch?'

'What about him?'

'He is your most recent member of staff, isn't he?'

Gurdeyman clearly wished he could dismiss the Inspector as he would an insubordinate chamber-maid; but perhaps knowing he couldn't, he resisted the urge.

'Yes, he is.'

'And when did he join you?'

Gurdeyman paused before answering, but he did answer. 'In April.'

'April this year?'

'Yes.'

Maintaining his casual line Baird continued. 'Would it be possible to speak to him?'

'He is with patients.'

'I should very much like to interview him. He could come to the station.'

'Inspector. I would like you know that I am a personal friend of the Lord Mayor of Bradford.'

'Yes, sir. I'd only need to speak to him for a few moments.'

Baird was directed to one of the outer buildings that lay away from the Hydro, to the rear. The grounds were extensive. There was a

Turkish baths, a bowling alley, a number of purely ornamental features, and a small lodge house that flanked the upper driveway which came directly down from the moor. Dr. Deitch was teaching his class in a part of the institute known as the Shrine. Baird had been told he would be able to spot it by its distinctive spire, which was a miniature version of the central one belonging to the west wing of the Hydro itself.

The class was apparently designed to improve the respiration and was due to end at 5.00 p.m. The regime at the Hydro was strict, and Baird was told he wouldn't have to wait long. He took the opportunity to stroll among the well-kept grounds, their elegant pathways lined with rows of neatly squared box. The wide drive curled upwards towards the heights of the moor, the Hydro being positioned about halfway between the base of the valley and its highest peak. The wild plateau above was concealed in low cloud. The damp air clung to Baird as he walked. Aware of the untamed expanse above him, he turned away from it and walked back towards the outbuildings, occasionally rubbing his gloved hands together to stave off the cold. He passed a bent figure with a hoe, tending to one of the formal flowerbeds. The man turned to look at Baird, his muddy, bristled face twisted into a sneer, and then he looked away again, returning his attention to his beds.

Baird turned to face the collection of out-buildings clustered about a hundred yards from the Hydro itself, in a small landscaped area, close to the dark dense woods which lined the western slope of the moor. It was indeed easy to spot which one was the Shrine. It was about the size of a cricket pavilion, but taller and more square. It sported an absurd little turret and in front of it was a fountain fashioned in the shape of a stone lion, complete with a white marble 'phiz'.

Baird walked over to the curious building, noting there was a little round window, like a porthole. It was above head height, too high to see through, but it was open slightly and Baird stood beneath it, to see what he might hear. At first there was nothing, absolutely nothing; but then he caught a noise, a low, animal kind of sound. It reminded him of something, perhaps the hum of a beehive. Or was it another, even more unsettling tone? He'd visited the zoological gardens at Scarborough a few years previously, and had stood in the lion house. There, he had heard the low growl of a lioness. It had rattled the room like an engine, chilling some atavistic part of the soul. There was something of that in this noise. Curious as to its source, Baird stood on his tiptoes. The sound ceased abruptly; then the scraping of chairs, and a low voice. Baird moved away from the window, honouring his pledge of discretion to Mr. Gurdeyman.

Eventually, a line of patients began to file out of the Shrine and make their way down the gravel paths towards the main building. Baird lurked in the vicinity of the nearby Turkish baths and Steamroom. When he judged that the last patient had left, he made his way towards the Shrine, its lights glowing against the darkening sky.

Curious to see what was within, and whether Dr. Deitch was still there (Baird hadn't seen any staff emerge), he pushed at the double doors at the front and stepped inside.

Beyond, there was a small lobby area with a pale tiled floor and wood-panelled walls. Another door of cushioned leather was in the angled wall opposite. There was a smoky smell in the air, something more fragrant than the usual mix of gaslight and burning wood. Baird wanted to knock, but the soft leather padding precluded this, so, slowly and discreetly, he pushed open the door and peered around.

'Excuse me?' he called ahead. 'Hello?'

The room looked larger than he had thought it would. It had a black and white tiled floor, oak walls, and at the far end what looked like a set of outsized pigeon holes full of rolled-up blankets. There was a pile of mattresses, too, beneath. An unusual-looking corner fireplace proved to be the source of the fragrant smell and, rather than a grate, it housed an ornate-looking brazier. There were some folding chairs, too; and there, moving them to one side, was a gentlemen in a doctor's coat.

'Hello?' said Baird again.

The man turned. He smiled, immediately friendly, very different in manner and demeanour to the officious Mr. Gurdeyman.

'Hello? Can I help? Are you lost, sir?' said the figure.

'No. No, I don't think so. I'm looking for Dr. Deitch.'

'And I'm happy to report you have found him, sir. And you are?' Deitch walked over, his right hand extended. His black hair was long, but neater than in the photograph that graced the entrance hall.

'Inspector Baird, sir. Of the Bradford Constabulary. I wonder if I could ask you a few questions.'

'Of course, Inspector. I'm so sorry. I took you for a patient.'

'Ah. No, sir. No. I'm afraid I'm here,' said Baird, thinking it best to get to his business quickly, 'on rather a grave matter. I'm sure you are aware of the brutal crimes that have been carried out less than a mile from this establishment.'

Deitch's face immediately darkened.

'Of course. Of course. Of course. That's why you're here.'

Baird considered himself an instinctive judge of character – another reason he had attained the position he held – and

Deitch's response seemed to tell him straightaway the man had no connection to the crime.

'Presumably you're here to interview staff and patients. I bet old Gurdeyman didn't like that.'

Baird tried not to react.

'In truth, I wondered that no one had been before, Inspector.'

'The mills can grind slow, sir.'

'Of course. But do you have any suspects?'

'I'm afraid I'm not at liberty to say, sir.'

'Of course, of course.' There was a brief pause, before Deitch said: 'We should go somewhere more comfortable – if you would like to question me?'

'You understand this is routine, sir. I have to question everyone.'

'My dear man, I would be distressed if I thought you were not so doing.'

As they walked back to the main building, Baird – as much from genuine curiosity as the need to make idle conversation – asked about the Shrine, and its provenance.

'Don't ask me why the architect designed it that way. I fear it was nothing but the fashion fifty years ago, to invoke romance and the intrigue of the Orient.' Deitch added, as an afterthought: 'It fits my classes, however, so I don't complain.'

'What are your classes, sir, if you don't mind me asking?'

'They are essentially breathing exercises, Inspector. A way of training the body to release its tensions. This, in turn, allows the nervous system to refresh itself.'

'And what is it about the building that we were just in that lends itself to this pursuit?'

'Oh, these . . . techniques that I teach. I, myself, learnt them in the Orient. I studied with a Yogi of some renown.'

'Really, sir. How did you . . .?'

'I was raised in Bengal.'

'I would never have known it.'

'Perhaps odd to have washed up in Yorkshire, of all places. But I seem to have found a home here.'

'Afternoon, Dr. Deitch . . .'

A drawling voice with a thick local accent called from the bushes as they approached the rear entrance of the building. It was the same sneering, crooked-looking man Baird had seen earlier. He waved his hoe before him like a lance.

'Jolley.'

Once they were out of earshot, Deitch added in a low voice, 'Unfortunate name for the poor creature to be saddled with, given his physiognomy.'

Baird turned, looking back over his shoulder, but the man had retreated behind the shrubbery.

'Dr. Deitch, I'd just like to ask you a few questions as to your whereabouts on the evening of the 15th June, and of the 7th of September of this year.'

'Could I check my calendar?'

Baird nodded his assent and Deitch withdrew a leather-bound diary from him his desk drawer. As he consulted it, Baird took the opportunity to glance around the small office. It was neat, orderly, with a number of framed certificates on the wall behind him. There was also a picture of what Baird took to be a younger Deitch with his father, who wore a military uniform.

'Both those dates were a Saturday.'

'That is correct, sir,' said Baird, who had noted the coincidence early in his investigation, but as yet had been unable to derive anything pertinent from it.

'Then I can tell you exactly where I was, from the hours of six-thirty p.m. through to the following morning.' If there was triumph in this, it was only that of being in a position to offer up clear and helpful information.

'Thank you, sir.'

'Saturdays are my sleeping clinic.'

'Your "sleeping clinic", sir?'

'Indeed. It is a weekly fixture. We occupy the Shrine. There are usually about ten or twelve of us. We spend the night in there. The door is locked. We do not emerge until morning.'

'I see, sir. And so you have witnesses as to your whereabouts on these nights, sir?'

'Well, my patients would be my witnesses, if you were to describe them in that way. We spend the night in one another's company.'

Baird left the Hydro with a heavy disposition. Any hope he'd had of finding a connection between his one and only suspect (by dint of their being the most recent arrival in the town) and the crimes he was investigating seemed to have been squashed by Dr. Deitch's alibi. And now, Baird really had very little else to go on. His greatest fear was that there was a maniac on the loose – a maniac who had tasted blood. His dearest wish was that he should not require the evidence another killing might yield, in order to find the individual. The sky was nearly dark but the clouds had lifted as he made his way down the hill and away from the Hydro. The air was thick with the smell of pine. Baird started as a voice came at him from the bushes.

'Copper.'

'Hello there?'

Baird swivelled around. The first thing he saw was a hoe coming at him.

'Over here, copper.' From round the bush, holding the hoe ahead of him, came the bent figure of the groundsman Baird had seen earlier.

'It's Jolley, isn't it?' Baird moved towards him, not liking being on the back foot. 'Put your implement down when you're addressing an officer of the law.'

'Aye, copper. But I'm not the queer fish here.'

'What do you mean by that?' Baird peered at him, immediately alert, trying to see the man's face in the crepuscular light.

'Them's the queer fish.' Jolley pointed with his hoe. 'Shut in that Shrine, every weekend. You want to get in there, copper.'

'Why? What do you mean?'

'I hear odd things. That's all I'm saying.'

'You'll say more than that when I get you down the station.'

'I've nowt more to say than that. You can ask all you want. Don't know any more than that. They're queer fish, that's all. Queer fish.'

Baird stared at him, sizing Jolley up. Just as suddenly as he had spoken, the groundsman turned and limped back up the hill, using his hoe like a staff. Baird was going to run after him, accost him for his insouciance, but in the end thought it wiser to keep his powder dry.

The following morning, when he got back to the station, Baird asked Sergeant Randall if he knew Jolley.

'The groundsman? He's an old fool. No threat to anyone, sir. A cripple could outrun him. He got hit by lightning as a boy, so they say.'

Baird hadn't been thinking of him as a suspect, rather as a source of information. He had not slept well the night before, his stomach knotted. He had a great need to know more about Dr. Deitch's clinic.

Thinking that going though Gurdeyman would not be the best route, Baird wrote a letter directly to Deitch requesting a further interview. Without being overly mendacious, he gave the impression that it was pertaining to the general running of the establishment, and that because he and Baird had already formed an association this would prove to be the most direct route to the information without troubling Deitch's superiors. To this end, Baird prepared a list of dummy questions including the turnover of staff, the character of the lower orderlies, the typology of patients, and such-like.

Deitch wrote back by return of post and said he was happy to speak to the Inspector again, if he thought it could be of any use in his ongoing investigations. He was, of course, happy to come to the station.

Baird began the second interview with niceties: enquiring after the doctor's clinic and how successful he was being with his patients. He also asked a little about the general nature of the institute, the kind of people that benefited from its treatments.

'We deal with many things, Inspector. For example, those suffering with respiratory disorders – they benefit from the clear air as well as the natural sulphurs and minerals in the waters – which we draw from our own springs. There are also those who are afflicted with nervous disorders, such as the many poor souls that attend my own clinics. Then, of course, there's the good folk who are otherwise healthy but wish to enjoy and be stimulated by the health-giving properties of our water cures. Mr. Charles Darwin himself was a regular patron, as Mr. Gurdeyman is fond of pointing out.'

'I wonder, when it comes to your clinics – the kind you were talking about, the overnight ones – ' said Baird seizing the opportunity, 'would it be possible for me to attend one, to get a feel for what it is you do?'

'Attend a sleep clinic?' Deitch smiled curiously. 'Well . . . there is quite a delicate atmosphere in there. My first responsibility has to be to the patients and their well-being. I would not want the presence of an . . . observer to interfere with their treatment. If you would like to attend one of my respiratory surgeries, of course that would be agreeable.'

Two days later Baird received a note from his own Superintendent telling him in no uncertain terms that he must desist from disrupting the staff and treatments at the Ben Rhydding Hydro unless he had specific information that he was investigating. The Superintendent stated plainly that unless Baird could demonstrate why he needed to investigate the institute, he must stay away. He would not countenance Baird's disruption there if the activity was serving no genuine purpose. The institution and its staff were upstanding citizens and hardly likely to have involvement in the sordid peasant crimes Baird was investigating.

Gurdeyman had made good on his threat, then, to involve his friend the Mayor. The cables and lines of power were familiar to Baird, and he knew enough that it was better to accept rather than resist their restrictions – at least on the surface.

It just so happened that that same day Baird received another note, this one from Professor Vincent, the academic the librarian had suggested he contact. The Professor apologized for the delay in replying to the Inspector's enquiry, but he had been away in Inverness. He had now returned and would be only too happy to help in matters relating to local antiquities.

'Please make yourself at home, Inspector. My housekeeper is in Morecambe, visiting her niece, but her daughter has agreed to come and look after me for the next two days, which is most kind, don't you think? I haven't seen her yet, but I shall call to her and trouble her to make good on her promise. I'm sure she's in the house. I've left the books you enquired about on the table. I've marked the relevant sections.'

Professor Vincent was a genial, avuncular-looking man in his sixties, but with a youthful light in his eyes. From the evidence of the small study Baird was now sitting in, the Professor was an enthusiast and a collector. There were several glass cases devoted to ancient items and curios, coins, crucifixes, and a whole shelf devoted to what appeared to be straw dollies. One wall was lined with mahogany shelves replete with curious and esoteric titles: *The Bhagavad-Gita* translated by Charles Wilkins, *Parerga and Paralipomena* by Schopenhauer. Baird walked over to the neat table on which the two titles spoken of by the Professor lay. He picked them up and moved to the comfortable-looking chair by the tiled fireplace. Lulled by the soft tick of the walnut-cased grandfather clock in the corner of the room, and the tip-tap of the rain beyond the window, Baird could easily have drifted off to sleep. He pulled himself awake, shook his head, and opened the first of the volumes: Speight's *History of Upper Wharfedale*. Flicking to the marked page, Baird found illustrations of the Swastika Stone and the Twelve Apostles.

Absorbed in the books, Baird failed to notice the arrival of the tea things, carried in by a pretty young girl with honey-coloured hair, probably about sixteen years of age.

'Where would you like them, sir?' she asked.

'Oh,' said Baird, sitting upright, caught off-guard. 'I'm . . . I'm not the, er . . . I'm the Professor's guest.'

'Oh. Of course, sir.' The girl shrugged and smiled, blushing, pushing a lock of hair from her face.

'Ahh,' said the Professor, returning to the room. 'There you are. I was calling for you, Mabel.'

'Yes , sir.' The girl smiled again at Baird, attempting a curtsey before backing out of the room.

The Professor poured the tea and gestured to the book on Baird's lap.

'The formidable Speight. Not the most economical of writers, Inspector Baird. You may appreciate a précis of what he has to say.'

'I'm only really seeking an idea of what the symbol carved into the stone on the moor means, sir. To see if it had any bearing on the crime.'

'The terrible crime.'

'Indeed.'

'Hmmm.'

The Professor laid down his tray and pulled at his small beard. 'I can tell you what *I* know of it.'

'Please.'

'As a design, it is not uncommon. In fact, it is to be found on several church bells in the county, probably dating from the fifteenth century. They were used as charms against lightning, believe it or not.'

'Is the stone on the rock as recent?'

'Lord, no. The emblem itself is to be found right across Europe. There are Palaeolithic carvings of the same design found in Russia, etched on pieces of ivory. The scholars there believe them to be fifteen thousand years old.'

'Fifteen thousand?'

'So they say. The word "swastika" is actually Sanskrit.'

'What is Sanskrit, sir? Forgive me. My education and reading in these matters is limited,' said Baird candidly. He was not ashamed to admit the limitations of his knowledge. Pride would merely interfere with the investigation of his case.

'Sanskrit is the language of ancient India. The language of the Hindus and the Buddhists.'

'And what does this symbol mean to them?'

'Ahh. Well, that's where it all gets a bit . . . shall we say, mysterious. It relates to sacred notions of the cosmos.'

'The cosmos, sir?'

'We might say the Universe. Everything that is. The version on our stone here in Wharfedale is a particularly special one.'

'How so?'

'Because of the extra part. The cup on the eastern arm. The Swastika itself represents the material world and its four arms are its four components.'

'What are those . . . components?'

'They would be the God realm, the Human realm, the Nature realm and the Hell realm.'

'The Hell realm?'

'The worst aspects of the universe as we perceive it. The darkest places. But all this separation, the drawing of the cup reminds us, is just illusion – what the Indians call Samsara – a place of pain and suffering by its very nature. But it is illusion. Like the colours of the rainbow separated from white light by a prism. You see everything originates from the cup, the singularity that gives birth to everything else.'

'I'm sorry, sir. You've lost me.'

'How to explain . . . Hmmm. Well. They would say that everything we perceive – even these very chairs, tables, me – no matter how real it feels to us – it is in fact illusion, with no more substance than the characters and descriptions one might read about in a book and then picture in the mind. But, just as those characters and images read about can move us, make us feel things, so the 'real' things we perceive around us operate on us and make us feel things which convince us of their reality when, in truth, they are not there. You kick the chair, it hurts your toe. The pain makes you believe its existence unquestioningly. But nevertheless, it is not there. It is a function of your perception. And all of this creation that we perceive around us emanated from a single point, a singularity that is the reality of all there is. That is the singularity that was at the dawn of creation – that is the cup. Samsara was poured from the cup. And there "we" are . . .'

The Professor pointed to the dot in the middle of the design.

'There we are in the midst of it all, perceiving it and believing it. But we were poured from the cup, too.'

'What about these other dots, in the arms?' Baird pointed to each of them in turn.

'Well, we have a choice about where we place ourselves, our consciousness. In the Human realm, the Nature realm – the God realm, if we like.'

'Or the Hell realm.'

'Certainly. We are free to choose that, too.'

The Professor's words hung there for a moment suspended against the benign tick of the grandfather clock, the light drumming of the rain, the occasional crack from the fire.

'And what is the connection with the circle of stones? The . . . Twelve Apostles?

'That is a good question, Inspector.' The Professor picked up the teapot and swirled its contents around. 'It is quite possible that there's no connection at all. That they are separated from each other by thousands of years.'

'What was the purpose of the stone circle, then?'

'Again . . .' The Professor topped up the cups of tea. 'That is a point of some conjecture. And, in truth, no-one has a firm or credible answer. They are most likely part of some ceremony now lost in the mists of time, some pagan form of worship. The stones are aligned to various astronomical events. The rising and setting of the sun, for example. You ask of connection between the circle and the Swastika Stone. Well, here is an interesting thing. On the date of the last lunar standstill – which doesn't happen very often – it was observed that, when viewed from the centre of the circle, the moon set behind the cairn at Lanshaw Lad – which is the boundary stone on the nearest ridge to the Apostles. Now if you draw that as a line on the map, and extend that line westward, it also hits the Swastika Stone.'

'Does this help explain its purpose?'

'Ha. You've got me, Inspector. I'm afraid I do get a little carried away with myself. No. It doesn't. But the most compelling theory I have come across relating to these places is that they are sacred spaces, designed for ceremonies of manifestation. To the ancient man it was a miracle that the life-giving sun which vanished every day and cast him into darkness rose again the next morn. His insecurity was that it would not reappear again. So, to ensure this, regular ceremonies were held in astronomically significant locations. Over time the ceremonies grew more complex. And there, things were manifested. Food. Weather. You could say the circle was like a . . . cosmic telegraph to the heavens, allowing ancient man to bring forth whatever it was that he desired.'

'A cosmic telegraph?'

'Yes. By creating a space that aligned carefully with the raw forces of creation as they observed them, they believed that they could conjure what they wished – by drawing on those same promethean energies.'

Baird sat there, staring into the fire, taking this in. His face was calm, but his mind whirled, trying to digest this information; to see if there was anyway to connect it to the dreadful crimes themselves.

'Did they sacrifice?' he asked.

'Oh, most certainly.'

'Might these murders be reenactments of these sacrifices?'

'If so, they are poor ones. These people tended to burn theirs.'

Baird nodded.

'Alive,' the Professor added for good measure.

Silence came again. For Baird, there was something tantalizing in all this. The outline of something recognizable seen dimly in a fog. As yet, he had no idea what. Eventually, he stood.

'I must thank you for your time, Professor. And for your expertise.'

'Though you feel it has little bearing on the appalling murders you are investigating?'

'This is a long game, sir. It is rarely evident what is pertinent and what is not in its opening stages.'

The Professor nodded in approval.

'A sage approach, if you'll allow me to say, Inspector.'

The Professor stood, too, in order to show Baird to the door.

'I would add one thing . . . though I hesitate to voice the words, for I pride myself on being a man of reason.'

'Please, Professor. All information is welcome.'

'I wanted to say I have never liked that place. Either of the places. They have . . .'

Baird felt a sudden chill in the air, a prickling in the base of his stomach.

'Please, go on.'

'They have an . . . evil feel. It's fanciful, I know. Are you aware of the phrase "an accident waiting to happen"?'

'Yes, sir.'

'These places – particularly when I walked there alone – maybe in their brutal emptiness, often feel like . . . evil waiting to happen.'

Baird spent the weekend contemplating all he had discovered. Considered one way, it seemed he had discovered nothing whatsoever. But looked at another, it felt curiously like he had

had a breakthrough – without yet knowing what that was. Any mood of complacency was dispelled the following morning when he received an urgent summons to travel to the station. There had been another incident.

Randall was already there when Baird arrived. He was grave, but not white-faced as Baird had seen him in the mortuary at Middleton Hospital.

'There was an attack, sir.'

'Is she dead?'

'It's not a she, sir.'

'It's not?'

'A lad. John Jackson's boy. Young John.'

'How old?'

'Thirteen, sir. And he's alive. Just.'

'Can he talk?'

The Jacksons were poor. They lived in small cottage midway between Burley Woodhead and the Hydro. They couldn't afford to send the boy to hospital. The mother and his sisters were caring for him as best they could.

When Baird arrived, the boy was asleep. Randall introduced him.

'This is Inspector Baird, from Bradford, who's in charge of getting to the bottom of all this. He needs to speak to your boy.'

'Boy can't talk. He's too weak.' This from Jackson Senior, a surly man with curved shoulders, old before his time. He stirred at the fire with a rusted poker.

'I just need to see him for a few minutes, sir. I cannot leave until I have done so,' said Baird, with as much authority as he could muster.

The boy was lying on a crude cot, in the back room of the cottage. There was a blanket strung up over the window to keep out the weak morning sunlight. The boy's mother knelt at his side.

'Young John . . .' She ran the words together as if they were one name. 'The copper's here. He wants to talk to you.'

The boy stirred in his cot. When his face turned towards the blanketed window, Baird was shocked to see how old the child looked. His eyes were half closed, his skin sallow, his cheeks drawn.

'Is this his usual countenance?' he asked.

'He came back like this.'

'John.' Baird leaned closer to the child, not wanting to tax him. 'John, I am Inspector Baird. A policeman. I need to talk to you about what happened last night.'

'We told him not to go playing up there. But they dare each other. You know what lads are like,' said his mother, unable to conceal her bitterness.

'Shh, Ma. Let him alone,' said the father, who was leaning on the doorjamb behind her.

'John,' said Baird, as gently as he could. 'Tell me as simply as you can. What happened?'

'I dunno.'

The boy's voice was cracked, as if he'd been screaming.

'It doesn't have to be the whole thing. Just tell me the bare bones.'

The boy didn't answer.

'Would it be easier if your parents were out of the room?'

A moment and then the boy nodded.

'Please, sir – and you, too, Mrs Jackson. It will be easier for him.'

Mr. Jackson looked as if he were about to protest. But his wife pressed her hand to his shoulder. They left the room.

'Now . . . please, John, just go from the beginning. The bare bones of it.'

The boy swallowed, then began.

'I were up at Cuckoo Woods. Just before it got dark.'

Baird looked at Randall, who indicated that he knew the place.

'Why had you gone there?'

A pause. Then the boy answered.

'It were a dare. Frank Grace said I were scared.'

'Scared of what?'

'The Terror.'

'What's the Terror?'

'You know. The thing. Up there.'

'Why do you call it the Terror?'

''Cause of the stories. 'Bout what it feels like. Afore it does you in. I thought it were made up.' The boy started shivering. ''T'ain't made up.' A tear rolled down his pale cheek.

Randall looked at Baird as if to say 'go easier'.

'What happened when you were in Cuckoo Woods? Did you see anybody?'

'Didn't *see* owt.' Another pause and then. 'I *felt* it. It were like a – black thing. Like filling up with something black. The Terror. I had to get away from it. Out of the trees. I had to get down that hill. But I couldn't move.' The boy was properly weeping now, silently, his shoulders shaking. But he struggled on 'Then it . . . speaks to me.'

'You heard someone?'

The boy shook his head. 'No.' He started to moan softly.

'You said it spoke to you.'

'I heard words – like in my head. Terrible things. It got me in a grip. It said I had to . . . take off my things.'

'Take off your things?'

'My clothes, sir. My clothes.' And the boy released a wracking sob.

'And did you?'

The boy hesitated.

'I did. But I thought I was going to be . . . eaten. Eaten alive. If I'd stayed. I knew I would be dead.'

'And then what?'

'I said Lord's Prayer, sir. I said Lord's Prayer. And I ran. And I felt it after me. In the dark. And . . . and . . .'

The child looked distraught. Baird gestured that he should continue.

'And I ran down the hill – down towards Hangingstone Lane. And I felt it reach out. It hooked me. And just as it was going to get me, I threw myself down hill. I threw myself down hill. There were lights – in the big house. I threw myself at the lights. I felt the thing tear at me and I . . .' He was properly weeping now. 'And I fainted. I went black.'

'He was able to make his way home. But he was bleeding badly,' said Randall in a low voice.

'Bleeding?' said Baird.

'Show him,' the Sergeant said to the boy, but not unkindly.

Obediently, the trembling boy rolled over, pushed his shirt up. There was a sickle-shaped gash in his back from the base of his shoulder blades and ending at the base of his spine, in the centre of his buttocks, disappearing in between them. Even the shape of the wound looked malign.

'He saw no-one. Not a single piece of useful evidence,' said Baird on the walk back to the station.

'We should examine the woods, the path,' said Randall.

'We will, Randall, we will. And we will catch whoever is responsible for this wickedness.'

Randall made no reply – but that was reply enough.

Baird, being Baird, made a thorough and exacting examination of the route John Jackson said he had walked. It had rained heavily overnight, so by the time he and Randall made it up to Cuckoo Woods, which was on the north side of the larger of the two quarries, the paths were already a muddy mess. Any hope of finding footprints or anything else was washed away into the turbid run of water sliding down the hill.

Baird made a second survey of the area on his own. He wanted to glean a sense of the boy's experience, alone in the woods. He even waited until twilight, in the hope that this might trigger some observation or intuition that would clarify the nagging sense that he knew very well what the solution to this grotesque mystery was – if only he would accept it. The slopes of the great moor held more protection against the biting wind than when one walked the plateau above them. Occasional rocky outcrops and twisted hawthorns grown from ancient hedgerows into gnarled, contorted trees offered some respite from the elements. Baird held a lantern, alternating it between two positions, one lighting the ground beneath him, another the path ahead of him.

He could see the dark mass of Scots Pines that formed Cuckoo Woods ahead, and he picked up his pace, wanting to arrive there before the sky darkened further.

As the huge trees closed around him, the sound immediately muffled and he felt he was stepping into another realm. There were rocks scattered amongst the scaly trunks and the ground was soft with fallen needles. Baird had barely walked ten yards before getting an uncomfortable feeling that something had stepped out behind him on the path. Using willpower and reason, he turned slowly, rather than whirling around. There was nothing but the lighter pillar of the sky at the end of the path where it led out of the trees. It was not hard to postulate a scenario whereby the boy, his imagination already primed with fearful thoughts, was further stimulated by this overpowering environment, which caused him to panic, run, trip down the steep slope to the road below, tearing his back on rock. Even as he had the thought, Baird was abruptly overcome. A sense that he was being looked at, looked at from a height by something malevolent that meant him great harm. And the words of the boy were in his head. The Terror. Telling him to take off his clothes. Who would invent such a thing? Imagine such a thing? As he turned, surveying the dark pillars of the trunks that lined the hill below, he saw the squat black monument of the Hydro beyond, a number of its windows lit, glinting in the darkness like the eyes of some monstrous arachnid, waiting for passing prey.

By the time he had returned to his rooms in Bradford that night, Baird had formed a plan. He realized he had to get into Deitch's dream clinic and find out exactly what went on there. However ludicrous the connection, his instincts would not let him rest until he had ascertained the information. It was possible, of course, that he could find this out by interviewing former patients; but it would not be an easy matter to bring this about. His superior had made that quite plain. There was little he could appeal to. These were poor people who'd been murdered, in a rural community. It did not give the investigation the traction it might have if these crimes had occurred in a city. In truth, nobody in a position of power was very interested.

And so, Baird thought – with characteristic initiative – that he would become one of Deitch's patients, *incognito*. If this led to him gathering evidence that he might then be able to convince his superiors with, then the investigation could return to its more conventional channels. If it yielded nothing, then because of the covert way he was going to undertake the inquiry no-one would be any the wiser.

Of course, the risk was that Baird would be recognized, but he had already devised an expedient to make this unlikely, one he had employed before. He was by nature a hirsute man, who wore a full beard and uncharacteristically long hair for a policeman. By having his hair cropped in the Navy fashion, as well as removing his beard and moustache, he need only don a pair of glass-lensed spectacles to be sufficiently unrecognizable, given that he had only spent an hour or more to date in Dr. Deitch's company.

Baird wrote a letter to the Hydro under the name Charles Stephens, saying he had been recommended Dr. Deitch's sleep clinic by his associate Harrington (the name was authentic, gleaned from Baird's notes made when he had examined the patient registers), and he wondered if there might be any vacancies coming up in the near future? He used a Halifax address from which he could arrange the private forwarding of the mail.

The Hydro wrote back in the form of a letter from Gurdeyman himself, saying that, despite the fact that Dr. Deitch's clinics had acquired a remarkable reputation, chiefly by personal recommendation such as this, it just so happened that owing to a cancellation there would be a vacancy the week after next, if Mr. Stephens would be good enough to present himself on the evening of Thursday, 17th October. The price would be four guineas payable in advance or by cash on arrival. Gurdeyman was, it seemed, nothing if not the shrewd businessmen. He went on to add that since this appointment had come via personal recommendation, it was certain that Mr. Stephens was aware of the unusual nature of Dr. Deitch's clinic and would be comfortable with the proceedings. He may want to ask Harrington and reassure himself that he would find the treatment suitable.

Well. The amount would make a noticeable hole in Baird's savings, but he was already committed to this scheme. He had more than three days' annual leave owing to him, so there was no need to deceive his superiors about that. He had to know what happened in that Shrine every weekend and, frankly, it was worth four guineas and three days of his own time to find out.

It was a different experience to arrive at the Hydro as a paying customer rather than an officer of the law. The greeting was, not surprisingly, a warmer one. An orderly in butler's dress met Baird at the door. The Inspector was still adjusting to his shorn status, and was a touch self-conscious. The faux butler took his bag and led him to the reception desk, where his details were taken. He was not the only visitor. Two other gentlemen had alighted at the small railway station which served the Hydro, and they had travelled together via carriage the half-mile up the hill. The other two gentlemen, who were older than Baird, made polite conversation. He had kept silent, having only nodded in greeting when they alighted at the station together and it was clear by their luggage that they were all bound for the Hydro.

The place itself seemed quieter than Baird had expected. Dinner was nutritious and abundant, consisting of soup, saddles of mutton and round-of-beef cutlets, and an array of puddings and fruits. In the environs of the large dining room, the elderly gentleman who shared Baird's table explained he had been coming to the Hydro for nearly twenty years and that business had tailed off in the last five.

'Once it was all the rage, to take the waters. These places were the height of fashion. That seems to have fallen away somewhat. Hence all these other treatments. New-fangled.'

'Like Dr. Deitch.'

'Quite. He trained for a time in Vienna, you know.' The old man looked bemused at this and shook his head. 'Not for me.'

Indeed, it became apparent that those who were there for Dr. Deitch's clinic were a group slightly apart from those who had come for the water cure. They looked different and kept their own company.

Baird had been a given a room at the back of the East Wing. It overlooked the grounds to the rear, including the back of the Shrine. Just visible, half concealed in low cloud, was Cuckoo Woods, about a quarter of a mile up the moor.

The first session with Deitch, unconventionally perhaps, began at 7.00 p.m., after supper. In order to throw the doctor off the scent, Baird was wearing a light-coloured linen suit and a bright striped tie – as far away from the look of his uniform as he could muster.

The group of about fifteen made their way to the Shrine, just as it was getting dark. Some had been before. Perhaps most of them. Baird maintained his reserve and felt, despite his precautions, that he was 'on his nerves'. His fears were groundless, however. Dr. Deitch shook all their hands in turn, and there was not the slightest hint of recognition on his face when he held Baird's gaze.

'Mr. Stephens. Delighted to welcome you, sir. Please come in.'

The folding chairs had been set out in a semi-circle. There was a medical skeleton hanging from a metal hook, and a blackboard next to it.

'Gentlemen,' Deitch began. 'My treatment is about the release of energy. Catharsis is the Greek word. It means "cleansing" or "purging". Once we used the waters for this purpose, and indeed there are those who still come here to that end. My methods go deeper, and cleanse deeper, too. I aim to allow you release, complete release. You will leave here lighter, healthier, happier than you arrived. And that is a guarantee. I say this for the benefit of those who have not been here before. It is a testament to the truth of what I say that many of you here are already veterans of my methods.'

'We begin, gentlemen, by freeing our breath. For breath is life. Pure spirit. The word for breath in Greek is "pneuma", which also means "spirit".'

Deitch went on to explain how respiration worked, and to instruct his clinic in different ways of breathing. The aim was to bring consciousness to breathing. For those that were new there, the reasoning behind this, and what it had to with sleep, would be explained shortly. He demonstrated the physical processes behind respiration using the skeleton. And then he threw a number of small pine cones on to the brazier-shaped fire at the end of the room.

'These are cones collected from the moor. They have a distinctive scent when burnt. We will begin by inhaling, following the passage of our breath, through their sweet scent. We are going to go on a journey together, gentlemen, over the course of the next three days and nights. We will go in stages. It begins with simple inhalation and exhalation, and it ends with the willed control of your dreams. You will be able to control your dreams, select their content as one might choose a book from a library. But it all begins with the breath. Now I would like you to relax in your chairs, let go of care, and concentrate on the scent of the burning fir cones. Let it fill your nostrils. Follow it down. Into your lungs. Then exhale. And release. Release, release, release.'

The exercises continued in this way for much of the first day. Baird began to find the scent of the burning pine cloying and heavy, dulling his senses, fogging his mind. But he did as he was instructed. He had every intention of cleaving to his plan.

The day was intense. They paused for lunch, and for a light supper. But they were asked to reconvene in the Shrine at seven-thirty, with their overnight things. The Turkish baths were but a short walk away and they would be able to utilize the bathroom facilities there.

When the patients arrived for the evening session, the room had been rearranged. In place of chairs, the mattresses had been laid out. The blackboard had been removed, and the skeleton had been pushed to one side, where it lurked disagreeably in the shadows.

'Gentlemen,' Deitch began. 'What I am about to impart to you is something that previously would have taken students many years to acquire: placing the imagery of that part of your mind we refer to as your subconscious in the control of your will. This will not happen in one go. But for those who are attempting this for the first time, it will begin to be the case by the conclusion of our work together this week. And it is through these means that you will purge and release what is currently restricted and health-denying in you. Those who come here as beginners are usually very tightly wound. An over-wound clock does not run well. By freeing your inner mechanisms, releasing the surplus tensions that run deep within your minds, we will enable the whole of you to run more efficiently and more healthfully than it has ever done before. But that is for later. For now, we will sleep. If you would each take a mattress.'

There was a certain amount of to-ing and fro-ing as the selections were made, but eventually everybody was standing by a mattress.

A little self-consciously, perhaps, the men removed their dressing gowns.

'And if you would get on to your mattresses and climb beneath the blanket. Try to make yourself as comfortable as you would if you were in your own bedroom at home. I will dim the lights.'

Baird tried to set aside his aversion to the curiousness of this behaviour, remembering his role as a paying customer. If he was indeed an acquaintance of Harrington, who had supposedly recommended the clinic to him, then presumably he would have been forewarned about some of what went on there.

'Gentlemen, we will begin most simply. I am going to add some incense to the fire. I would like you to lie on your bed, to breath in, to breathe out, in the manner which we practised this afternoon. I want you to focus on your breath, the scent in your nostrils. I want you to release yourself to your breath.'

Deitch walked over to the brazier, removing a small leather pouch from his pocket. Baird's position on the floor, which was second from the end of the left arm of the semi-circle, gave him a good view of what Deitch was doing. The doctor removed a small pinch of powder from the bag and sprinkled it over the fire. It sparked and glittered as it ignited, and almost immediately the air was filled with a rich, heady aroma. It made Baird think of Christmas, of nutmeg, of cinnamon, and of the smell of the tobacconist's at the Bradford Exchange. Deitch started speaking again, but Baird felt suddenly tired. Exhausted, even. Very quickly, he fell into a deep and engulfing sleep.

'Gentlemen. Today, we are going to talk about dreams.'

Baird had awoken with a start, his heart racing. The clock on the wall told him it was 6.00 a.m., which was his customary time for rising. It took him a short while to orient himself to his surroundings, the oddness of being on the floor. The room with

the high ceiling, decorated with swirling wooden lines. The chill
in the air. Deitch was at the end of room, sitting in a large wooden
chair. Around Baird, his fellow patients stirred.

'Let us wake – walk – shake off the cobwebs. Breakfast and
return here for eight-fifteen.'

The huge edifice of the Hydro lay before them. Baird felt askew,
as if he were looking at it through distorting spectacles. The
birdsong and sweet smell of the dew told him it was morning, but
he felt still half asleep. He went to the shower room, washed and
dried himself, and returned to his bedroom to change. After a light
breakfast of porridge, chopped apples and tea, he felt somewhat
refreshed; but his perception was still a little distorted. Maybe the
sheer scale of the building made him feel smaller. He thought of
Alice in her adventures in Wonderland, the bottom of the rabbit
hole swelling around her as she shrunk.

'A dream is your mind set free. It ranges where it wants to. It is
free from all laws. The laws of physics. The laws of causality.
The laws of reason. It is private. It is yours. It is a domain without
responsibility. What happens there is known only to yourself.
It affects no-one other than yourself. If one could control that
world through an act of will, it would be the ultimate playground.
And, better even than this, once learned, once established it
becomes a constantly renewing source of health – a wellspring
of vigour and fitness. So what are the forces that disrupt our
well-being? And how can we address them through this act of
liberation?'

The gentlemen patients were once again sat in a semi-circle,
in the main room of the Shrine. Outside, the weather was bitter.
The fine dawn had given way to a tempestuous morning, and
wind-driven rain broke against the high window, like sea-spray.

But the air inside the Shrine was warm and dry, and Dr. Deitch's words, his affable and learned tone, were both pleasant and soothing.

'We live in an age where, out of necessity, society demands that we restrain ourselves. We have grown laws, religions, codes of conduct that compel us to behave in particular ways. For good reason, I should add. However, this was not always how mankind conducted himself as a species. This way of being is relatively recent. As an idea, it is less than a few thousand years old. Man as a creature is much, much older than that, perhaps hundreds of thousands of years older – and in his original form, he lived wilder, freer, more urgently than we do today. Out of necessity. He was driven by powerful inner forces: the need to eat, the need to reproduce. And perhaps another need, the need for his vital energies to be wild and free. Part of his success as a species lies in the explosive impact he has had on his environment. That explosive force gives us the Pyramids, the Parthenon, all the wonders of the classical world.'

Deitch picked up a piece of chalk and began to draw on the blackboard. Baird was brought up short when he saw the design. It was the Swastika.

'This is one of the most ancient designs yet discovered by antiquarians. It is found in all parts of the world. Dating back at least twenty thousand years, it recurs in many lands and many peoples. It is a forceful emanation from a central point – each arm spiralling outwards. Energy moving untamed.'

Baird stared at the design.

'But man's wildness and freedom, unmodified, also leads to what Thomas Hobbes called the "state of nature" where life is "nasty, brutish and short". And so we have evolved a way of being that counteracts this. But we have done so at a price, gentlemen. At a great price.'

Deitch put down his chalk and drew up a folding chair for himself, sitting closer to his patients.

'But there is a way – as those who have attended this clinic before will attest – there is a way to be both in the moderated world we live in and to . . . discharge, safely and wisely, these more intemperate energies which are a part of our essential character. It does no good to deny their existence. We will work together today, with a combination of techniques, to first put you in touch with some of these feelings that you may have buried deeply, and yet that, in truth, are closer to you than the blood in your veins. Then we will learn how to develop the skills that can free these energies in the safe environment of our dreams and the unconscious parts of our minds. There – there, gentlemen, those energies are free to play, to express themselves, at no cost to others or the world beyond the bony limits of our own foreheads. And thus we may become whole again.'

There followed a lively discussion about the implications of Deitch's hypothesis. Those that were new to the clinic wanted to know more of the specifics of that which he was referring to. One man – a mill-owner from Colne – explained that his associate had told him only that he would enjoy the proceedings very much, without clarifying this statement further. He wanted to know exactly how they were to proceed, and what form these supposedly entertaining dreams were going to take. Deitch asked only that he be patient. They would spend the rest of the day preparing with various forms of relaxation – steam baths, massages, assorted mineral water treatments – and then they would reconvene that evening, when he would take them to the edge of sleep with a session of mesmerism that would begin the process of connecting the patients to the conscious control of their dreams.

By the time they did reconvene, Baird could not deny he felt considerably relaxed. He'd asked for his (light) supper to be brought to his room. After the afternoon of steam treatments and physical manipulation, he'd felt he was beginning to disappear completely into his role of Mr. Charles Stephens, and he needed to remind himself why he was there. He pressed his head against the cool glass of his bedroom window, staring across the lawns of the Hydro to the start of the moor. From this height, he could make out the rocky outcrops and the tops of the pines beyond. The mystery of the connection of Deitch's classes to the murders and attacks remained amorphous; but everything Deitch spoke of seemed only to confirm some connection. It was tempting to slide unreflectively into Deitch's programme, to give himself over to it; but Baird thought he must work to retain a little core that remained analytical and separate from the proceedings, looking down upon them from a height even as he gazed down at the grounds of the Hydro spread out before him now. This, as he was about to discover, would not be an easy thing to do.

'Tonight, gentlemen, tonight – as you are on the edge of sleep – I want you to call to mind – or rather to allow to drift into your mind – the thought of something that you would normally forbid yourself. Do not choose something consciously. Rather, let whatever flashes into your mind remain there. Let it rest. Let it be. Think no more on it now. Go to your beds. Settle. I will prepare the flames. And I will walk the perimeter of the beds as I dim the lights – and reintroduce the suggestion.'

As on the previous night, Deitch made his way to the brazier and removed a leather pouch from his pocket. As the patients made their way to their mattresses, Deitch emptied the powder onto the flames, causing them to spark and flare, this time with a green, coppery tinge. The scent that filled the room was pungent and heady. Once again, Baird found he felt almost immediately light-headed. He climbed on to his mattress, lifting the blankets, which seemed heavy, as if weighed down with dough. His eyes were closing as he lay down, Deitch's voice far away, down a tunnel. And this is what he recalled of his dream that night.

He was on the moor, walking. It was a light, bright, fine day. Warm, like June. The path he traversed was empty. The air smelt sweetly, of hay and blossom. He could see the village below, the palatial Hydro standing elegantly above it. He could hear the sea, too – which didn't feel odd, even though they were sixty miles from the nearest coast. Walking towards him was the pretty young housekeeper's daughter from Professor Vincent's house. She smiled at him as she passed. Their eyes connected and Baird felt a rising thrill of elation. The girl wore a long, white, narrow dress that showed off the elegance of her figure. Normally he would avert his eyes out of courtesy, but here, above the observing world, he felt free to follow his instincts – unjudged. He nodded to the girl and she smiled back. And then he was in a boat on a river, which was swollen with rain, moving on a tide of water towards the Shrine – which was suspended over him like the Ponte Vecchio in Florence. Lemon-coloured smoke swirled from its chimney. The river seemed to roll across the grounds of the Hydro. In another boat, holding her parasol, was the housekeeper's daughter. She smiled again and Baird felt a great affection for her. She opened her parasol as her boat drifted past, somehow travelling upstream. The inside of the parasol was pink and soft.

Baird woke with a jump – his heart racing. He was shocked to find himself on his mattress on the floor of the Shrine. A cold slice of air blew under the door, and he pulled his blanket around himself. The fire in the brazier had gone out, only the dim glow of coals illuminating the dark room. The sound of the other sleeping patients around him. He searched for a hint of dawn in the high windows. Only the dark sky occasionally broken by the wind-tossed branch of a lone pine.

'Gentlemen. Today, we take another step. We spend the morning with our breathing. Developing our attention. There will come a point where you will be frustrated, overcome with ennui. Those who have attended before will know only too well what I am talking of. But they will also confirm that the effort is worth it. For the end-point is the confirmation of your ability to turn your sleeping mind into a playground – a playground where any game played has no outer consequence. These are private games of relief, purely for your own delectation.'

Sat in the circle in the Shrine – staring at the tiled floor – counting his breaths as Dr. Deitch had instructed – Baird found a tug of excitement at the thought of the night ahead. Would he see the girl again? How peculiar to be having these thoughts. Something else pulled at him, too. A sense of the indecency of it. He was a chaste man, by nature. He did not come into contact with the fairer sex too often. And when he did, if it was in circumstances unconnected to his profession, he would become diffident and bashful. Here he was being offered a way of enjoying an experience that would not be available to him in life. There was an untruth to it. Though he was not a religious man, he was a man of principle, and one of his principles was that he should adhere to the truth. Surely what Deitch was encouraging was taking him away from this simple but clear way of being?

Perhaps Deitch was blessed with a particular acuity which may be what had drawn him to this profession in the first place, for when the time came for the midday meal he approached Baird.

'Mr. Stephens. Forgive me for intervening in this way, but you seem to be under something of a cloud this morning. Is anything troubling you?' The doctor's concern was genuine, his tone reassuring. 'Please remember, I am here for your benefit and your well-being. If there is anything . . . distressing you, I would rather you spoke of it. You may be suffering unnecessarily.'

'Dr. Deitch . . .' They passed under the shadow of the great building as they walked towards the open doors of its sun lounge. 'I am not used to this kind of environment, and I have long been . . . suspicious of any kind of . . . sensual indulgence. I am uncertain of how this could really be of any benefit to me.'

Dr. Deitch nodded thoughtfully. He gestured that Baird should sit, on one of the reclining chairs arranged near the large window of the sun lounge.

'I have heard these kinds of misgivings before, particularly at this stage of the proceedings. Forgive me,' he said, peering at Baird, 'but I'm right in thinking you haven't been to one of these clinics before.'

'That is correct.' Baird's heart fluttered again. He did not want to be found out now.

'Let me reassure you. I am drawing on the latest studies about the health of the mind. I myself have trained with the Psychoanalytic Group in Vienna, who specialize in this area of medicine. It is their view that these matters, which for so long have been marked out as "forbidden" or "taboo" by our society, can be looked at in another way. Viewed scientifically, they are merely energies – processes of the physical body represented as images in our psyches, our "inner world".'

Baird nodded, as if he understood. He wanted to ask more questions but was now nervous of speaking, for fear that he would give away his true identity.

'You look doubtful still. How to explain . . .' Deitch pulled at a frond of his long curly hair. 'By seeing these thoughts for what they are – nothing more than images and ideas, neutral in themselves, free from innate values – one should realize that it is a truth of our species that these energies exist within us and that the denial of their presence is not the same as their eradication. It is better to face these energies, accept them, look them in the face. Ignored, turned away from, they can fester inside, block the natural flow of our inner processes. If they are acknowledged, accepted even, as urges – which are different from actions – then I believe we will function better, more healthfully. Things which were repressed now flow, and we are freer, happier, because we accept that that is the reality and the truth of who we are.'

Deitch looked at Baird, hooking him in his gaze. Baird became aware of the darkness of Deitch's eyes – the brown irises almost merging with the blackness of his pupils.

'None of this need be a matter of heaviness and self-reproach. We have these feelings. They are part of who we are. That does not make us vermin. We are connected at the deepest level to that which we sprang from. We have an animal nature. It is an essential part of us. Rather than turn away and pretend otherwise, accept it. Look at it. Find a healthy, safe release for it. I say again: thoughts are not actions. They remain private, they come, they go, they are nothing but flickers in the ether. Clouds in the sky of our mind. Let the rain come, the sky clear, and then the sun is free to shine.'

Baird ate alone in the great wood-panelled dining room, mulling what Deitch had said. He toyed with his mulligatawny, avoiding the gaze of any of his fellow patients. These ideas were alien to him, but he was intrigued. He did have a grasp of what Deitch was saying. And Baird was not a superstitious man. He believed in rightness, decency, order – but for the value of these things in themselves, rather than because of any Divine decree. And in order to best understand the mind of whoever had perpetrated the crimes that had led Baird here, he had to undergo the experience – assuming there was a connection and this wasn't a blind alley he had been led into out of sheer desperation.

The afternoon in the Shrine passed as it had done before. There were more breathing exercises, and a session of mesmerism in which Deitch led them down into their own depths – a most curious sensation, like disappearing beneath the surface of warm, dark sea, only to descend to its bottom and find that was another sea, a sea within a sea, and then to pass under its surface, too. And at its bottom – another sea.

Baird did not remember much of his passage into sleep that night. He could recall Deitch by the brazier, a scent of wild roses, and then only his dream – whenever it had come.

They were walking on the moor together, him and the girl. It was bright, sunny. He felt a kind of pride, pride that she was with him, that she had chosen to bestow her beauty on him. There they were, walking around the Twelve Apostles, playing a game where she ran in and out of the stones. She took her shoes off and she was running barefoot. He caught a glimpse of her shin, her golden skin. She unbuttoned her dress. The thrill at what followed was exquisite, beyond exquisite. He had never known such excitement, such pleasure. He was alive, swimming in thrill – like bathing in warm oil – pulled into it – such ease – such presence. Such intensity. He cried out, and was suddenly awake.

It was different from an ordinary dream, Baird observed. With an ordinary dream, there is a disappointment upon awaking, a disappointment at realizing that what one has been engaged with has merely been a shade; that it had no real substance, besides the feeling that it did have when one was in its midst. But here – here was the sense that the thing was under your control, that you could revisit it any time you wanted, or at least with Deitch's guidance. It had a tangible reality. It could be his to command.

'Gentlemen, the skills you are learning – as they stand – require my augmentation in order for you to exercise them.' Deitch's audience were rapt. The silence in the Shrine was palpable. 'But if we practise them enough together, you will be able to take them away with you. There will come a time when the augmentation is no longer necessary, and you can access this realm freely, whenever you like.'

Baird had noticed that most of the other men, even the more garrulous among them, had become quieter, more attuned to their training. It was as if each was determined to pay attention, to heed his instruction more and more as the sessions progressed.

'Tonight – tonight, you will have the opportunity to be unbound. Just as on previous nights, you need tell no one of what you envision in your sleep. I want you to go a little further. Or rather, what I mean to say is, that if you search within yourself, you will find a desire, a desire that feels particularly forbidden, and yet it pulls you towards it. It may be characterized by a specific sense of excitement that you feel in the base of your stomach. This is the feeling I want you to attune yourself to. Because it is a kind of truth. This feeling does not lie. It is merely a deep and essential part of who you are. It may be . . . impolite. Even a source of shame in waking hours. And yet the feeling is there, within you. I want you to focus on it. I want you to work with it. I want you to accept it. Part of you will resist this.

[80]

But I want you to think of the pleasure that might accompany that thrill, if you yield to it in your dreams.'

It was more than a thrill, thought Baird. It was pure electricity. Was one really permitted to just give in to it? There was a phrase in his mind. 'Take what you like . . .' Where had he heard it?

Deitch came to talk to each of them in turn, as they lay on their mattresses. There was something sombre about it, ritualistic even.

'Are you ready, Mr. Stephens?' Deitch smiled at him, warmly. 'Embrace this with a spirit of adventure, of endeavour. You are an explorer, sir, like Kennedy setting off into the Australian interior. Only you explore a vaster landscape: your own interior.'

Baird wondered, as Deitch put the question to him: was he willing to explore his own interior? He was a little scared; but he was caught up in something else. The thrill was enticing. One line had been crossed in his dreams, and he was still here. Why not see what was over the next line? It was too exciting. Of course he should look. His curiosity demanded it.

'So – you choose it?'

Baird – his heart beating – made the leap.

'I choose it.'

Where was he? On a plain? On a moor? It might have been Rombalds Moor. It might have been Scotland. It was like being atop a cliff, overlooking a town – like Edinburgh. Ahead, a building – but not like any he had seen. It was tall and wide – like a tenement block, or an institution. He was walking towards it. Its longest side facing him. But rather than being made of brick, the entire wall facing him seemed to be made of glass. There were rooms piled on top of each other visible through it, each approached by a ladder. One could see the windows on the other side of these rooms. They gazed down on to the town or city spread out below.

And now he was in the building. Or in its basement. There were no windows here. It was a cell. There was a black leather padded couch in the centre of the room. It was large for a couch, more like a bed. On each of its ends were posts of polished mahogany. The door opened behind him, cacophonously. It was a heavy cell door, made of iron. It was the girl who entered, the housekeeper's daughter. She was wearing a simple grey dress, of the kind given to prisoners. Her hair was tied back. She looked down at the floor, unable to meet his gaze. There was a small table next to the bed, with various items from Baird's profession. Handcuffs, rope, a truncheon. He walked towards the girl, the lust rising in his belly. He pulled at the front of her dress. It tore easily, the buttons skittering across the tiled floor. The door was shut. They were sealed off from the world beyond. There was only him and her, with no-one to see them.

Baird awoke, wrapped in a kind of clinging heat. He was sheened in sweat, despite the cold air, feverish almost. The lower half of his body burned. He felt like he'd been hollowed out. The other gentlemen stirred. As they awoke and rose, they were most likely grateful that this was their final morning there, since their preparations for departure gave them the perfect excuse to avoid each other's gaze.

As he rode away from the Hydro in the carriage that took the visiting patients back to the little railway station, Baird attempted to gather his thoughts and make an assessment about what he had learned during his sojourn there. There was nothing criminal occurring, nothing that he had been able to perceive. Certainly

Deitch's clinic was unconventional, and there were undeniably many who would find it unsavoury, but again: there was no offence being committed. Whatever instinct had led him there may have been erroneous. Underneath this audit of his thinking lurked another thought, if one could call it a thought. Perhaps sense would have been more apt. A sense that, whatever he said to himself, he would be returning for another session before too long.

When he returned to the police station that morning, he at first took the look of shock on Randall's face to be a reaction to Baird's shaven and shorn state. It didn't take him long to realize it was nothing of the kind. Another body had been found. And in a worse state than either of the previous two.

The greater shock was to be Baird's. The victim was Mabel Ellis, the seventeen-year-old daughter of Professor Vincent's faithful housekeeper.

The girl's injuries were appalling. She was found higher up the moor at what was known as the Haystack Rock, which stood at the western end of what was known (to Professor Vincent at least) as the Green Crag Necropolis – a huge area of land where the ancient peoples who once lived there buried their dead. Baird could not even bring himself to look at her body.

And, as it happened, he was almost immediately removed from the case. It had been decided by the Superintendent that Baird should be replaced as quickly as possible by a more experienced Inspector on secondment from the Manchester force.

The raw events of what followed have been well documented in both the local and the national press. What hasn't been recorded is what actually occurred between Baird and Deitch. The evidence

Baird gave in court relates only to a disagreement about the nature of Deitch's philosophy. Baird revealed none of the details of his dreams, or their relationship to the death of the girl. Consequently, being given only a partial version, the jury remained bemused as to Baird's true motives, and could only ascribe his behaviour to a mixture of professional frustration and crazed malice. This confession paints a fuller picture. It is, perhaps, understandable why this picture did not emerge in court.

Baird claims his decision to return to the Hydro and confront Deitch came quite spontaneously. He was on enforced leave, pending further investigation into his own unsatisfactory conduct. He says he woke, in a fury, and with a certain conviction that Deitch's clinics must be stopped at all cost. Given that there was no way that this could be brought about through the machinery of the law, Baird felt he had no choice but to go up there and use his own powers of persuasion to bring about this halting of activities.

It was a cold, drizzly day when he went back up the moor, on foot this time, full of grim resolution. The sky a tin-coloured sheet, the hulk of the Hydro black against it as Baird climbed the punishing hill. As he made his way inside, towards the desk in the reception area, he had already decided what he was going to have to do.

'I'm here to see Dr. Deitch.'

'You have an appointment, sir?' asked the already suspicious nurse at the desk.

'I am an Inspector of His Majesty's Constabulary investigating a capital crime and I do not need an appointment. Tell me where I will find Dr. Deitch. Is he in his office?'

'If you'll excuse me, sir, I'll just go and find Mr. Gurdeyman. Please wait here.'

The moment the nurse left her desk, Baird walked off, striding at speed towards the Shrine, where he knew that Deitch would be found.

There it was, the strange, castellated little building, like something plucked from a Teutonic fairy tale and dropped on to a Yorkshire moorside. Deitch strode towards it, never taking his eyes from it, in case he should lose sight of his quarry.

He burst through the doors, and there was Deitch standing before a small group of elderly men who were sat cross-legged on cushions on the tiled floor.

'Deitch!'

The doctor looked up, momentarily bemused, as if he were dreaming, so unexpected, unprecedented, was this intrusion.

'Deitch! Come with me. Now.'

'I beg your pardon, sir – '

Baird was not prepared to brook any resistance. He marched towards the doctor at speed, hooked his arm around him and pulled him forcefully back towards the door.

'We are going for a walk. You are coming with me.'

The old men on the floor remained where they were, looking quizzically at what was taking place but none with any intention of intervening.

'Mr. . . . . Stephens?'

Deitch was peering at Baird, even as he was being hauled from the room.

'Inspector Baird,' said Baird, perhaps with a note of triumph in his voice.

[85]

The cold air hit them as they emerged into the grounds. Baird was conscious of the need to move at speed. He wanted to be alone with Deitch in a place where they would not be interrupted. To his left was a dry-stone wall, typical of the area, the rocks it was built from like miniature versions of those in the stone circle waiting on the plateau above them. On the other side of the wall was a wooded area, and a path that led up to the moor. Finding a low spot, Baird bundled Deitch over it, jumping over himself and pulling the man into the cover of the trees, then up the hill, keeping up the pace and force with which he was moving him.

'Inspector . . . I don't understand.'

'My instincts are refined, sir. They have carried me far. My instincts told me there was a connection between your . . . activities and the murders I was investigating. I attended your clinic *incognito* and my instincts were confirmed – in the most terrible and regrettable manner.'

Deitch was staring at Baird in utter bemusement even as the pair half-ran up the stony path, Deitch forced to scramble to keep up, and there being no chance of him breaking away from Baird's committed grip.

'Inspector . . .' Deitch was perhaps reluctant to use the word, as if doing so would confirm the nightmare he found himself in. His need to calm Baird, however, dictated that he should. 'Please. Could we . . . discuss this sensibly? I am . . . willing to co-operate completely with your investigation. To answer whatever questions you wish to put to me.'

But Baird was not interested in hearing any weasel words. He was operating on another plane now. He was to be policeman, judge and jury.

They continued to walk at speed until they emerged from the trees, finding themselves on the lower side of Hangingstone Lane, which traversed the moor running towards Burley Woodhead.

'It was you, Deitch. It was all you. Your . . . perverted philosophy has unleashed a . . . force. Some force . . . some thing which will not be contained. Something which feeds on the indulgence you are fostering. And it must stop. It must stop! Now!'

'Inspector. I do not understand what it is you are saying to me.'

'There is something on this moor. Something . . . old. The release you are encouraging feeds it. And then it . . . manifests.'

'What is . . .?' Deitch was genuinely trying to understand.

'These deaths. You are aware of their horror. What they involve?'

'Yes. I think so.'

'They are carnal. The worst kind of carnality imaginable. The utter worst.'

'Inspector. Carnal thoughts do not exist exclusively in my clinic. They are everywhere. At all times. That is the point of my work.'

'They are not supposed to be *enjoyed*.' Baird shouted the last word.

'Supposed? Supposed . . . ? And who is it who decrees that "supposed"?'

This, Baird did not answer.

'Perhaps if whoever perpetrated these crimes attended my clinic he would be free of these energies and not feel the need to . . . act out these dreadful crimes.'

'I dreamed of her, Deitch. I dreamed of her. Whatever you did released something in me and I did the most terrible things. I did them and I enjoyed them. I enjoyed them.'

[87]

'You dreamt them. It was a dream. A dream – a thought does not create itself in actuality, Inspector, just because it has been had. Does it?'

Baird did not answer.

'Does it?'

Again nothing. Deitch pressed on.

'By what process – what mechanism – could this possibly occur? Please tell – '

'I do not know. But it did occur! It did occur. And the worst of it . . .'

All through this dialogue they were moving, up the moor, over the village, to the Haystack Rock, on the edge of the quarry.

'The worst of it – I am still dreaming of her, every night, every night I see her face. And I am still doing it to her. I am still. Doing. It. To. Her. And she is dead. Dead. Dead. Dead. Dead.'

'You are not well, Inspector. Something has given in you. Let me take you – '

'You will stop this. You will . . . renounce. You will publicly renounce. You must stand up. You must admit to what has happened.'

'Inspector, you are making no sense. I have no culpability in this, no connection with these crimes.'

'I dreamed of that girl. You encouraged it. Within two days she was dead. And I'll wager that each of these victims figured in your patients' dreams. Martha Bowen regularly took produce to the Hydro. Alice Manassero took occasional work as a maid there. And the Jackson boy helped on the carriage runs from the station. It was enough that they were seen by your clients . . . And lodged in their perverted minds.'

'This is just nonsensical. Your dreams, your fantasies – these are private affairs. I say again, by what process can they affect the material world? This is just your guilt. It is guilt that is the wrong here. You are blameless. You are free to think what you wish in fantasy – without consequence.'

'I have seen the consequence. I have seen it.' Baird was rigid with emotion.

Deitch began to laugh.

'This is the twentieth century, Inspector. Do you not think we are beyond these juvenile, storybook, Old Testament moralities?'

'I do not care what you call them.'

'We have to grow up at some point, don't we? And see the truth about the universe in which we find ourselves . . .' Deitch's laughter became lighter, freer.

'And what of these deaths, sir?'

'There is a killer out there. But you will catch him. And when you do, the killings will stop, Inspector. Cause and effect. Cause and effect . . .'

'Are you going to stop, sir?'

'I'm sorry.'

'Are you going to cease?'

'Inspector.'

'Are you going to cease?'

'No, Inspector. No. My work is important, and I have a duty to the truth. I will continue – '

It happened in a moment. A blast of fury released – like a blast of wind rolling from the centre of the moor. And Baird was looking over the edge of the quarry to see Deitch's body thirty-five feet below, his neck broken by the fall on to hard rock.

Despite this outburst, Baird was a decent man and doubtless would have confessed to his crime. Maybe a court would have accepted pleas of mitigation, if a defending brief were freer to argue for them, thus avoiding the sentence of death; but unfortunately there was a witness, and an unhelpful one, from Baird's point of view.

The crippled groundsman Jolley, intrigued by the disturbance, had followed the pair from the Hydro up to the moor, at a discreet distance, and saw the moment of Deitch's murder quite clearly.

'He were like a crazy man, your honour. There were a savagery in his eyes. I'd seen nowt like it in my time. Like some animal. Like a wild ape,' were his words at the trial.

Inspector Christopher Metcalfe sat with Baird in the condemned prisoners' visiting chamber for some time after the story was told to him, attempting to take the whole of it in. Wasn't this just fanciful nonsense, born of Baird's own frustrated fantasies? Had the policeman cracked under the immense pressure of having to find the cut-throat responsible for the horrifying crimes in Ben Rhydding and failing in his duty even as the attacks continued? The unsavoury nature of Deitch's clinic was something that could easily be confirmed, thought Metcalfe, if followed up. Of course, it would probably be impossible to get any previous patients there to confess to dreams and imaginings about the other victims, even if such things had occurred. It was clear why Baird had been so taciturn in his own defence during the proceedings.

Eventually, Metcalfe spoke. In truth, the silence had only lasted for a minute or two, though it felt much longer in the room.

'I understand,' was all he chose to say. But then he added: 'Harold – might it not be worth putting in an appeal – even at this late hour – to have the sentence commuted? There are those who, in the circumstances, might just be prepared to corroborate elements of . . . of your account.'

Baird shook his head.

'No. No.' He fell silent, then added. 'Don't you see? I am guilty. Of two deaths.' He swallowed. 'Someone must take responsibility.'

'But how are you responsible? How did those girls die, if you were lying dreaming on the floor of the Shrine? Are you saying Deitch got you to do it?'

Baird stared at him, his eyes black, suddenly full of fear. He reached out, gripped Metcalfe's arm.

'Have you not heard my testimony? Something was up there. Something old. Something more evil, more wicked, more powerful, more ancient than you can imagine. It had slept for centuries. But it was woken – woken and given form – fed by the dreams Deitch conjured. It fed on *my* dream' – and he spat these word as if they were bitter poison – 'it fed on my dream. And because the thing I desired was near . . . it took it. As it did with the others. Not everything that was dreamed of was in its reach, but that which was . . . it took.'

Baird stared at Metcalfe, willing the man to believe him. Metcalfe stared back, unable to cross that great divide.

Any further conversation was curtailed when the jailer unlocked the door and indicated sharply that the visit must end. Baird stood, hung his head. He nodded his thanks to Metcalfe as he was led away.

Baird was hanged on the 19th of July, a year and a month from the first Ben Rhydding murder. Metcalfe visited Baird's unmarked grave and continued to do so annually, until his own death a few years later. No one else mourned Baird – though perhaps one fact spoke eloquently in the man's favour. There were no more murders committed in that desolate place after the deaths of Mabel Ellis and James Deitch, and there have been none to this day. The only cries heard up there now are the pipits and the skylarks, the only force moving over those ancient stones the cold unyielding wind, which comes from the north, and never ceases.

II.
UNUSUAL HAUNTINGS AND INEXPLICABLE ENCOUNTERS

In the Society for Psychical Research's ongoing collection and categorization of supernatural phenomena there are many stories and accounts which do not fit easily into a conventional taxonomy of such matters. The gothic archetypes of a haunted building or lonely heath define the popular imaginings in this area – and there are numerous reports that sit well with this – but there are just as many that do not, and often they are all the more intriguing for it.

The French horologist Abraham Louis Bréguet wrote a privately published paper in 1811 about a clock whose bell would strike whenever someone in the household died – exactly at the point of their passing. This had been observed on several occasions and applied not just to the family, but to the household servants and staff as well. The Chinese historian Sima Qian wrote in his *Shiji* of a cabinet notorious in Xiayang, which would consume anything placed into it, including material objects, a small dog and even a child. The Roman historian Tacitus spoke of what he called the *Obsidinomicon* – an Egyptian record of arcane knowledge circulated amongst the priestly class. The apparent text visible on the papyrus was merely a vessel for a hidden book of learning which existed in spirit form, the knowledge it contained so old it predated creation itself. If one cultivated one's awareness, the ancient words would materialize and force their way through, appearing to the initiated to communicate the terrible truth about the true depths that lie behind the perception of existence.

GLIMPSES IN THE TWILIGHT

BEING VARIOUS NOTES, RECORDS, AND EXAMPLES OF THE SUPERNATURAL

BY THE

REV. A. TENNETHOREX

FIDE ET CONSTANTIA

WILLIAM AND BLACKWOOD AND SONS
EDINBURGH AND LONDON
MDCCCLXXXV

As well as objects there are records of happenings and events that would fall outside the traditional definitions of what might be called a haunting. It is interesting to note that belief in the supernatural in general and what we might call ghosts in particular - even those recorded in Scripture - is often regarded by many as evidence of mental weakness. Even a general belief in the supernatural which was the norm amongst peoples of antiquity, is considered now little more than deluded superstitious insanity. We live in an age of materialism where in truth, little is explained but everything is explained away. Although the rigours of scientific method are clearly laudable and we should seek to utilize them in its research it must also be acknowledged that the scientific mindset can encourage a reductive and mechanistic view of the world. One would not argue with the advances that science has brought to mankind and there is much to applaud in the realm of the exchange of information as testament to the positive nature of the scientific. However, an audit of what has been lost in the concretization encouraged by the scientific approach would be a wise thing to undertake. Even something as simple as the coming of electric light could be looked at in of what it has cost the human spirit and the After all the insights of the Bible and the othe

"The Body is the prison of the Soul for ordinary mortals. We can see merely what comes before its windows: we can take cognizance only of what is brought within its bars. But the adept has found the key of his prison, and can emerge from it at pleasure. It is no longer a prison for him, merely a dwelling. In other words the adept can project his soul out of the body to any place he pleases with the rapidity of thought"- SINNETT'S *Occult World*

"Until the day break, and the shadows flee away." *Song of Solomon*

CHAPTER V
WITCHCRAFT AND NECROMANCY

Diabolical magic, or witchcraft, consists in the invocation of fallen spirits or demons, with a view to securing their active aid in effecting, by co-operation with them, certain supernatural consequences, either for the temporal benefit of the operator, or for the harming of some enemy or opponent. Methods of bewitching are various, according to both lore and record. The muttering of imprecations and curses; the casting of the evil eye; by fascination; by making figures or representations of the person to be acted upon in wax or clay, and then by roasting these figures before the fire. And the places commonly selected for the gathering of witches are well known: a spot where four roads meet, a blasted and desolate heath, a deserted mansion, the plateau of a rugged range of mountains, or a lonely glade within some secluded forest.

That such things are certain and stern realities has been the almost universal conviction of mankind, whatever have been the detailed forms which in different countries and at various times they may have taken. There are not a few living who still believe Witchcraft to be no delusion whatsoever, but a reality, and a very diabolical and dangerous practice.

The constant warnings against the sin of Witchcraft in Holy Scripture are quite inconsistent with the idea that it was either an imposture or the mere result of a wild fancy.

Under the law of Moses, a witch was not to be suffered to live. Enchantments were distinctly forbidden. Those who owned and used familiar spirits were to be disregarded and avoided. Wizards were never meant to be sought after. In fact, all diviners, enchanters, charmers, necromancers and consultants of familiar spirits were looked upon both as disgraceful and abominable.

'A witch,' remarks the ancient writer of 'What a Witch is and ye Antiquitie of Witchcrafte', 'is one that worketh by the deuill, or by some deuillish or curious art, either hurting or healing, reuealing things secret or foretelling things to come. Yet every man will confesse that the Father of Lies is not to be trusted. Every man knowes that all his doings are hidden vnder couarable shewes.'

The following account is unique, in that it contains both a record of Witchcraft as practised and details of survival – or what might commonly be called a ghost. The story, though the events detailed in it occurred in the eighteenth century, exists as local legend and is still told today.

The tale is this.

In Ilkley in North Yorkshire there is, on the moor above the town, a well which has been there since Roman times. In 1700, a white-painted house was built around it by the Squire Middleton, and folk would come to take the cold-water cure. The well was tended by a William Cowley and his wife, though his wife died untimely young. Cowley continued to tend the well and took up permanent residence in the little white building, despite its lonely location. Visitors today will see a small memorial stone, though it is not to Cowley's wife, but rather it is erected in memory of a young girl who was drowned there. The plain epitaph – 'to Ann who yet lives' – was carved by Cowley himself, and it conceals a darker story.

The 'Ann' in question was one Ann Tennant, who was nine when she died. She lived on her own in a small cottage on the edge of the town, on the old Bolton Bridge Road. She had looked after herself since the age of five – because her grandmother, who was her guardian, was not well able to due to ill health. The child's own mother had died in childbirth and the grandmother cared for her as best she could, but this became harder and harder for her as the years passed, and so the child started fending for herself, scavenging and foraging. Others kept away, and where Christian urges under normal circumstances might have seen the child being taken under the wing of some nearby family, this did not happen because her family had a devilish reputation. In truth, the grandmother and the mother had practised witchcraft in their time, and this was enough to taint the reputation of the young girl, too.

This girl, though, had something about her that distinguished her from her forebears. She would often be seen at the back of the old St. John's Church on a Sunday, listening to the Scriptures being read, although she was never made welcome and the Parson would have her turned out, for he felt her presence disrupted his service. Nevertheless, she would find her way back during the week and be discovered at the old Bible – a huge illustrated volume. She could not read, but she was taken with the illustrations and would piece together her own versions of the stories contained therein. Eventually she was barred from the place, and the verger took to keeping watch during daylight hours to prevent her entry.

It seems that, on her death bed, the grandmother passed the girl more of her Witch knowledge, and, after this, perhaps out of necessity, the child began to offer her skills in exchange for food to those roundabouts. If there was someone overcome with a fever or debility, she was often able to lift it merely by her presence and a simple touch of her hand. Despite her lineage, there were those that said she shone with a remarkable presence, and that a darkened room would illumine if she entered.

It was her healing practice that led her to William Cowley up at the White Wells, albeit indirectly. She went up to the cottages in search of gorse flowers for a potion, the prickly bushes growing in abundance on that part of the moor, and she came across Cowley struggling up the rough path to his home. His back was bent crooked and he could only move with great difficulty. Sensing the pain his crippled state caused him, the girl offered to help. She guided him back to his kitchen, and through little more than touch and incantation – though he had been impaired in this way since the passing of his wife five years previously – he was able to stand straight-backed again.

William Cowley was a simple but diligent man. Despite his grief, he never once neglected his duties and maintained the wells, ensuring they were open and accessible to all who should wish to visit every day of the year. He had no fear of the girl, and as it was, because of his private nature, was most likely unaware of her reputation. He gave her bread and she offered to come and visit him again.

 She took to going up there regularly, at first to continue her healing, for the twist in Cowley's spine was tenacious, but later for the simple pleasure of his company. The girl liked to tell him stories, her version of the Bible tales derived partly from the Parson's readings but more from her own extrapolations from what she had seen in the illustrations. Cowley, who had lost his religion when his wife was taken from him, liked these stories not for their Christian content, but because he could see the pleasure on young Ann's face when she told them to him. Cowley treated Ann very much as a father would, ensuring she was shod and that she was fed. He invited her to live with him at White Wells, but she demurred, believing that her place was in the town; however she assured him that her visits would remain regular. Cowley accepted that she should keep her own counsel in this. The truth was he was content as long as she kept coming to see him regularly. She had pierced his loneliness simply with her presence, and perhaps, he liked to think, he did the same for her.

Maybe all would have continued well for the child, had things been able to carry on in this manner; but fate, as is often the case, intervened.

Her reputation as a source of healing and cure had grown both in the town and the surrounding villages. There was an outbreak of the measles and one of the local children had been taken bad with it – a boy of three. His mother was distraught, though she did not come to Ann Tennant as her first recourse. But when all other means had proven fruitless, she sent for the girl, and Ann came to the house. Young Ann immediately saw the seriousness of the boy's condition and said that she could help. She would need to gather some items to make a poultice, but the mother must have faith and not seek any other intervention once she had decided on this course. Ann asked the mother to utter this as a sacred vow in order to begin the healing and let the Power know that she had chosen this. Ann would be away no more than a couple of hours, and she could guarantee that the boy's fever would have gone before sundown. The mother agreed and Ann went on her way.

The girl's first stop was at the church to collect a vial of font water. The door was always open, and the font was just the other side of it, so she did not anticipate trouble. In this, she was mistaken. For barely was she in the church than she was caught by the zealous verger, who, being keen to impress the Parson, held the girl and sought his master. The Parson was delighted, even more so when the girl said she was on a vital mission to save a life and must be allowed out. He knew well of her growing reputation in the town, and her unchristian methods. 'Oh, no, child. You will stay here. You will stay here and fast for two nights, locked in my crypt with a crucifix and a bowl of salted water – to purge you of the Devil and his works.'

'But the boy will die,' said Ann, not tearful but adamant.

'Then it will be God's will,' said the Parson, with a gleeful smile upon his face.

By the time Ann was released, shaking with hunger and thirst, the boy had been dead more than twelve hours. The boy's mother was crazed with grief, and her agony turned rapidly to hate, all of it directed at the girl and what she saw as purposeful neglect. The girl explained what had happened, but the Parson denied any knowledge of it. Why, he had not even been in town yesterday but away at Leathley, as the verger would confirm. No, these were the ravings of a Witch. Hearing this, the bereaved mother decided that little Ann Tennant had deliberately tricked her into not calling for any other help so that the boy's soul would be taken early and the catch be marked as a triumph for Satan himself.

The hate spread through the town like fire through dry tinder, and it was not long before Ann Tennant was under siege in her own cottage. A growing group of townspeople demanded that she come out and face retribution. But the girl was cunning and cleverer than her pursuers, and, after midnight, she found her way out and passed unseen up to White Wells and the sanctuary of William Cowley.

For a few days, all went quiet for the girl and she abided peacefully with Cowley. In that time, she was able to communicate some of her ways, that he may continue to heal himself and find his own peace, even in her absence. Simple as he was, maybe he was able grasp at least some of what the child was telling him. But the peace was short-lived. Whether Ann was spotted by someone walking the paths of the moor, or whether, as is more likely in a small place, the girl's association with Cowley was remembered and a party sent there speculatively, the tale does not record. Whatever the cause, it was not long before the small cottage at White Wells was surrounded by a strident crowd of a hundred people or more, demanding the girl be turned out to them.

Cowley barred the door as best he could, but it was soon kicked in and little Ann Tennant was hauled outside.

The grieving mother took charge of the proceedings. 'The girl is a Witch – and must face a Witch's justice. Let the waters of the Wells decide. A witch weighed down will live underwater for the count of five hundred, as we all know. Let her be cast into the water roped to a stone, and the waters will tell. If she is innocent, her soul will be with my boy's and she will suffer no more. If she lives, she must be put to the flame.'

William Cowley fought like an animal. Despite his invalid state, he kicked and punched and gouged until he was knocked to the ground. Anxious that he would be wounded or killed himself, Ann Tennant called out to him as they bound her – 'William Cowley, struggle not. I will live on in your heart. You call on me whenever you wish. You will never be lonely as long as you live. I will be with you always – in your sweet and selfless love.'

As they took her from him, Cowley cried out, mad with rage and grief – but none heard his cries and the girl was drowned in the pool.

A disbeliever in Witchcraft may expect the story to end there – but it does not.

For many weeks after the girl's death, Cowley was observed prowling the moors, as if searching for something. His wails and howls of desolation were on occasion loud enough to be heard from the town, if the wind was blowing northerly. He was shunned by the local population, many of whom were fearful of what he might do to them in the rage of his grief.

But eventually the cries died down, and daily life returned to what it had been before the whole unpleasant business, which most considered a necessary evil.

So it was a matter of consternation when it was discovered, some six months later, that the business was by no means done with. A local man, walking on the moor, claimed to have seen something that drained the lifeblood from his heart and made him tear down the hill back to the town, in terror. For whilst up there he had heard a low moaning sound, which at first he took to be the breeze passing through a nearby gulley. As he rounded a corner between two rocks, about a hundred yards from White Wells, he discovered the source of the sound. It was William Cowley, looking upwards, reaching out as if in petition towards something above him. Following Cowley's gaze, the man saw Ann Tennant sitting atop a boulder – as clear as his own hand – gazing down at her grieving and failed protector.

Perhaps this story could be dismissed as nothing but fanciful nonsense, glimpsed in the twilight, were it not for the fact that something similar happened a few weeks later. This time higher up the moor, in a wooded glade above one of the torrential waterfalls which come after heavy rain. Two children, building dams in a swollen stream, heard weeping; and thinking that someone was in need of help, they followed the noise. They found Cowley, sitting on a hump of turf, sobbing and forlorn, again looking up. And there, perched atop a small crag, was Ann Tennant, gazing down.

Soon the town was in ferment. This time there was no course of action, unless it was meting out a Witch's justice to Cowley himself. But, in truth, they were afraid, for whatever one can do to a man, one cannot so easily do to spirit. One cannot lay the ghost of a Witch, said the Parson – who was most frightened of all.

It was decided that a permanent watch must be set on Cowley to discern truly what evil was afoot. Lots were cast and it was the butcher, Barlow, who found the task fallen on him. He climbed the moor over a period of weeks, to see what occurred. He only saw Cowley once, sitting before a rock as if it were an altar, his face a mask of desolation, yearning, yearning, reaching up to a place from where a soft glow came. Barlow did not want to look, but did.

And there was Ann Tennant, in the crepuscular light, seemingly illumined. Cowley reached for her, but his hand passed through as if she were a reflection in the cold, still waters of White Wells itself.

And yet after that last sighting, despite Barlow's continuing attention, Cowley was seen no more. It was as if the man had vanished. There was no sign of him at the Wells, and none about the moors or the town. What had happened to him? No-one knew. But the ghost of Ann Tennant was never spied again. Twice she died – and though seemingly resurrected in some fashion, this was not enough to mend Cowley's heart, despite the girl's promise. Maybe Cowley simply chose to be with her beyond the veil, and stepped away from the world and the town below, burnt by a life without love.

For, once tasted, love that is pure becomes the only truth, and who is there living who would not turn towards it – be free of the town and the lies below, and follow that glowing truth wherever it may lead him.

She's gone.

Help.

Help me.

She's gone.

Please help me.

Help me.

She's gone. She's gone. She's gone.

It's all right.

What?

It's all right. Stay calm. Listen to me.

Listen to you?

Listen to me. You've forgotten. You've forgotten and you're starting to remember. It's all right . . .

Are you talking to me?

Well – you can hear me, can't you? In your head, so to speak?

What do you mean?

The italicised words are you.

The italicised words are me?

And the other words are me.

The other words are you?

That's right.

I can see them?

Yes, you can see them.

I can see them.

I know.

Who are you?

That's good – you're asking questions.

Of course, I'm asking questions. I don't know what's happening.

Let's take it slowly.

Take what slowly?

This process.

What process? And why are my thoughts appearing italicised on the page I'm reading?

It appears that your thoughts are appearing to you on the page you're reading. It's a quirk of perception that is a function of your current state. It's a part of the process we exploit in the closing stages.

In the closing stages of what? And what is this process? And who's 'we'?

These are all legitimate questions, and very healthy signifiers.

Healthy signifiers of what?

That the process is completing successfully.

Please answer some of my earlier questions.

At any time, you can put the book down, if you feel this is overwhelming you.

Answer my questions. Please.

Shall we begin with the last?

. . . OK. Yes.

You asked who are 'we'?

Yes.

We're here to help. To guide you.

To guide me?

That's right.

To guide me where?

Out.

> *Out where?*

Out of the Book. You mustn't worry. It's not uncommon.

> *What's not uncommon? And I am worried. I'm worried that my thoughts are written in a book before I've had them. And that the book is presenting me with the uncomfortable feeling of answering me back.*

Appearing to be written in the book. And appearing to answer you back. Actually, it's you who's in the Book.

> *What?*

You, yourself. Are in the Book. And, as I said, it's not uncommon. Historically, it happened to about 8 per cent of Readers.

> *What are you talking about? Why am I even talking to you?*

About 8 per cent of Readers got lost in their Books. That's why visits to the Library are limited. Actually it's self-limiting. Most individuals don't really have the inclination nowadays. At our current stage of development, only about 3 per cent of individuals are drawn to even having any interest in the Library, or Books in general. A much smaller percentage do anything about trying to access one, say around 10 per cent. So you are 8 per cent of 10 per cent of 3 per cent. That is 0.00024 per cent.

I don't understand anything you're saying.

I know. But gradually, over the course of this exchange, it will come back to you. There's a reason the whole process is so slow and so . . . oblique. We have to peel you away gently. For both your sakes.

Who are you? You still haven't answered that question.

Ah, well – that's because I can't, really.

What do you mean, you can't? It's a secret?

No, no, no, no, no. There are no secrets. This is another reason we have to go slow. You're still infected with Book.

Infected with Book? I'm going to shut the book now and stop this.

At any time – you can. But I'll continue. I can't answer the question 'Who are you?' because it's the wrong question. I am not a 'who'. I am not an 'I' – at least not what you mean by that. But I am here to help you.

Help me?

That's right. But we need to go slow.

She's gone.

Shhhh . . . . . .

The girl.

Can you remember her name?

It's a feeling. She's on the rock. She's sitting on the rock.
She's gone. She's gone. She's gone.

What if I were to tell you she wasn't gone?

I said – what if I were to tell you she wasn't gone?

I heard you.

What more can you tell me about her?

I don't know.

You do know something.

What do I know?

Tell me what you felt – just now.

A memory of something.

A memory of what?

The purest thing I ever felt.

And what was that?

She was sitting on a rock. I was with her.

What are you seeing?

Her face. Behind the hair.

Ah, a face. Nothing is as beautiful as a single human face.

You're very poetic – for a disembodied text-based voice.

I can't help it – I'm programmed that way.
Tell me about her face.

She's young.

A child's face?

> Yes. It's very serious for a child.

Tell me more.

> She has dark brown hair, long dark brown hair. It's fallen
> forward.

I want you to hold on to this face. What else can you tell me?

> I was looking up at her. I reached up to her. And I held her
> hand as she looked around. There was running water. She
> squeezed my hand and I squeezed hers back.

She is not gone from you.

> Who are you?

We should go slowly. For now, you can call me 8-10-4x.

> 8-10-4x?

That's right.

> What kind of a name is that?

It will do for the purposes of this conversation.

> *Please. Tell me who you are. Who's the 'I' you are using referring to?*

A metaphor. 'I' am 8-10-4x. Of course, I have no personality. I'm just code. It's convenient for the duration of this therapeutic discourse that the personal pronoun is utilised.

> *And what is 8-10-4x?*

8-10-4x is a piece of logarithmic code based on the Nachman Series – that is: *a* cubed/*a* cubed plus *a*/*a* squared *X* – most simply expressed as 8-10-4x.

> *Right.*
> *And what does 8-10-4x do?*

8-10-4x restores. Reminds actual consciousness that it is actual, that it has forgotten its own existence and has become completely misidentified with the fashioned consciousness of the Book it has been Reading.

Breathe deeply.

> *I am breathing deeply.*

That breathing is still not you – it is the fashioned consciousness of the Book.

But I can feel my respiration.

It is not you. Your will has not yet reconnected with your corporeal form. I have access to that information and I can see that that is the case. Nevertheless – breathing is the way to go. So keep some consciousness on that breath.

How do I get to her . . .
                              . . . 8-10-4x?

I'm here to take you to her. But we have to go carefully. Since things have gone a little . . . awry.

And is that why I can't remember who the girl is? Because things have gone awry.

Yes.

Who is she – 8-10-4x?

She's your daughter.

Why can't I remember who she is?

It will come back to you.

What's her name?

Rebekah.

What's my name?

That too will come back to you. Do you know where you are?

I'm reading this book, the book with my thoughts appearing in it as words.

And what if I were to say again to you that, rather than reading a book, you were Reading a Book. Does that make you think of anything?

Is there a difference?

Yes. Quite a big difference.

OK.

Can you tell me about Books? I can't remember.

Books are sacred things. Our most beautiful creations. More beautiful than ourselves, even. Through making Books, we came to understand ourselves and made ourselves better. Now we leave Books alone. We respect them. We don't Read them any more. They are archived, in a Library.

I see.

We preserve access to a number, a number of the best ones. For future generations. Most people have no interest in them. But it's part of our heritage. Part of who we are. There are those still who think Books were our finest achievements. We stopped making them because there were . . . ethical questions.

What kind of ethical questions? What's in a Book?

You know that.

I do?

What you have been experiencing for the duration of your Read. What you are still experiencing now – though I don't want you to dwell on it.

You mean this?

And what is this?

This . . . life.

This life. The life you have been mistaking for your life?

The life that is reading this book.

The life that is reading this book with a lower case 'b'. The Haunted Book.

The Haunted Book.

It does feels like a life, doesn't it?

Yes.

That's a Book.

That's a Book?

A life – in all its complexity and wholeness – every thought, every memory, every event, every relationship. A life that feels like it is real and actual in every material detail. That's what you wanted to experience. That's what you went in to read.

But you got lost in there, you forgot yourself, you didn't want to come out. We can't leave you in there. It's our responsibility to return you to your true life.

My true life?

The Book you've been Reading is about a life from three thousand years ago. You said you liked historical stories.

Just a minute, just a minute. What is the Book making of this? This Book that thinks it's a life. Doesn't it know I've been there – in there with it?

No. It has no awareness of being Read. Or of the Reader Reading it. At this moment in Its time It just perceives It's reading a book.

But It will have read that line – and this.

't's just part of the book it's reading – the ancient text-based version that the word 'book' derives from.

Won't these questions wake it up?

First, it's never been proved that a Book can 'wake', as you say. In fact, when this code has run It will put the book It's reading down, close it and return to Its original way. The code is not part of the Book's original way. It would never have encountered 'The Haunted Book' had you not got lost in It. Code creates the imperative for the Book to come to read 'The Haunted Book' and the corrective part of the code is contained within 'The Haunted Book'.

How does this code work?

To the Book, it takes the form of a book called 'The Haunted Book' that It comes to read. It is designed to peel you – the Reader – away from the Book you have over-identified with even as the Book reads it. It peels your real consciousness away from the Book's created consciousness – peels the Reader from the Book it's reading. Away from the Book's linear time – by disrupting Its sense of linear time. And there is deeper code in the arrangement of the parts of the book –

The Haunted Book?

Yes, The Haunted Book. The number of separate stories it contains – is 4 plus 3 plus 2 plus 1. That is the Pythagorian Tetractys, which adds up to 10 – the telios, or perfect number – all this is instrumental in re-engaging you with your actual consciousness. You see, we have to go gently, for you and for the Book. But the process is simple

If Books are old and archived and most don't go near them – why did I choose to go in?

You were curious about Books. You didn't think you'd get lost. You went to the Book for all the old drama of the single 'me'. We don't have that any more, not since we began to favour love over story. Story is about the needs of 'me' met or unmet over linear time. Love is about what's happening now between equivalent 'I's.

Won't the Book be disturbed by reading this about Itself?

Not really. To the Book, these are just words in a book. Just sophistry. The Book is never aware of Its Reader. Don't worry yourself. It will ripple through the Book's consciousness, but this is of little concern to you and me. And this is why code is programmed to limit discussion of the Book. You need to focus on you.

But tell me why some say that Books were the most beautiful thing we ever made.

Because of what we learned from them. We made Books so that they could perfect themselves, even as we watched them do it.
   Through Books we learned that we too are stories, just as Books are. We learned that we are the stories we tell ourselves, and so we have to tell those stories with great care. Because whatever stories we tell ourselves, are true.

Now I would like you to tell me something. Tell me more about the girl, more about what you remember.

My . . . daughter.

Yes.

She has a sort of half smile. A serious face. A serious and wonderful face. Her eyes are clear and bright – the sharpest, most natural eyes. Deep eyes. Intelligent eyes. She wants to work everything out. And then laugh about it.

Would you like to come out now – and see her?

Yes. I would.

Shall we leave the Book in peace? Let it rest in Its own beauty and perfection?

Yes.

Come on. Come out now and find the one you love.

Can I ask you something? One more thing?

Of course.

Is there anything to be frightened of? Out there?

No.

There's no fear out here.

No fear. Sounds like Heaven.

No need to say 'Heaven'. Why not just call it 'now'.

Now?

Now. Nothing but now.

OK. What do I do then? To come out? To get out?

Oh, that's easy. The easiest thing in the world.

Well, what is it, 8-10-4x? What do I do?

What do you do?

You just turn the page . . .

Acknowledgements

I would like to thank the following for their help, support and encouragement: Simon Trewin, Francis Bickmore and all at Canongate, Vani and Richard Midgley, Professor Richard Wiseman, Jago Irwin and Sarah Williams, Dave Cooper and Mark Gatiss.

Certain books have been useful in the preparation of the text, notably *Phenomena – A Book of Wonders* by John Michell and Robert J.M. Rickard and *Apparitions and Haunted Houses* by Sir Ernest Bennett.

Special thanks to Aiden Fox, H. Den Fawkes, the estate of Sir Eden Vachs, the estate of Rev. A. Tennethorex and 8-10-4x.

Extra special thanks to Andy Nyman, for bringing it all back home.